Theory and Interpretation of Narrative
James Phelan and Peter J. Rabinowitz, Series Editors

IMAGINING MINDS

The Neuro-Aesthetics of Austen, Eliot, and Hardy

Kay Young

THE OHIO STATE UNIVERSITY PRESS

Columbus

Library of Congress Cataloging-in-Publication Data

Young, Kay
  Imagining minds : the neuro-aesthetics of Austen, Eliot, and Hardy / Kay Young.
      p. cm.—(Theory and interpretation of narrative)
  Includes bibliographical references and index.
  ISBN 978-0-8142-5174-4 (pbk. : alk. paper)—ISBN 978-0-8142-1139-7 (cloth : alk.
paper)—ISBN 978-0-8142-9238-9 (cd)
  1. English literature—19th century—History and criticism. 2. Consciousness in litera-
ture. 3. Other minds (Theory of knowledge) 4. Mind-brain identity theory. 5. Austen,
Jane, 1775–1817—Criticism and interpretation. 6. Eliot, George, 1819–1880—Criticism and interpretation. 7. Hardy, Thomas, 1840–1928—Criticism and interpretation.
I. Title. II. Series: Theory and interpretation of narrative series.
  PR468.C66Y68 2010
  823'.809353—dc22

                                                    2010022225

This book is available in the following editions:
Cloth (ISBN 978-0-8142-1139-7)
Paper (ISBN 978-0-8142-5174-4)
CD-ROM (ISBN 978-0-8142-9238-9)

Cover design by Janna Thompson-Chordas.
Text design by Jennifer Shoffey Forsythe.
Type set in Adobe Bembo.
Printed by Thomson-Shore, Inc.

♾ The paper used in this publication meets the minimum requirements of the
American National Standard for Information Sciences—Permanence of Paper for
Printed Library Materials. ANSI Z39.48-1992.

9 8 7 6 5 4 3 2

CONTENTS

ILLUSTRATIONS & TABLES

PROLOGUE

"Nor praise the vermilion in the rose," she read, and so reading she was ascending, she felt, on to the top, on to the summit. How satisfying! How restful! All the odds and ends of the day stuck to this magnet; her mind felt swept, clean. And then there it was, suddenly entire; she held it in her hands, beautiful and reasonable, clear and complete, the essence sucked out of life and held rounded here—the sonnet.

—Virginia Woolf, *To the Lighthouse*

To read literature, to commit the mind to imagining to and through how a work of literature imagines, means to know something of the unbound, something of the expansion that moves us beyond the pressing immediacy and presence of the world—to know the life of the mind. But I think, too, it means to know something of a great longing for the world and to know our place in it—as a means of having our selves. Teaching a seminar of graduating seniors what has become for me a life-defining work of literature, George Eliot's *Middlemarch,* I asked why the novel suggests we wonder and search for that which is beyond ourselves, why the most expansive minds of the text—Lydgate, Will, and maybe most of all Dorothea—never feel self-satisfaction, always reach out for that which is beyond themselves. We came to see that the search for attachment—to a person, an object, a work of art, an idea—held open the possibility of feeling not alone, of feeling that one fits with or in relation to, of knowing the meaning of expansive connection between self and world.

Literature holds open that possibility of feeling the meanings of attachment and expansion because of how it calls upon us to imagine. In Alan Bennett's *The History Boys,* a remarkable moment of quiet exchange happens between the literature teacher Hector (surely named for the *Iliad*'s

Trojan warrior) and one of his students, Posner, the one who will himself
become a teacher of literature. They meet in a place of shared meaning
through the poem "Drummer Hodge" by Thomas Hardy:

> *Hector:* Uncoffined is a typical Hardy usage. It's a compound adjective,
> formed by putting "un" in front of the noun or verb, of course.
> Unkissed, unrejoicing, unconfessed, unembraced—it's a turn of phrase
> that brings with it a sense of not sharing, being out of it, whether
> because of diffidence or shyness, but holding back, not being in the
> swim of it. Can you see that?
>
> *Posner:* Yes, sir. I felt that a bit.
>
> *Hector:* The best moments in reading are when you come across something,
> a thought, a feeling, a way of looking at things that you'd thought
> special, particular to you. And there it is set down by someone else, a
> person you've never met, maybe even someone long dead. And it's as
> if a hand has come out and taken yours.

The life of the mind was my father's life. It is to him that I write a thought,
a feeling, a way of looking at things—these words. His is the hand that I
seek across death, across time. It is to him, my best reader, my best teacher,
that I dedicate this book.

TO MY FATHER
Stanley J. Young
(1925–2007)

INTRODUCTION

The Integrated Mind

1. THE MYSTERY OF MIND

A schoolboy, on the way to becoming a writer, notes on the inside cover of his poetry anthology:

1) What is the meaning of the poem and what is the experience?
2) What thought or reflection does the experience lead us to?
3) What mood, feeling, emotion is stirred or created by the poem as a whole? (Didion, *The Year of Magical Thinking* 41)

As readers of literature, we understand the young John Gregory Dunne's questions to be ours, too, because they address what the work of literature creates—meaning, thought, reflection, mood, feeling, emotion—and because they prompt us to wonder how it is possible that literature creates that which consciousness creates: experience.

A philosopher of mind notes about the physical nature of mental experience:

If we acknowledge that a physical theory of mind must account for the subjective character of experience, we must admit that no presently available conception gives us a clue how this could be done. The problem is unique. If mental processes are indeed physical processes, then there is something it is like, intrinsically, to undergo certain physical processes. What it is for such a thing to be the case remains a mystery. (Nagel, "What is it like to be a Bat?" 447)

And as minded beings, we understand Thomas Nagel's question to be ours, as well: how can a physical theory of mind account for the subjective character of experience?

David Chalmers calls this "the hard problem of consciousness":

> The hard problem . . . is the question of how physical processes in the brain give rise to subjective experience. This puzzle involves the inner aspect of thought and perception: the way things feel for the subject. When we see, for example, we experience visual sensations, such as that of vivid blue. Or think of the ineffable sound of the oboe, the agony of an intense pain, the sparkle of happiness or the meditative quality of a moment lost in thought. All are part of what I am calling consciousness. It is these phenomena that pose the real mystery of mind.[1]

The "easy problem of consciousness" for Chalmers is understanding the brain functions that can be measured, studied, and located organically and behaviorally through cognitive and neuroscience testing, that which defines *objective consciousness:* the ability to discriminate, categorize, and react to environmental stimuli; the integration of information by a cognitive system; the reportability of mental states; the ability of a system to access its own internal states; the focus of attention; the deliberate control of behavior; the difference between wakefulness and sleep ("Facing" 200). However, what the study of brain function has yet to reveal is why we have *subjective consciousness,* meaning how is it possible for subjectivity to arise from the physical processes of the brain? Why do we have internal lives? Beyond the processing of information, as in visual or auditory sensation, how is it possible that we have the *felt-quality* of seeing or hearing, the experience of feeling or thinking about our aliveness? Experience, point of view, orientation, ego, subjectivity, consciousness—these are the words that hold the idea of "mind." This, as Chalmers puts it, is "the real mystery of mind." Acknowledged in the neurosciences, the mystery of mind, according to the

---

1. David Chalmers, "The Puzzle of Conscious Experience," 62. For his extensive discussion of this puzzle, see Chalmers's *The Conscious Mind: In Search of a Fundamental Theory.* Other recent important contributions to the literature on consciousness and the nature of mind include *The Journal of Consciousness Studies;* Paul Churchland's *Matter and Consciousness;* Paul and Patricia Churchland's *On the Contrary: Critical Essays, 1987–1997;* Francis Crick's *The Astonishing Hypothesis: The Scientific Search for the Soul;* Daniel Dennett's *Brainstorms: Philosophical Essays on Mind and Psychology* and *Consciousness Explained;* Gerald Edelman and Giulio Tononi's *A Universe of Consciousness;* Richard L. Gregory's *The Oxford Companion to The Mind;* Colin McGinn's *The Mysterious Flame: Conscious Minds in a Material World;* Thomas Nagel's *The View from Nowhere;* Steven Pinker's *How the Mind Works;* David Rose's *Consciousness: Philosophical, Psychological and Neural Theories;* and Adam Zeman's *Consciousness: A User's Guide.*

neurologist Antonio Damasio, is

> a major gap in our current understanding of how neural patterns become
> mental images. The presence in the brain of dynamic neural patterns (or
> maps) related to an object or event is a *necessary* but not sufficient basis
> to explain the mental images of the said object or event. We can describe
> neural patterns—with the tools of neuroanatomy, neurophysiology, and neu-
> rochemistry—and we can describe images with the tools of introspection.
> How we get from the former to the latter is known only in part, although
> the current ignorance neither contradicts the assumption that images are
> biological processes nor denies their physicality . . . At the level of systems,
> I can explain the process up to the organization of neural patterns on the
> basis of which mental images will arise. But I fall short of suggesting, let
> alone explaining, how the last steps of the image-making process are car-
> ried out. (*Looking* 198)

What is the process by which the organization of neural patterns becomes
the image-making process, what Damasio calls the movie-in-the-brain, what
Chalmers calls the consciousness of experience, what Nagel calls the subjective character of experience?

Since their emergence in the nineteenth century, the mind-brain disciplines have testified to advances made in understanding relations of mind
and brain and to the power of the ongoing mystery of those relations.
Writing at the cusp between the nineteenth and twentieth centuries, as an
American founder and defining practitioner of those mind-brain disciplines,
and as an advocate of their integration, William James writes:

> [O]ur psychology will remain positivistic and non-metaphysical; and
> although this is certainly only a provisional halting place, and things must
> some day be more thoroughly thought out, we shall abide there in this
> book, and just as we have rejected mind-dust, we shall take no account of
> the soul. The spiritualistic reader may nevertheless believe in the soul if
> he will; whilst the positivistic one who wishes to give a tinge of mystery
> to the expression of his positivism can continue to say that nature in her
> unfathomable designs has mixed us of flame and clay, of brain and mind,
> that the two things hang indubitably together and determine each other's
> being, but how or why no mortal may ever know. (*Principles* I, 182)

This is a book about that mystery—the mind—and how a set of novels
tell the mind's story.

2. THE MIND WORK OF AUSTEN, ELIOT, AND HARDY

Imagining Minds explores the particular contributions of Jane Austen, George Eliot, and Thomas Hardy to the writing, understanding, and experience of mind. I consider how these three English novelists who span the nineteenth century reveal in their aesthetic practices modern, post-Cartesian conceptions of the integrated mind—as cognitive, affective, embodied, and relational—together. "I think, therefore I am" becomes in their telling varying displays of "I think and feel and am embodied and am in relation to others and the world, therefore I am." My fundamental claim is that the novel writes about the nature of mind, narrates it at work, and stimulates us to know deepened experiences of consciousness in its touching of our own integrated minds. Thinking more generally about the relationship between literature and the evolution of mind, Jonathan Bates, a Shakespeare scholar, asserts, "[L]iterature may have been genetically evolved to do cognitive work precisely by stimulating the emotions."[2] If the theories of mind generated by the mind-brain disciplines of philosophy, neurology, psychiatry, cognitive science, psychology, and psychoanalysis help explicate states of mind, the more purely cognitive mind-brain models and theories of these other disciplines cannot themselves *perform* what I call the novel's more fully integrated because embodied and emotionally stimulating "mind work"—mind work that prompts us to better know our own minds. The fantasy life of Emma Woodhouse, the loss of consciousness and its return as embodied feeling in *Persuasion,* the problem of other minds and its "solution" through sound as a physiology of empathy in *Middlemarch,* the embodied mind in *Daniel Deronda,* the moods of Sue Bridehead, the dissociative waking dream states of Tess—these are the mind states I address in this book in my desire to assert that the novel narrates the integrated mind and writes experience into being.

    It's not hard to imagine that by reading Jane Austen's novels I am

---

    2. Emily Eakin, "I Feel Therefore I Am," *The New York Times,* Saturday, April 19, 2003, A19. While Bates hypothesizes here about the existence and evolution of literature because of its capacities to stimulate emotion and the cognitive work that results from that stimulation, Mark Turner suggests that our minds are literary by nature—that we think in parables because of the evolutionary advantages such open-ended thinking structures engender—in his pathbreaking *The Literary Mind.* For further study on emotion and the brain, see the neuroscientist Joseph LeDoux's important *The Emotional Brain: The Mysterious Underpinnings of Emotional Life.* For a philosophically inflected, psychoanalytic account of emotion, see Donna Orange's *Emotional Understanding: Studies in Psychological Epistemology.* Other remarkable philosophic treatments of emotion and its relation to the arts include Sue Campbell's *Interpreting the Personal: Expression and the Formation of Feelings;* Susan L. Feagin's *Reading with Feeling: The Aesthetics of Appreciation;* Philip Fisher's *The Vehement Passions;* and Martha Nussbaum's *Upheavals of Thought: The Intelligence of Emotions.* For a literary historicist account of emotion in eighteenth- through early-nineteenth-century English thought and the verbal arts, see Adela Pinch's *Strange Fits of Passion: Epistemologies of Emotion, Hume to Austen.*

reading her mind. Sometimes over the course of these pages, I address the authors' minds—as presences embodied in the words of their novels—that I imagine as I do other minds. However, novels create a felt-consciousness beyond their reflectiveness of the author's mind. When we read a novel, we enter a world that in its verbal representations expresses multiple states and layers of subjective and intersubjective experience, mind-inflected states of consciousness to which we bring our own. "Character minds" set in relation to "context minds" (by which I mean narrative contexts that bespeak themselves as "minded beings") are guided and defined by "narrating" and "authorial" (stated and implied) minds. Together, I would argue, these verbal subjectivities—author, character, context, narrator—create a reading experience of multiple "mindedness." The novel is a minded world brought to consciousness through our reading minds. Meeting the mindedness of a novel happens in our understanding of and emotional identification with its narrative account of experience. When we read a narrative, we imagine we too are going through the experiences it describes because those descriptions evoke our emotions and set off the mental processing of empathy.[3] The Austen scholar Wendy S. Jones writes, "When we respond strongly to literature, the emotional components of our neural maps become active: neurons fire along pathways within and between emotion centers of the brain, thereby altering our feelings, our thoughts, our moods—and perhaps cumulatively, our actions and characters" (338). By actuating the frontal lobes of the brain—the neuroanatomic substrates of "other minds"—the act of reading novels connects with the emotional networks in the brain. Neurologists account for our capacity to feel empathy in part through their discovery of "mirror neurons."[4] When we read of specific somatic and neural states that are felt by the novel's characters, context, or author/narrator, we, too, can have those responses, similar and neural-evoked within us. Lakoff and Johnson call this mental process "enactment":

> When we imagine seeing a scene, our visual cortex is active. When we imagine moving our bodies, the pre-motor cortex and motor cortex are active. In short, some of the same parts of our brains are active in imagining as in perceiving and doing. We will use the word *enactment* for dynamic

3. For an extended discussion of the relation between novel reading, empathy, and altruism, see Suzanne Keen's fine *Empathy and the Novel*.

4. Mirror neurons have now been recorded in human beings, not only in motor regions of the brain (as expected), but as well in regions involved with vision and memory. See Christian Keysers and Valeria Gazzola's report of Dr. Itzhak Fried and Roy Mukamel's breakthroughs of neurosurgical research in "Social Neuroscience: Mirror Neurons Recorded in Humans." I write more about mirror neurons and their relation to empathy in my chapter on *Middlemarch*.

brain functions shared both during perceiving and acting and during imagining. (*Metaphors* 257)

Novels name emotional experiences: their naming evokes their state. Reading the named emotional state, we must decode the word's meaning, and that evokes our own associations and experiences with the word and hence its feeling. William James writes about feeling an emotion from thinking it as one of "all-overishness": "[T]he emotion both begins and ends with what we call its effects and manifestations. It has no mental status except as either the vivid feeling of the manifestations, or the idea of them" (*Principles* II, 458). Reading novels leads to a feeling of "all-overishness," to the dynamic brain function of enactment, to the firing of mirror neurons, and in turn to our understanding of and identification with their narrated experiences, experiences that become shared. We read novels for our lives—we lend to their reading our own aliveness and come away from their reading more alive. It is from this position and this understanding of the novel that I write.

Jane Austen's work introduces to the novel sustained, self-conscious reflection on the nature of the *self's mind*—the subject of Part I. If Emma in chapter 1 comes to consciousness of what it means to be self-conscious, Anne Elliot and Frederick Wentworth in chapter 2 discover what it means to return to full consciousness after knowing its early, devastating loss. In Part II, I consider how George Eliot's writing brings to full embodiment in the novel reflections on the nature of the *other's mind*. Chapter 3 explores how Dorothea, Will, Lydgate, and Caleb Garth come to "know" another through hearing and holding the other's sounds, while Daniel Deronda in chapter 4 comes not just to know another but to imagine being another and in so doing to be (an)other. Hardy's characters don't just resist self-conscious thought about their own minds or the minds of others: they simply cannot, it seems, sustain or sometimes even have such thoughts. I consider in Part III how self-conscious knowledge or other-conscious knowledge in Thomas Hardy's novels happens mostly through *nonintrospective states of mind*. I explore the impulses and moods of Sue Bridehead in chapter 5, and the waking dreams and other forms of dissociation of Tess in chapter 6—states that produce forms of what I'm calling nonintrospective knowing. The hard cognitive work of analysis that yields forms of knowledge in the works of Austen and Eliot essentially disappears as a mental strategy or possibility with Hardy: "I think, therefore I am" does little in Hardy's universe to solve the problems of mind or anxieties of existence. Throughout the book I imagine the mind not as split between the conscious and unconscious, but as integrated between multiple complementary conscious and unconscious mind states that function always and simultaneously in relation to one another. I'm interested in exploring how Hardy's unanalyzed automatic states reveal for instance what Damasio defines as "core consciousness," or how Eliot writes the mental processes of imagining the unimaginable, or how Austen writes the experience of what the analyst Christopher Bollas calls the "unthought known" not only as manifestations of the unconscious mind, but as integral to the mind as a whole. No one novel tells the mind's whole story. Each chapter stands alone and can be read alone for its particular discussion of the mind's story as told in its narrative universe. Each chapter, therefore, functions as a discrete entity, discrete in its account of the presence, forms, and methods of mind work each novel engages and creates—and yet the chapters are related. When studied together, I believe, the novels of Austen, Eliot, and Hardy help to make the idea and work of the integrated mind more apparent to us as their readers because of our discovery of the variety of different but related mind-imagining strategies, accounts of mind, and experiences of mind they represent and evoke in us as their readers.

Included here as a coda to the book is "The Neurology of Narrative," a piece I co-authored with the neurologist Jeffrey Saver, which suggests we think in narrative because our brains are hardwired to do so, that offers some ideas about why, and that looks at autobiography in light of these claims. I began work on the relation of the mind and narrative with "The Neurology of Narrative." Though situated at the book's close, it was its origin: the chapters that precede the coda are the results of the thinking I've done since on the relations of mind and the novels of Austen, Eliot, and Hardy. While the coda is distinct in its attention to autobiographical narrative and its sustained analysis of the neurobiological underpinning of narrative in human cognition, *Imagining Minds* is the subject of what followed—a working-through of how to mind narrative and how to narrate the mind—call it "the neuroaesthetics of narrative and the narrative aesthetics of neurology." Damasio presents his theory of mind in terms of a theory of narrative. He writes in *Looking for Spinoza: Joy, Sorrow, and the Feeling Brain:* "The mind exists for the body, is engaged in telling the story of the body's events and uses that story to optimize the life of the organism" (206). I read these novels as individually and together telling the mind's story, as narratives that make states of mind present to us. This is what I mean by the novel's "mind work"—and it's part of what narrative art, by its nature, makes. My assertion is that the novel by nature can't help but write our embodied/feeling minds and minded/feeling bodies. One of the earliest but still foundational works of narrative theory that seeks to understand fictional consciousness, Dorrit Cohn's *Transparent Minds: Narrative Modes for Presenting Consciousness in Fiction,* defines the rhetorical taxonomy of its structures.[5] And more recently, Lisa Zunshine draws on cognitive science to explore in *Why We Read Fiction: Theory of Mind and the Novel* how reading fiction trains our minds to better read the minds of others, while Alan Palmer's *Fictional Minds* brings cognitive science to the novel to help elucidate the nature of fictional minds.[6] I'm working on how fiction makes present the nature of our minds—our minds' embodiments—as real minds embodied in fictional flesh. I understand these novels to reflect, enact, and present in very different ways narratives of the integrated mind. *Imagining Minds* is about my desire to understand more fully how and why that is—how the novels of Austen, Eliot, and Hardy make the reader feel his or her own experience of mind more deeply.

Spanning the English nineteenth-century literary landscape, Austen, Eliot, and Hardy write into being accounts of the self-conscious, other-conscious, and nonintrospective conscious mind, remarkable accounts of mind, in relation to which other novels (English and beyond, nineteenth-century and beyond) can be read and better understood for their mind work. So although the writings of Sir Walter Scott are not an object of my study because his texts most often keep us outside the inner workings of his characters' minds in order to show how the conditions of a character's life and times contribute to his or her makeup, I think we can better understand Scott's radical break with some inherent notion of "character" by studying how far Hardy will take that radical break internally. Likewise, the particular nature of the work of the Brontës on the nature of the auto/biographical mind grows clearer by understanding their novels in relation to Austen's defining work on the fantasizing mind and embodied feeling. And Dickens's mysterious uses of metonymy, for instance, grow somewhat less mysterious when set in relation to Eliot's uses of metaphor as an embodied pathway between minds. The models of mind states I describe from my readings of Austen, Eliot, and Hardy will, I hope, open the way for others to explore and expand on those models of mind with regard to the novel as a genre

---

5. Predecessors of Cohn include Henry James, Mikhail Bakhtin, Wayne Booth, Franz Stanzel, and Gérard Genette.

6. Other recent studies on the relation of art/narrative/the novel to consciousness and subjectivity include Nancy Armstrong's *How Novels Think;* George Butte's *I Know That You Know That I Know;* William Cohen's *Embodied;* Gary Fireman, Ted McVay, and Owen Flanagan's edited collection *Narrative and Consciousness;* Patrick Colm Hogan's *Cognitive Science, Literature, and the Arts;* Jonah Lehrer's *Proust was a Neuroscientist;* David Lodge's *Consciousness and the Novel;* Elaine Scarry's *Dreaming by the Book;* Gabriele Schwab's *Subjects Without Selves;* Michael R. Trimble's *The Soul in the Brain;* Mark Turner's *The Literary Mind;* and James Wood's *How Fiction Works,* to name a few.

at large, in particular with regard to the modern novel which, with self-conscious design, makes the nature of mind its fundamental topic.

While the emergence of the minding of the nineteenth-century English novel must in ways be related to the corresponding rise and development in the nineteenth century of the mind-brain disciplines, this is not the line of argument I pursue in the book.[7] *Imagining Minds* is not a work of intellectual history. Instead, it is a work of neuroaesthetics. I attribute to their pioneering work on the relation of the visual arts to the visual cortex of the neuroscientists V. S. Ramachandran, William Hirstein, and Semir Zeki the creation of this new field of inquiry.[8] Imagining neuroaesthetics to be a study of future knowledge not just of the visual brain and the visual arts, Zeki states: "The future field of what I call neuroaesthetics will, I hope, study the neural basis of artistic creativity and achievement" ("Artistic Creativity and the Brain" 52). *Imagining Minds* is a response to that hope. When read in relation to the research and far-reaching, transformative accounts of the mind-brain, primarily of William James and Antonio Damasio, the novel embodies and informs through its very nature as narrative art their accounts. My fundamental claim is this: *the novel is an aesthetic map to and experience of the nature of the mind-brain.* The ideas and their expression of James and Damasio when set next to those of Austen, Eliot, and Hardy make evident their connection—where James and Damasio describe in ways that shift the paradigm for how we understand the nature of mental processing, the novelists in remarkably different ways bring that processing to embodied, feeling, relational narrative life. The book operates, therefore, through a principle of resonance—the principle of listening and looking for compelling resonances in language, meaning, and representation shared accounts of the

7. Such thinkers in the nineteenth-century mind-brain disciplines include the psychologists Herbert Spencer, George Lewes, Alexander Bain, Hermann Helmholtz, Wilhelm Wundt, and of course William James; the neurologists Joseph Gall, Pierre Broca, J. H. Jackson, J. M. Charcot, and G. B. Duchenne; and Freud and the birth of psychoanalysis. Intellectual historians of the nineteenth-century mind-brain disciplines include Robert Young, Rick Rylance, Thomas Dixon, G. Stanley Hall, William R. Woodward, Mitchell G. Ash, Edwin Clarke, and L. S. Jacyna. For fine instances of such work that traces the influences and confluences of nineteenth-century British or American literature, psychology, and neuroscience see, in particular, Jane F. Thrailkill's *Affecting Fictions: Mind, Body, and Emotion in American Literary Realism;* Nicholas Dames's *Amnesiac Selves: Nostalgia, Forgetting, and British Fiction, 1810–1870* and *The Physiology of the Novel: Reading, Neural Science, and the Form of Victorian Fiction;* and Alan Richardson's *British Romanticism and the Science of the Mind* and *The Neural Sublime: Cognitive Theories and Romantic Texts.* Andrew H. Miller's "Reading Thoughts: Victorian Perfectionism and the Display of Thinking" is striking for how it weaves together historicism with a Stanley Cavell–inflected reading of how Victorian writing displays the mind in dialogue with itself.

8. See in particular V. S. Ramachandran and William Hirstein's "The Science of Art: A Neurological Theory of Aesthetic Experience," and Semir Zeki's, "Art and the Brain," both of which appeared in the first special feature issue on "Art and the Brain" of *The Journal Consciousness Studies* in 1999.

integrated mind. In the way that no one novel tells the mind's whole story, neither does no one theory of mind-brain wholly define it. In addition to drawing throughout on the work of William James and Antonio Damasio, I turn at moments to other remarkable philosophic, psychological, physiologic, psychoanalytic, psychiatric, and neuropsychiatric perspectives to help me see and understand differently because of their different perspectives the states of mind the novels write—of George Lakoff and Mark Johnson on the embodied mind; Elaine Scarry and Jean-Paul Sartre on the literary imagination; Charles Darwin on the expression of emotion; Christopher Bollas on the transformational object; Hermann Helmholtz on the sensation of tone. Part III of *Imagining Minds*—on Hardy's movement away from introspection—brings with it an accompanying movement toward the mind-brain perspectives in particular of the psychiatrist Kay Jamison on mood, the neuropsychiatrist J. Allan Hobson on dreaming, and the psychoanalysts Heinz Kohut on narcissism, Adam Phillips on kissing, and Philip Bromberg on dissociation. Feeling the exchange between what I understand to be a novel's mindedness and my own prompted me to turn to mind-brain theorists, not because of their historical connection in time or place, but because of their compelling resonances in meaning and significance to their fields of research over time. It as well led me to seek to write a book in response to these novels that mirrors the reading experience I am having of them, meaning that is cognitive, but that is also feeling and embodied and relational. Sometimes when I read a cognitively informed approach to a literary text, the felt-quality of the reading experience of the literature is lost. In particular, when emotion is concretized into a graph of arrows and boxes, it becomes something cognitive rather than something emotional. While I don't attempt to intuit the effects of the representations of consciousness on the reader's mind, I do attempt in the writing of *Imagining Minds* to elicit the felt-quality of my reading experience in my readers—to bring to embodied, relational, feeling, and cognitive consciousness those effects on a sentence level in the reader's mind.

Years of reading and thinking about and feeling how these novels move through me, affect me, and live in me led me to want to understand through introspection how my own sense of experience, which is to say, my own sense of self, shifted from their reading. At first I imagined I pursued this study to help me grasp how these novels display consciousness at work, but the more closely I made contact with the felt-experience of each novel, the more I began to consider the novels themselves to be the elucidators of how consciousness works. I found myself wondering again and again the kinds of questions that make this a study of neuroaesthetics: How and why does a novel have at its core what I experience as "mindedness," or felt-consciousness? How does that narrative consciousness address my own, enter it, change it? Is this true for all experiences of art? Is this what art does? Is this how art moves us? Or, is it particularly true of verbal narrative art because of its word-based, storytelling medium, a medium, I'm claiming, that mirrors the most central medium of our minds? The novel, the great verbal art form of the verbal mind, is for me most of all the aesthetic of consciousness, the aesthetic that tells the mind's story. I seek to bring to consciousness how novel-imagining creates what no neuro-imaging can map—*the experience of how we mind.*

3. THE WORKS OF MIND OF DESCARTES, JAMES, AND DAMASIO

Why always Descartes? To think about the nature of mind, what brings me back to the Cartesian "I"? And why for others who work on the mind is there no getting away from the "*cogito*"?[9] At the core of the *Meditations on First Philosophy* is Descartes' central premise—the "essential self" is the mind. We are haunted by the *Meditations* for good reason. Our most intimate, profound, defining experience of being alive is the experience of mind. Were we not to be minded, we would not experience. "I think, therefore I am" means to Descartes "I am my experience of 'I am'"—a mind that thinks.

Descartes' *Meditations on First Philosophy* (1641) and its famous *cogito ergo sum* inaugurated a tradition in epistemology that understood mind split from body, and privileged mind over body, reason over emotion—a tradition that I believe continues to cast a long shadow. For me, the great nineteenth-century work on mind, William James's *The Principles of Psychology* (1890), and the current research of Antonio Damasio when studied together address and seek to answer the mind/body problem with the notion of "the integrated

9. The historian of neuroscience Robert Young, for instance, discusses the effects of Cartesian dualism on the development of the mind sciences in *Mind, Brain, and Adaptation in the Nineteenth Century* when he writes, "The price paid for the scientific revolution in the physical sciences was the isolation of mind from nature and of the study of purposive behaviour from the advance of the scientific method. The fragmentation of the world into primary and secondary qualities, outer and inner, body and mind, and the exclusion of final causes from science have plagued the study of mind and behaviour at least since Descartes [. . .] Cartesian dualism supplied an ontological basis for the separation of mind from body, while the theory of representative perception separated the knowing mind from its external object for knowledge" (2). And other works, *Descartes' Error* by the neurologist Antonio Damasio and *Philosophy in the Flesh* by linguist George Lakoff and philosopher Mark Johnson, are explicitly revisionist accounts of the Cartesian self and Cartesian dualism. Lakoff and Johnson begin *Philosophy in the Flesh* with a summary of the findings of cognitive science on the nature of mind: "The mind is inherently embodied. Thought is mostly unconscious. Abstract concepts are largely metaphorical . . . When taken together and considered in detail, these three findings from the science of mind are inconsistent with central parts of Western philosophy . . . What would happen if we started with these empirical discoveries about the nature of mind and constructed philosophy anew?" (3).

brain and mind"—embodied, feeling, and reason-making together. Simply put, the work of William James and Antonio Damasio revise the Cartesian "I."[10] Throughout *Imagining Minds* I integrate theories of mind with novel writings of mind. Before coming to the blended novel-theory discussions in the chapters to follow, I offer here discrete accounts of the Cartesian "I" and of the (re)visionary theories of mind of James and Damasio, to those who would find some sustained attention to their ideas, separate from the novels, beneficial.

a. "A thinking thing; that is a mind, or intellect, or reason"

Who is this Cartesian "I"? "I am sitting here near to the fire, wearing my

10. I don't mean to suggest that James and Damasio were the first or only to hypothesize about the integrated brain and mind; rather, they've described what are for me its most compelling accounts. The other great seventeenth-century Western philosopher to whom Damasio attributes some of the origin of his own theories, Benedict de Spinoza, writes in the *Ethics* a philosophical bringing together of mind and brain and emotion in "Of the Nature and Origin of the Mind" and then in "On the Origin and Nature of the Emotions": "[T]he human mind is the very idea or knowledge of the human body"; "That the mind is united to the body we have shown from the fact, that the body is the object of the mind" (102); "The human mind perceives not only modifications of the body, but also the ideas of such modifications" (103); "The mind does not know itself, except in so far as it perceives the ideas of the modifications of the body" (103); "The human mind does not perceive any external body as actually existing, except through the ideas of the modifications of its own body" (105). Many of the nineteenth-century British, American, French, German, and Austrian philosophers and scientists who emerged as the founders of modern psychology, neurology, and psychoanalysis came in their work to propose forms of mind/body/emotion integration. They include Charles Darwin (*The Expression of the Emotions in Man and Animals*), Alexander Bain (*The Senses and the Intellect, The Emotions and the Will, Mind and Body*), Herbert Spencer (*The Principles of Psychology*), George Lewes (*The Physiology of Common Life, Problems of Life and Mind*), J. H. Jackson (studies in neurology), William James (collected works), J. M. Charcot (collected works), G. B. Duchenne (*The Mechanism of Human Facial Expression*), Sigmund Freud (collected works), Herman Helmholtz (*On the Sensations of Tone, On the Origin of the Correct Interpretation of Our Sense Impressions*), Eduard Von Hartmann (*Philosophy of the Unconscious*), Wilhelm Wundt (*Principles of Physiological Psychology*). I believe the development of these more integrated, "whole" visions of mind/body interactions can be understood as reflective of the nineteenth-century penchant for not shying away from the desire to discover "the key" to all knowledge, that which would replace the role of the divine. Hegel's phenomenology of spirit, Darwin's theory of evolution, Marx's economic theories, even Casaubon's "key to all mythology" are instances of how nineteenth-century thinkers sought integrated models of knowledge. Therefore, the idea of an integrated understanding of being would be more easily embraced than a more compartmentalized model that separated mind from body, cognition from emotion. The desire for and even belief in integrative models of knowledge have, I think, suffered in the twentieth and twenty-first centuries: as knowledge has grown more complex, advanced, and vast, thinking has grown more compartmentalized and analytic, less associative and synthetic. Living on the cusp between the nineteenth and twentieth centuries, Henri Bergson addressed this growing split between analytic knowing and synthetic knowing (a knowing we experience through time as "la durée") in his work. I understand the emergence of phenomenology in the twentieth century as the philosophic heir to the desire for integration and synthesis in its emphasis on experience, specifically with regard to the mind/body problem. As Merleau-Ponty in *Phenomenology of Perception* writes: "I am, I exist embodied in the world." And: "Being in truth is indistinguishable from being in the world" (395). And: "I am bound with my body, bound with the world" (408–9).

winter dressing gown, and I am holding this sheet of paper in my hands"
(14). Such a cozy, inviting self-portrait in words of "I am my body in the
world" is undone by a question. "But on what grounds could one deny
that these hands and this entire body are mine?" (14). Descartes' *Meditations on First Philosophy* is a work devoted to that denial, which is to say
to the radical act of imagining away reality. Descartes makes the thinking
away of everything about which he cannot be wholly certain in pursuit of
that which he can be certain the subject of his meditations. If Descartes'
expressed desire is for the indubitable, his pathway there is through doubt,
not belief. His claim at the opening of the *Meditations* in his letter of dedication is to prove to unbelievers that God and the soul exist. What belief
cannot persuade an unbeliever to know, reason, Descartes asserts, can. And
so through doubt—our rational capacity not to believe—Descartes embarks
on meditations to discover what is beyond doubt.

To meditate one's way into complete doubt sounds like a joke. Who
really doubts reality? Wouldn't believing such doubt require losing one's
mind? And it's this—his mind—that Descartes realizes he cannot doubt
away. His mind, he asserts, constitutes "mine," that is, what enables him to
know he exists. The *cogito*—"'I am, I exist' is necessarily true every time I
utter it or conceive it in my mind" (18)—is for Descartes the one certain
truth upon which all else rests because it is beyond doubt.

> Here I make my discovery: thought exists; it alone cannot be separated from
> me. I am; I exist—this is certain. But for how long? For as long as I am
> thinking; for perhaps it could also come to pass that if I were to cease all
> thinking I would then utterly cease to exist—this is certain. At this time I
> admit nothing that is not necessarily true. I am therefore precisely nothing
> but a thinking thing; that is a mind, or intellect, or reason. (19)

"I am; I exist" means to Descartes, "I am thinking." And if thinking is "I,"
then "I" am my "mind, intellect, or reason," that which for Descartes means
"I, a thinking thing." What Descartes can doubt, what is not "I am; I exist,"
is his body. "*I am not that concatenation of members we call the human body*"
(emphasis mine, 19), Descartes writes, because his body and its senses, reason
tells him, can deceive him: "[A]ll these images—and, generally, everything
belonging to the nature of the body—could turn out to be nothing but
dreams . . . Moreover, I realize that I must be most diligent about with-
drawing my mind from these things so that it can perceive its nature as
distinctly as possible" (20). That he may be dreaming are the grounds on
which Descartes can doubt that "these hands and this entire body are mine."

He must work hard to draw his mind away from his body to perceive his mind as itself, as himself. If mind is "mine," body may not be:

> I know that I exist, and that at the same time I judge that obviously nothing else belongs to my nature or essence except that I am a thinking thing, I rightly conclude that *my essence consists entirely in my being a thinking thing.* And although perhaps (or rather, as I shall soon say, assuredly) I have a body that is very closely joined to me, nevertheless, because on the one hand I have a clear and distinct idea of myself, insofar as I am merely a thinking thing and not an extended thing, and because on the other hand I have a distinct idea of a body, insofar as it is merely an extended thing and not a thinking thing, it is certain *I am really distinct from my body, and can exist without it.* (Emphasis mine, 51)

Descartes' thought experiment—"to raze everything to the ground and begin again from the original foundations . . . to establish anything firm and lasting" (17)—comes to this strange conclusion. Though "very closely joined to me," my body is not "I." "I," a "thinking thing," can exist without it. A mind split from body, a mind that can exist without a body, a mind privileged over a body—who or what would such a Descartes be? He would not be the man who sits by the fire in his dressing gown holding the sheet of paper in his hands. He would not be the man who attempts to doubt all that he once held to be certain and true. He would not be the man who discovers the certainty of his own self-conscious thought. Descartes would not be himself, would not have a human self were this description of his essential self to be true.

A disembodied self is a nonentity: the language of the *Meditations* reveals this. If Descartes' thoughts experiment with an understanding of mind split from body, his language cannot. "To raze everything to the ground" or "I will apply myself earnestly and unreservedly to this general demolition of my opinions" (13) are embodied accounts of what it means to doubt and how the mind attempts to do so. To get to the idea of a disembodied truth, he uses the embodied idea of physical destruction: Descartes' language "acts" differently than his argument does. He depends on physical language as he attempts or as the means to let go of it. From metaphors of demolition, Descartes at the end of Meditation One and beginning of Meditation Two uses similes to compare his attempt to think his way into disembodiment ("I will regard myself as not having hands, or eyes, or flesh, or blood, or senses . . . But this undertaking is arduous, and a certain laziness brings me back to my customary way of living") to embodied states of imprisonment and drowning.

First:

> I am not unlike a prisoner who enjoyed an imaginary freedom during his
> sleep, but, when he later begins to suspect that he is dreaming, fears being
> awakened and nonchalantly conspires with these pleasant illusions. In just
> the same way, I fall back of my own accord into my old opinions, and
> dread being awakened, lest the toilsome wakefulness which follows upon a
> pleasant rest must be spent thenceforward not in the light but among the
> inextricable shadows of the difficulties now brought forward. (17)

And then:

> Yesterday's meditation has thrown me into such doubts that I can no lon-
> ger ignore them, yet I fail to see how they are to be resolved. It is as if I
> had suddenly fallen into a deep whirlpool; I am so tossed about that I can
> neither touch the bottom with my foot, nor swim to the top. Neverthe-
> less I will work my way up and will once again attempt the same path I
> entered yesterday. (17)

Descartes does not just think doubt; he feels it and its effects through his
body. His experience of doubt leads him to imagine how it resembles
other states, not just of the reasoning mind, but of his whole person. The
prisoner who yearns to stay asleep to feel his freedom in his dreams rather
than face his harsh reality is like the Cartesian "I" who dreads waking up
to this state of oppressive doubt and the shadows of uncertainty those
doubts yield. The tossed-about Cartesian "I" who has suddenly fallen into
a deep whirlpool and can neither touch bottom nor swim up is like the
Cartesian "I" who feels thrown into such doubts that he can neither ignore
them nor discern how to settle them. Descartes' doubt, that which he calls
a method of reason, depends on its embodiment in language for definition and for some disclosure of its terrifying effects on him. All of these
moments reveal seemingly multiple "I's" who are Descartes. Doubting his
way to the essential "I" who thinks uncovers other "I's" who imagine and
feel. Doubt, Descartes' language reveals, is not just a form of reason: doubt
suggests how reason is linked to the imagination, the senses, and emotion.

What is not for Descartes' argument clear and distinct—his body—is
what creates clarity and distinction in Descartes' language and, therefore,
the possibility of its clarity and distinction for his readers. "Let us take,
for instance, this piece of wax. It has been taken quite recently from the
honeycomb, it has not yet lost all the honey flavor. It retains some of the
scent of flowers from which it was collected" (21). As much as Descartes

understands the all-pervasive presence of his subjectivity—"I am a thinking mind"—to be that which is most clear and distinct because it is the
"mind" beyond doubt, how much more clear and distinct is the wax to
us, his readers? When Descartes meditates on the greatest of abstractions,
what he calls "the idea of God," his most abstract thought cannot abandon
its embodiment: "I want to spend some time contemplating this God, to
ponder his attributes and, so far as the eye of my darkened mind can take
me, to gaze upon, to admire, and to adore the beauty of this immense light"
(emphasis mine, 35). What is an "I am"? What is a "thinking thing"? How
am I to know the Cartesian "I" who thinks? How much more easy it is
for me to think of the Cartesian "I" who tastes honey and smells flowers and sees an immense light, or who imagines himself in a whirlpool
when he doubts all existence, or who feels like a prisoner who dreams
of freedom and wishes not to awake to his cell of doubt. What Descartes'
skepticism claims to raze—sensory knowledge—is for me what emerges as
the groundwork of his argument and of my ability to imagine it and hold
it in my mind. To be his mind—for himself, for me to imagine—depends
on how Descartes' mind thinks (however unacknowledged) with emotion
and imagination through his senses, meaning through his body.

b. *"This palpitating inward life"*

William James's *The Principles of Psychology* is a work so vast in scope, learning, introspection, and imagination that it must be read for itself to get a
sense of its intellectual and emotional magnitude, prescience, and influence.
It is to psychology what Proust's *À la recherche du temps perdu* is to the
novel—its *magnum opus*. But I can only excerpt moments to give a sense
of its ideas and qualities which radically revise Descartes' account of mind
and presage many of the paths psychology, psychiatry, and neurology will
eventually follow. In offering these moments, I hope to reveal something
of its wide-open spaces of thought, innovation, and imagination, and how
it invites us to address its words and ideas with our own experience of
mind. At its opening, James reveals the intellectual design of *The Principles*—
a working-through of one essential postulate—"The fact that the brain is
the one immediate bodily condition of the mental operations is indeed so
universally admitted nowadays that I need spend no more time illustrat-
ing it, but will simply postulate it and pass on. The whole remainder of
the book will be more or less proof that the postulate was correct" (I, 4).
James was in a unique position to draw his work from this postulate. As a

medical student, James studied neuroanatomy; *The Principles of Psychology* (based on his long course of lectures on psychology delivered at Harvard) refer throughout their pages to what was known and not known in 1890 about the human brain and nervous system. As a philosopher, James may have felt tempted to move toward what he calls the metaphysical, but he holds himself to this limit: "This book, assuming that thoughts and feelings exist and are vehicles of knowledge, thereupon contends that psychology when she has ascertained the empirical correlation of the various sorts of thought or feeling with definite conditions of the brain, can go no further—can go no farther, that is as natural science. If she goes farther she becomes metaphysical" (I, 4). Understanding our thoughts and feelings as products of a deeper source—the Soul, God—are metaphysical explanations James refuses to consider as elements of psychology. James neither models his *Principles* on Scholasticism's turn to the Soul as a means to unify and make sense of the variety and complexity of mental phenomena nor on Associationism's construction of a psychology without a soul "by taking discrete 'ideas,' faint or vivid, and showing how their cohesions, repulsions, and forms of succession, such as reminiscences, perceptions, emotions, volitions, passions, theories, and all other furnishings of an individual's mind may be engendered. The very Self or ego of the individual comes in this way to be viewed no longer as the pre-existing source of representations, but rather as their last and most complicated fruit" (1). Neither Descartes' reliance on God as the ultimate source of mind nor the Associationists' (Locke, Hume, Mills, Spencer, or Bain—the reigning British philosopher-psychologists of the eighteenth to latter nineteenth century) reliance on the association of ideas as the source of mind are the theoretical frames that guide James's work.[11] Instead, the brain and in a larger sense the body are for James the groundwork of mental states and must be studied in their relation to the mind and the mind in relation to them:

> Bodily experiences, therefore, and more particularly brain-experiences, must take a place amongst those conditions of the mental life of which Psychology need take account. *The spiritualist and the associationist must both*

---

11. Here's James on Spencer, for instance: "On the whole, few recent formulas have done more real service of a rough sort in psychology than the Spencerian one that the essence of mental life and bodily life are one, namely, 'the adjustment of inner to outer relations.' Such a formula is vagueness incarnate; but because it takes into account the fact that minds inhabit environments which act on them and on which in turn they react; because, in short, it takes mind in the midst of all its concrete relations, it is immensely more fertile than the old-fashioned 'rational psychology,' which treated the soul as a detached existent, sufficient unto itself, and assumed to consider only its nature and properties" (I, 6).

be "cerebralists," to the extent at least of admitting that certain peculiarities in the way of working their own favorite principles are explicable only by the fact that the brain laws are a codeterminant of the result.

Our conclusion, then, is that a certain amount of brain-physiology must be presupposed or included in Psychology.

In still another way the psychologist is forced to be something of a nerve-physiologist. Mental phenomena are not only conditioned *a parte ante* by bodily processes; but they lead to them *a parte post.* That they lead to *acts* is of course the most familiar of truths, but I do not merely mean acts in the sense of voluntary and deliberate muscular performances. Mental states occasion also changes in the calibre of blood-vessels, or alteration in the heart-beats, or processes more subtle still, in glands and viscera. If these are taken into account, as well as acts which follow at some *remote period* because the mental state was once there, it will be safe to lay down the general law that *no mental modification ever occurs which is not accompanied or followed by a bodily change.* The ideas and feelings, *e.g.,* which these present printed characters excite in the reader's mind not only occasion move-ments of his eyes and nascent movements of articulation in him, but will some day make him speak, or take sides in a discussion, or give advice, or choose a book to read, differently from what would have been the case had they never impressed his retina. Our psychology must therefore take account not only of the conditions antecedent to mental states, but of their resultant consequences as well. (I, 4–5)

The general law from which *The Principles of Psychology* operates—"no mental modification ever occurs which is not accompanied or followed by a bodily change"—defines James's fundamental theory of the mind as embodied because brain-based and body-based and the body as minded because mentally inflected or driven. And his description of what became my own desire to write about his work from its physical impressing on my retina—"the ideas and feelings . . . which these present printed characters excite in the reader's mind not only occasion movements of his eyes and nascent movements of articulation in him, but will some day make him speak"—defines James's method of bringing introspection to inspection. Observing that mental states occur simultaneously with changes in blood flow, heartbeats, glands, and viscera leads James to conclude that mental states are embodied and are forces that "live" beyond the moment of their embodiment, that they have "resultant consequences." Further, James's general law of the mind's embodiment/the body's mindedness and his method of introspection from inspection lead him to stay present to *his own experience* of the variety of mental states he discusses, to report them in general and subjective terms, and to call upon his readers to do so as well:

> *Now can we tell more precisely in what the feeling of the central self consists?* . . .
> I think I can in my own case; and as what I say will be likely to meet with opposition if generalized (as indeed it may be inapplicable to other individuals), I had better continue in the first person, leaving my description to be accepted by those to whose introspection it may commend itself as true, and confessing my inability to meet the demands of others, if others there be.
> I am aware of a constant play of furtherances and hindrances in my thinking, of checks and releases, tendencies which run with desire, and tendencies which run the other way. Among the matters I think of, some range themselves on the side of the thought's interests, whilst others play an unfriendly part thereto. The mutual inconsistencies and agreements, reinforcements and obstructions, which obtain amonst [*sic*] those objective matters reverberate backwards and produce what seem to be incessant reactions of my spontaneity upon them, welcoming or opposing, appropriating or disowning, striving with or against, saying yes or no. *This palpitating inward life is, in me, that central nucleus which I just tried to describe in terms that all men might use.* (Emphasis mine, I, 299)

This description of James's mind working on the mind—"this palpitating inward life is, in me, that central nucleus"—creates a space of mental openness and invitation. James's mind grants to his readers as deep and as present a "central nucleus" as he does to himself, and asks his readers to reflect on their own experience of this "palpitating inward life."

From understanding all mental states to be brain- and body-based, James derives two fundamental principles about the mind to which he returns throughout *The Principles of Psychology*. First: "Knowledge about a thing is knowledge of its *relations*. Acquaintance with it is a limitation to the bare impression it makes. Of most of its relations we are only aware in the penumbral nascent way of a *fringe of unarticulated affinities* about it" (emphasis mine, I, 259). The underlying assertion here is that nothing exists in isolation, separate and intact, without concrete relations. What he calls "rational psychology" "treats the soul as a detached existent, sufficient unto itself, and assumed to consider only its nature and properties" (I, 6). James's principles of psychology understand "minds [to] inhabit environments which act on them and on which in turn they react" (I, 6). The mind for James is by nature relational and integrational—inhabiting, acting upon, and reacting to the brain, body, and world beyond the organism.

Our access to the knowledge of anything and in particular our knowledge of the mind is limited, he claims, to the "fringe of unarticulated affinities about it." Study the brain, body, and world of the mind; only then will knowledge of the mind begin to be manifest. But to engage in that study of relations requires feeling or happens through feeling: "[F]ew writers have admitted that we cognize relations through *feeling*" (emphasis mine, I, 247). For James, it is the feeling of relations that enables our cognition of anything, which leads him to this second fundamental principle and revision of the Cartesian "I":

> For the central part of the Self is felt . . . it is at any rate no mere *ens rationis,* cognized only in an intellectual way, and no mere summation of memories or mere sound of a word in our ears. It is something with which we have a direct sensible acquaintance, and which is as fully present at any moment of consciousness in which it is present, as in a whole lifetime of such moments. When, just now, it was called an abstraction, that did not mean that, like some general notion, it could not be presented in a particular experience. It only meant that in the stream of consciousness it never was found all alone. But when it is found, it is *felt;* just as the body is felt, the feeling of which is also an abstraction, because never is the body felt all alone, but always together with other things. (I, 298–99)

The Jamesian "I" is not just "a thinking thing, that is a mind, or intellect, or understanding, or reason." What is for James the central part or nucleus of the self is a found presence physically feeling in relation to other things, "something with which we have a direct sensible acquaintance," and a presence never found all alone in the stream of consciousness, "but always together with other things." Further, the central part of the "me," James writes, "is the feeling of the body and of the adjustments in the head; and in the feeling of the body should be included that of the general emotional tones and tendencies, for at bottom these are but the habits in which organic activities and sensibilities run" (I, 371). In James's telling, the "I" is not only a physically feeling presence but is as well an *emotionally feeling presence.* The mind for James feels emotions, comes to acquire "general emotional tones and habits," and makes them its habits from the body's sensorimotor responses to the object world: "Objects do excite bodily changes by a preorganized mechanism . . . the changes are so indefinitely numerous and subtle that the entire organism may be called a sounding board, which every change of consciousness, however, slight, may make reverberate" (II, 450). James's theory of emotion, its central role in the nucleus of the self, and its very nature, follows from his understanding of the mind as brain- and body-based—that emotion is bodily change—"Our natural way of thinking about these coarser emotions is that the mental perception of some fact excites the mental affection called the emotion, and that this latter state of mind gives rise to the bodily expression. My theory, on the contrary, is that the bodily changes follow directly the perception of the exciting fact, and that our feeling of the same changes as they occur *is* the emotion" (II, 449).[12] To grant emotion not just a central part of his conception of mind, but to make emotion be a province of science, a field for future empirical study, was cause for scientific protest. James writes in *The Principles* that for the biologists of his day, "The desire on the part of men educated in laboratories not to have their physical reasonings mixed up with such incommensurable factors as feelings is certainly very strong . . . *[F]eeling constitutes the 'unscientific half of existence'*" (emphasis mine, I, 134–37). For James to understand the "unscientific half of existence" as the essential half of existence and for him to seek to do so scientifically reveals part of what's so astonishing about *The Principles of Psychology.* And for James to seek to understand the mind in relation to the brain and the body, in fact as the mental formulation of brain and body, to seek to explore the mind in relation to all its capacities, not as would a rational psychologist or philosopher as "Soul" detached and sufficient unto itself, and to understand the "unscientific half of existence"—emotion—as an essential half of consciousness and as necessary and deserving of scientific inquiry meant for James to *reinvent* how to study the nature of the mind and how to *reimagine* the mind. Working at the intellectual crossroads between medicine, philosophy, and psychology at the dawning of the twentieth century, James defines a modern account of the integrated mind-brain, as his thinking and writing embody it. *The Principles of Psychology* presents a remarkably original model of mind—as embodied and feeling—of a remarkably original mind. Since James, over a hundred years of advances in neuroscience have helped clarify and reveal the relations of mind and brain. However, James's recognition of the "unscientific half of existence," what meant for James emotion and consciousness, continued to remain outside the purview of scientific research until fairly recently. James acknowledges throughout *The Principles* that it would be for later researchers to elucidate how our mental structures are connected to our

12. James's theory of emotion is often referred to as the "James-Lange theory." James acknowledges Lange's work in the opening pages of his chapter on emotion, cites where their theories correspond, and as well notes where their thinking diverges. James claims something of the original-author role of the theory when he writes, "Now the general causes of the emotions are indubitably physiological. Prof. C. Lange, of Copenhagen, in the pamphlet from which I quoted, published in 1885 a physiological theory of their constitution and conditioning, which I had already broached the previous year in an article in *Mind*" (II, 449).

nervous system and concludes this massive work of mind/on mind which seeks to define what we know about that connection with closing words about how little we know:

> The causes of our mental structure are doubtless natural, and connected, like all our peculiarities, with those of our nervous system. Our interests, our tendencies of attention, our motor impulses, the aesthetic, moral, and theoretic combinations we delight in, the extent of our power of apprehending schemes of relation, just like the elementary relations themselves, time, space, difference and similarity, and the elementary kinds of feeling, have all grown up in ways of which *at present we can give no account.* Even in the clearest parts of Psychology our insight is insignificant enough. And the more sincerely one asks to trace the actual course of *psychogenesis,* the steps by which as a race we may have come by the peculiar mental attributes which we possess, the more clearly one perceives "*the slowly gathering twilight close in utter night.*" (Emphasis mine, II, 688)

c. "The presence of you is the feeling of what happens"

James's "night," what we don't know in 1890, "the steps by which as a race we may have come by the peculiar mental attributes we possess," Antonio Damasio's research and theories on mind–brain integration help elucidate. Damasio summarizes an evolutionary account of how brains generally emerge from bodies, and then begins to suggest how a mind may develop from the brain:

> Brains can have many intervening steps in the circuits mediating between stimulus and response, and still have no mind, if they do not meet an essential condition: the ability to display images internally and to order those images in a process called thought. (The images are not solely visual; there are also "sound images," "olfactory images," and so on.) My statement about behaving organisms can now be completed by saying that not all have minds, that is not all have mental phenomena (which is the same as saying that not all have cognition or cognitive processes). Some organisms have both behavior and cognition. Some have intelligent actions but no mind. No organism seems to have mind but no action.
>
> My view then is that having a mind means that an organism forms neural representations which can become images, be manipulated in a process called thought, and eventually influence behavior by helping predict the future, plan accordingly, and choose the next action. Herein lies the

center of neurobiology as I see it: the process whereby neural representations, which consist of biological modifications created by learning in a
neuron circuit, become images in our minds; the process that allows for
invisible microstructural changes in neuron circuits (in cell bodies, dendrites
and axons, and synapses) to become a neural representation, which in turn
becomes an image we each experience as belonging to us.

To a first approximation, the overall function of the brain is to be well
informed about what goes on in the rest of the body, the body proper;
about what goes on in itself; and about the environment surrounding
the organism, so that suitable, survivable accommodations can be achieved
between organism and environment. From an evolutionary perspective, it
is not the other way around. If there had been no body, there would have
been no brain. (*Descartes' Error* 89–90)

What Damasio describes is an emergence of mind from body. From an
evolutionary perspective, without the body there could be no mind because
no brain. Single-cell organisms without brains produce behavior in response
to their environment. In response to the environment and its objects and
as an increasingly better response to promote survival, organisms develop
brains and then minds to aid in their survival. Damasio advances his sense
of how neural representations become the "images" that become thought
that becomes subjectivity in his discussion of object representation:

[C]onsider all the ingredients I have described above—an object that is
being represented, an organism responding to the object of representation,
and a state of the self in the process of changing because of the organism's
response to the object—are held simultaneously in working memory and
attended, side-by-side or in rapid interpolation, in early sensory cortices.
I propose that subjectivity emerges during the latter step when the brain
is producing not just images of an object[,] not just images of organism
responses to the object, but a third kind of image, that of *an organism in the
act of perceiving and responding to an object.* I believe the subjective perspective arises out of the content of the third kind of image. (Emphasis mine,
Descartes' Error 243)

Damasio proposes that subjectivity results from how the brain processes and
represents the interaction of the body with object to body being changed
by interaction with object. All of this unconscious processing/representing/
imaging by the brain of how the body is being affected by what is outside
of it becomes the groundwork for the emergence of mind. *The Feeling of
What Happens: Body and Emotion in the Making of Consciousness* is Damasio's

more sustained working-through of this hypothesis:

> The sensory images of what you perceive externally, and the related images
> you recall, occupy most of the scope of your mind, but not all of it. Besides
> those images there is also this other presence that signifies you, as observer
> of the things imaged, owner of the things imaged, potential actor on the
> things imaged. There is a presence of you in a particular relationship with
> some object. If there were no such presence, how would your thoughts
> belong to you? Who could tell that they did . . . I shall propose that the
> simplest form of such a presence is also an image, actually the kind of
> image that constitutes a feeling. In that perspective, *the presence of you is the*
> *feeling of what happens when your being is modified by the acts of apprehending*
> *something.* The presence never quits, from the moment of awakening to
> the moment sleep begins. The presence must be there or there is no you.
> (Emphasis mine, *The Feeling* 10)

Damasio rewrites Descartes' *cogito* as a question: "If there were no such
presence, how would your thoughts belong to you?" However, the Cartesian
self of a "thinking thing," "a mind, or intellect, or reason," in Damasio's
telling is "the feeling of what happens when your being is modified by
the acts of apprehending something." Not thought, *a priori,* separated from
all else, supreme essence of what constitutes "I," but feeling the "I" change
apprehending something else—an "I" feeling in relation—is what, like James,
Damasio claims defines the essential self, subjectivity. Drawing on his years
of clinical research on patients with prefrontal damage, in particular on his
work with his patient "Elliot," Damasio makes scientific the importance of
emotion in our understanding of being. Surviving damage to the prefrontal
lobe, Elliot is no longer Elliot. Drawing perhaps most directly on the work
of James, Damasio states:

> I turn now to emotion and feeling, central aspects of biological regula-
> tion, to suggest they provide the bridge between rational and nonrational
> processes, between cortical and subcortical structures. (*Descartes' Error* 128)

> I see the *essence* of emotion as the collection of changes in body state that
> are induced in myriad organs by nerve cell terminals, under the control of
> a dedicated brain system, which is responding to the content of thoughts
> relative to a particular entity or event. Many of the changes in body state—
> those in skin color, body posture, and facial expression, for instance—are
> actually perceptible to an external observer. (Indeed the etymology of the
> word nicely suggests an external direction, from the body: *emotion* sig-

nifies literally "movement out.") But there is more to emotion than its essence . . . I leave out of emotion the perception of all the changes that constitute the emotional response . . . I reserve the term *feeling* for the experience of those changes. (Emphasis mine, *Descartes' Error* 139)

Damasio understands emotion and feeling as the bridge between rational and nonrational processes, between cortical and subcortical structures. *Descartes' Error: Emotion, Reason, and the Human Brain; The Feeling of What Happens: Body and Emotion in the Making of Consciousness; Looking for Spinoza: Joy, Sorrow, and the Feeling Brain* are about what Damasio calls the "feeling brain," the scientific elucidation of emotion and feeling, and the uncovering of their role in the construction and work of consciousness and culture. He writes:

[F]eelings are just as cognitive as any other perceptual image, and just as dependent on cerebral-cortex processing as any other image.

To be sure, feelings are about something different. But what makes them different is that they are first and foremost about the body, that they offer us the cognition of our visceral and musculoskeletal state as it becomes affected by preorganized mechanisms and by the cognitive structures we have developed under their influence. *Feelings let us mind the body*, attentively, as during an emotional state, or faintly, as during a background state. They let us mind the body "live," when they give us perceptual images of the body, or by "rebroadcast," when they give us recalled images of the body state appropriate to certain circumstances, in "as if" feelings . . .

I see feelings as having a truly privileged status . . . [B]ecause of their inextricable ties to the body, they come first in development and retain a primacy that subtly pervades our mental life. Because the brain is the body's captive audience, feelings are winners among equals. And since what comes first constitutes a frame of reference for what comes after, feelings have a say on how the rest of the brain and cognition go about their business. (Emphasis mine, *Descartes' Error* 158–59)

If James's *Principles of Psychology* and Damasio's research on the feeling brain write *why* "I feel, therefore I am," Jane Austen, George Eliot, and Thomas Hardy write "I feel, therefore I am the mind's story"—embodied, thinking, feeling, and relational. *Imagining Minds* is an integrational exchange on the nature of mind between six imagining minds—Jane Austen, George Eliot, and Thomas Hardy set in relation to William James, Antonio Damasio, and me. We are six minds caught, like Descartes, in a state of wonder that "I am," six minds, like Descartes, who must find a way to express the mystery of mind.

PART I

Jane Austen and Self-Consciousness

CHAPTER 1

"A Mind Lively and at Ease"

Imagination and *Emma*

1. FORD'S DOOR

There's a moment in chapter 27 of Jane Austen's *Emma* in which Emma withdraws briefly from Harriet's side to go to the door of Ford's shop to see what stretches out before her eyes:

> **Emma went to the door for amusement.—**
> **Much could not be hoped from the traffic**
> **of even the busiest part of Highbury;**
> —Mr. Perry walking hastily by, Mr. William Cox
> letting himself in at the office door, Mr. Cole's
> carriage horses returning from exercise, or a stray
> letter-boy on an obstinate mule,
> **were the liveliest objects she could hope to**
> **expect; and when her eyes fell only on**
> the butcher with his tray, a tidy old woman travel-
> ing homewards from shop with her full basket, two
> curs quarrelling over a dirty bone, and a string of
> dawdling children round the baker's little bow-
> window eyeing the gingerbread,
> **she knew she had no reason to complain,**
> **and was amused enough; quite enough still**
> **to stand at the door.**
> (Emphasis mine, 241)

I pause over this moment because it is unlike any other in *Emma*. Nowhere else in the novel does Austen list the objects before Emma's eyes. And it may be that nowhere else in Austen's writing does she create such a list of things set before her heroine's viewing and thinking consciousness. The objects listed are framed between three sentences that tell us something of why Emma seeks them with her eyes. At the top of the passage, like the top of the door's frame itself, Austen writes: "Emma went to the door for amusement." Emma looks out the door at the objects it frames because it holds the possibility of her delight. The first half of the list is not composed of objects she actually sees, only those she could expect to see, those from which "much could not be hoped"—the expected known of the traffic of Highbury—Mr. Perry walking, Mr. Cox at his office door, Mr. Cole's horses, a stray letter boy on a mule. Austen's dividing middle phrase of the framing door, "the liveliest objects she could hope to expect," reiterates both why Emma would go to the door—to seek enlivening—and why she would be disappointed—only *these objects* and *this level* of accompanying liveliness. The bottom of the frame, "she knew she had no reason to complain, and was amused enough; quite enough to stand at the door," tells us what she actually sees—the butcher with his tray, an old woman with her full basket, two dogs quarrelling over a bone, and children hanging about the baker's window—unexpected though known objects—are *enough* for Emma, in that they draw her attention and cause her to feel amused. At the conclusion of the passage, we arrive at a sentence that at once stands back from Emma at the door and takes us inside its meaning: "A mind lively and at ease, can do with *seeing nothing,* and *can see nothing* that does not answer" (emphasis mine, 241). In a scene of viewing and in a sentence that reflects back on its meaning, Austen frames the nature of Emma's viewing consciousness, which is to say, the nature of Emma's mind.[1]

The neurologist Antonio Damasio hypothesizes that for there to be consciousness, an exchange must occur between an organism and an object, the exchange that prompts change, what he calls "the feeling of knowing"—

1. For other recent perspectives on Austen's writing the nature of Emma's mind and imagination, see Juliet McMaster's "*Emma:* The Geography of a Mind." Without prior knowledge of each other's work, McMaster and I have written on the nature of Emma's mind with an uncanny similarity of attention to passage selection. Though our analysis differs, what we share is recognition of Austen's topic. As well, for further exploration of the relation of the imagination to reason see Carroll Fry's "'The Hunger of the Imagination': *Discordia Concors* in *Emma*"; and Barbara Moore's "Imagining the Real: The Development of Moral Imagination in *Emma.*" Drawing on aesthetic theory and brain-based research, Wendy S. Jones in her fine "*Emma,* Gender, and the Mind-Brain" explores how Emma learns to see sympathetically rather than artistically. Reading *Emma* "neurologically," Jones works to show how Austen writes sympathy as a "universal and central human capacity, and one, moreover, that we are morally obligated to cultivate" (318).

the experience of mind. Though wordless, this process follows uncannily Austen's description of what happens to Emma standing at the door. Here's Damasio:

> How do we ever begin to be conscious? Specifically, how do we ever have a sense of self in the act of knowing? We begin with a first trick. The trick consists of constructing an account of what happens within the organism when the organism interacts with an object, be it actually perceived or recalled, be it within body boundaries (e.g., pain) or outside of them (e.g., a landscape). This account is a simple narrative without words. It does have characters (the organism, the object). It unfolds in time. And it has a beginning, middle, and an end. The beginning corresponds to the initial state of the organism. The middle is the arrival of the object. The end is made up of reactions that result in a modified state of the organism. (*The Feeling* 168)

Emma at the door expects "objects" outside her body's boundary—the known landscape of Highbury's businessmen. From the initial state in time of the "organism" Emma seeking objects for amusement, to the middle state of the objects' actual arrival outside Emma's perception—the surprise appearance of the unnamed though recognizable figures of Highbury busily engaged in their own object pursuits, to the end state of Emma changed by the exchange—Emma amused—plots one narrative of how Emma experiences the feeling of knowing or having a mind: "A mind lively and at ease . . . can see nothing that does not answer."

But what of the first half of Austen's description of what it means to have a mind lively and at ease, "a mind lively and at ease, can do with seeing nothing"? We learn from the opening words of *Emma* that no real restraint or limit has been imposed on Emma, in fact, that by nature and upbringing nothing stands in her way: "Emma Woodhouse, handsome, clever, and rich, with a comfortable home and happy disposition, seemed to unite some of the best blessings of existence; and had lived nearly twenty-one years in the world with very little to distress or vex her" (37). Without a mother to check her development and act as a model, with "a most affectionate, indulgent father" (37) who dotes on her and himself acts the part of the child, and with a governess who comes to assume the part of friend "who had such an affection for her as could never find fault" (38), Emma "seems" to "unite some of the best blessings of existence." The moral lessons of the novel focus on the uncovering of "seems," why Emma's blessings are not yet "best." The aesthetic lessons of the novel focus on what happens to a clever mind when it develops unchecked and roundly supported by almost all other minds to believe that it is "best," even "perfection."[2] Such a mind is "lively and at ease." Such a mind, Austen claims, "can do with seeing nothing." However like all conscious organisms Emma is in Damasio's terms, the character Emma is apparently distinctive in that her mind can do with seeing nothing, can do without objects, which means can do with or make do with (only) itself. How is this? Or, what might Austen add to Damasio's "simple narrative" of the mystery that is consciousness?

2. MISS EMMA WOODHOUSE IS *NOT* A GREAT READER

Emma Woodhouse has a fantasy life. Mr. Knightley describes how Emma's tendency toward fancy informs the qualities of Emma's mind: "She will never submit to any thing requiring industry and patience, and a subjection of fancy to understanding" (66). Emma's liveliness makes her not patient and her ease requires no industry. Meaning to improve Harriet's mind, Emma's mind finds "it was easier to chat than to study; much pleasanter to let her imagination range and work at Harriet's fortune, than to be labouring to enlarge Harriet's comprehension or exercise it on sober facts" (95). Such a moment of dramatized consciousness takes us *inside* Emma's *mind* and keeps us *outside* to question its *character*—to better know her resistance to labor and sober facts, her ease with "chat," and the predominance of her imagination as it "ranges" over the moment. Is there any cause for an exertion past what comes easiest and most naturally to Emma? Thinking about why Emma's mind is the way it is, Knightley continues: "And ever since she was twelve, Emma has been mistress of the house and of you all. In her mother she lost the only person who could cope with her. She inherits her mother's talents, and must have been under subjection to her" (66). Knightley claims, therefore, two forms of "subjection" missing in Emma's experience: the self-experience of fancy made subject to understanding and the other-experience of self made subject to another. Austen writes in Emma a subjectivity not made subject, a mind free of other minds and free of the accompanying urge to try to understand those

2. Harriet's exclamations most of all support Emma's world-viewing consciousness, as in her response to how Emma imagines Elton's feelings for Harriet: "'Whatever you say is always right . . . and therefore I suppose, and believe, and hope it must be so; but otherwise I could not have imagined it. It is so much beyond anything I deserve'" (100). The crisis of the novel occurs when corroborating support for the worldview of Emma's mind is called into doubt—at Box Hill. Emma must, in almost the same breath, hear herself named "perfection" by Mr. Weston and "unfeeling" by Mr. Knightley. For Emma to experience Mr. Knightley's doubt is to know a crack in her self-consciousness. The other mind has broken in . . . .

other minds. Austen writes into being a character, I want to suggest, who has an imagination, an imagination that more often than not "can do with seeing nothing" (certainly with not seeing a "sober fact"), an imagination that defines in fundamental ways her particular inwardness, which is to say her self-consciousness. Emma claims an understanding of others' minds—that she can imagine how others imagine—as in particular about Mr. Martin and in general about all men, "A man always imagines a woman to be ready for anybody who asks her" (87); or about Mr. Elton and Harriet's portrait: "It is his companion all this evening, his solace, his delight. It opens his designs to his family, it introduces you among them . . . How cheerful, how animated, how suspicious, how busy their imaginations all are!" (83). Not made subject to others' minds and not made subject to her own sense of reason, Emma's imagination ranges freely—happy, fluent, unbound. Damasio writes, "The fluency of ideation is reduced in sadness and increased in happiness" (*Looking* 92). With no critical judgment from within or without to make her unhappy or to check her, Emma's imagining powers of ideation are "lively and at ease."

Don Quixote's madness, his living out his desire to fantasize, grows out of his voracious reading habit. Feeding on books leads, Cervantes tells us, to a mind that no longer knows the difference between the "real" and the "imaginary." Likewise, another Emma, Madame Bovary, spends her early years in the convent reading the romances that shape her self-fantasies that lead her to desire the fulfillment of these read and then adopted fantasies. And another Austen heroine, Catherine Morland, believes *The Mysteries of Udolpho* to be more true in its depiction of what constitutes an abbey than the actual Abbey that meets her eyes. Reading creates a fantasy, or an imaginary conception that precedes a sensory reality for Catherine and that holds her consciousness until ongoing encounters with what we are to imagine being a perceptually present object to her—Northanger Abbey— leads her consciousness to a new understanding. The nineteenth-century novel, rife with readers inside its texts, uses the figure of the reader as a literary embodiment of its actual consumers, the genuine readers, who find in these mirrored companions descriptions of how their consciousnesses imagine from reading images. Perhaps such imagining leads to a brief refusal to know from perception, or perhaps to radical redefinitions of self: "I am a romantic heroine"; "I am the knight of the woeful countenance." Yet, in all instances, the imaginary reader reading inside a novel reflects back to us the engagement, play, even transformation of consciousness because of the mind's encounter with narrative language. These inscribed readers perform in their reading of novels and romances what it is George Bluestone tells us the novel is about—the making of the hidden life of consciousness. For Bluestone, in his classic work on adaptation, *Novels into Film*, the novel presents states of mind "which are precisely defined by the absence in them of the visible world. Conceptual imaging, by definition, has no existence in space" (382). Whereas we perceive the image of the visible world in space, we conceive the reading image in mind. Bluestone writes on the word as a phenomenon distinct both from the objects of the physical world and from the sign of other signifying systems, such as pictures. He draws our attention to the word's capacity to create the consciousness of fantasy.

Which brings me back to Emma Woodhouse. Austen's Emma does *not* read. Mr. Knightley says of her, "'Emma has been meaning to read more ever since she was twelve years old. I have seen a great many lists of her drawing up at various times of books that she meant to read regularly through. . . . But I have done with expecting any course of steady reading from Emma'" (66). Knightley tells Miss Taylor[3] in no uncertain terms that Emma's mind has not been shaped by the written word, has not been shaped apparently by any force stronger than itself. Whereas other novelists make the desire to read novels be the etiology that accounts for their protagonists' fantasy lives, Austen makes the proclivity toward fancy be the first feature that distinguishes the self-consciousness of Emma—makes it, that is, be the constituent feature of her consciousness *by nature* as opposed to *by reading*.

Emma fancies things about herself as the early means of constructing her knowledge of herself and her world. About the marriage of Miss Taylor and Mr. Weston she declares in the first chapter: "I made the match myself. I made the match, you know, four years ago; and to have it take place, and be proved in the right, when so many people said Mr. Weston would never marry again, may comfort me for anything" (43). Emma plays with this fancy in her mind because it gives her, she claims, "joy" and "comfort." But she believes herself to have this power because experience has taught her so: Emma claims she imagined the match and thus it happened. Her wish was not just granted but made true by her power. Austen writes that in part Emma's imagining herself to have such powers comes from Emma's disposition "to think a little too well of herself" and her lived experience as "having rather too much her own way" (37). For much of the novel, Emma understands that the world exists as she experiences it in her imagining consciousness; she fancies that it moves and responds to her design

3. While it is true "Miss Taylor" becomes "Mrs. Weston" from the opening pages of *Emma*, like Mr. Woodhouse (probably because of Mr. Woodhouse), I am never able to stop thinking of her as "poor Miss Taylor" and so call her here by her given name, her name before the "origin of all change" changes her.

because she has yet to learn that it does not. This is the narcissism of her imagining; it is what distinguishes her mind's self-consciousness. In Emma, Austen writes a character who fancies the world to be a reflection of her mind's imaginings of it. Using the figures about her who exist almost as blank slates onto which Emma can project, Emma imagines *ideas* about their natures (that Miss Taylor and Mr. Weston should wed, that Harriet was "exactly the young friend she wanted—exactly the something which her home required" [56], that Harriet should marry somebody—Mr. Elton or Frank—but not Mr. Martin and certainly not Mr. Knightley), and then models her actions to fulfill those visions because she understands objects and events in the world to corroborate her imagining visions of it. According to William James, "Fantasy or imagination are the names given to the faculty of reproducing copies of the original once felt. The imagination is called *reproductive* when the copies are literal; *productive* when elements from different originals are combined so as to make new wholes" (emphasis mine, II, 44). Emma's imagination is productive in that she brings to her mental copy of the other her idea of him or her, combined to make a new whole. Emma's mind cannot do wholly with seeing nothing, therefore. James writes, "Sensations, once experienced, modify the nervous organism, so that copies of them arise again in the mind after the original is gone. No mental copy, however, can arise in the mind, of any kind of sensation which has never been directly experienced from without" (44). "The original once felt" must be before or be remembered to her imagining consciousness. Unlike the inventing mind of Austen the novelist, Emma the character needs to have at least seen or even just heard, it seems, of Miss Taylor and Mr. Weston and Harriet, but she needs not much more than that to be able to combine these images with her fantasizing energy. Emma's capacity to combine together in new ways what she has seen or heard, what for James constitutes "productive imagination," is for Damasio "the images of recall." About this Damasio writes: "The images that we reconstitute in recall occur side by side with the images formed upon stimulation from the exterior, the images reconstituted from the brain's interior are less vivid than those prompted by the exterior. They are 'faint,' as David Hume put it, in comparison with the 'lively' images generated by stimuli from outside the brain. But they are images nonetheless" (*Descartes' Error* 108). And all of them—Hume, Damasio, and James—follow Aristotle's line of thought on the nature and power of the imagination in *De Anima* in which he describes imagination as "sensation without matter." Aristotle writes: "As sight is the most highly developed sense, the name *phantasia* (imagination) has been formed from *phaos* (light) because it is not possible to see without light. And because imaginations remain in the organs of sense and resemble sensations, animals in their actions are largely guided by them."[4] It is significant that Aristotle makes the imagination be a power of mind informed by light and the visual—by what can be perceived visually—*without* its being what is actually perceived—"sensation without matter." For Damasio, all of our mentation is done in "images," by which he means not just visual markers of the seen but all somatic markers of the sensed. Emma's imagination is pleased both by the actual lively images before her and those less-lively recalled sensations in mental reformulation. Recalled image-sensations enable her to create something new formed out of something old. How different Emma's mind work is from that of Mr. Knightley, whose keen sense of discernment comes from the careful observation of what in reality stands before him in space and time. The nature of Mr. Knightley's mind—his empirical bent, his realism—has everything to do with his attention to how others behave and the deductions and conclusions he draws about them from observation over time. As an empiricist who does not impose his image on the world, but rather who seeks to discern the objects as they are, in themselves, and from this come to an understanding of the world outside him and his relation to it, Mr. Knightley works from the object in, whereas Emma works from her mind out. However noble and benevolent he may be, Mr. Knightley is distinctly unimaginative. Or perhaps it is more just to say that his is, in James's terms, the "reproductive" imagination of a scientist or a detective, not the "productive" imagination of an artist or a novelist.

3. "AN IMAGINIST, LIKE HERSELF"

Like Emma, the language of Austen the novelist resists the seen as the requirement for image-making or imagining. Jean-Paul Sartre asserts too broadly that this is true of all novels. He writes in *The Psychology of Imagination*: "[I]mages appear apart from the reading process itself, that is, when the reader is thinking of the events of the preceding chapter, when he is *dreaming over the book,* etc. In short, images appear when we cease reading, or when our attention begins to wander. But when the reader is engrossed, there are no mental images" (emphasis mine, 90). How are we to picture

---

4. Like the philosophers to follow him, Aristotle is clear to distinguish between the imagination that makes images of what it directly senses, what he calls "sensitive imagination" and attributes to all animals, and what he calls "deliberative" or "calculative imagination." For Aristotle deliberative calculation is less about the recalled image and more about imagining an intended future. I am drawing here from Arnold H. Modell's references to Aristotle in his useful compendium of visions of the imagination and its role in meaning-making in *Imagination and the Meaningful Brain* (211).

Emma? "Emma Woodhouse, handsome, clever, and rich." But there is no attempt at visual particularity in these words.[5] Sartre asserts, like Bluestone, that words by their nature do not "picture." Words do not make images. Of course, they are wrong. Concrete words such as "flower" or "apple" do immediately activate images. But the more abstract descriptors that Austen chooses are not of this type, and do not immediately and irresistibly call up particular pictures. We do, Sartre writes, make images when our eyes leave the written text and we go into a state of reverie about the narrative when we are no longer reading the actual narrative. He does not, then, take words to be wholly divorced from what leads us to imagine, as Sartre later writes: "They represent the area of contact between us and the imaginary world . . . the reader is in the presence of a world" (90). Austen has no real interest in a material language, in a language that translates the experience of seeing phenomena into the semiotic system of words. As James Wood describes it, Austen gives birth to the novel's capacity to write inwardness, or to the "discovery of how to represent the brokenness of the mind's communication with itself" ("Heroic Consciousness" 25). This is why the scene of Emma's looking out the door at Ford's shop at the objects before her stands out. What Austen writes more generally has everything to do with the making up of a world—call that Emma's "large mental chamber" (Wood 27)—or her self-consciousness of "fancy" joined to her mapping of how the world external to her fancy holds or seems to correspond to her ideas of it. Admiring Harriet's soft blue eyes as she imagines how to improve Harriet, Emma basks in "the real good will of a mind delighted with its own ideas" (54). Emma's imagining fancy is most defined not by word-depictions, but by word-thoughts. I associate this distinction with how the psychologist Stephen Kosslyn defines the human brain's two fundamental modes of representation of mental imagery, as depictive and propositional. He writes in *The Case for Mental Imagery:*

5. While there is no visual particularity in "handsome, clever, rich," there is some it seems in Miss Taylor's description of Emma in chapter 5 when she discusses Emma's nature with Mr. Knightley: "'Can you imagine any thing nearer perfect beauty than Emma altogether in face and figure?' . . . 'Such an eye!—the true hazel eye—and so brilliant! regular features, open countenance, with a complexion! oh! what a bloom of full health, and such a pretty height and size; such a firm and upright figure. There is health, not merely in her bloom, but in her air, her head, her glance. One hears sometimes of a child being "the picture of health"; now Emma always gives me the idea of being the complete picture of grown-up health. She is loveliness itself'" (67–68). Here, Austen sees Emma through Miss Taylor's eyes—eyes that render Emma concrete through one particular—hazel eyes. Otherwise, what is "perfect beauty," "regular features," "open countenance," "bloom of health," "loveliness itself"? However gesturing toward description these phrases are, they do not render a particular picture of Emma. Instead, they make Emma the ideal woman in face and figure—loveliness itself—not someone we can see, but an idea we might imagine of the "ideal." "'Can you *imagine* any thing nearer perfect beauty?'" Miss Taylor asks of Mr. Knightley and of us.

[D]epictive representations make explicit and accessible all aspects of shape and other perceptual qualities (such as color and texture), as well as the spatial relations among each point. In contrast, propositional representations make explicit and accessible semantic interpretations, which can include aspects of shape and other perceptual qualities. Depictive representations of shape must also incidentally specify size and orientation; propositional representations only specify what was specifically included when the representation was created. Depending on the precise task at hand, one or the other format may be most useful. (14)

We read in the door scene how Emma constructs *depictive* representations in her mind—that list of objects, what they look like to her viewing eye—not mental pictures of color, shape, and size, but depictions nonetheless ordered by sequence, age, and activity. We know the door moment of mental representation is rare because of its contrast to how Emma mostly engages in the mental imagining of *propositional* representation-making. Like Austen, Emma's capacity for "fancy" is itself a capacity to compose *semantic propositions* about the nature of the world, propositions that are later tested in the world that is apart from her imagining construction of it.

Perhaps most vividly, Emma conceives a fancy for Frank Churchill because of the "sound" of Frank Churchill and the "idea" of Frank Churchill and of his seeming already to belong to her because of the connections between families. This conception will guide her later experience of Frank Churchill. Austen writes of Emma's imagining mind:

> She *heard* enough to know that Mr. Weston was giving some information about his son; she *heard the words* "my son," and "Frank," and "my son," repeated several times over; and from a few other *half-syllables* very much suspected that he was announcing an early visit from his son. . . .
>
> Now, it so happened that in spite of Emma's resolution of never marrying, there was something in the *name,* in the *idea* of Mr. Frank Churchill, which always *interested* her. She had frequently thought—especially since his father's marriage with Miss Taylor—that if she *were* to marry, he was the very person to suit her in age, character and condition. He seemed by this connection between the families quite to belong to her . . . [S]he had a great *curiosity* to see him, a *decided intention* of finding him pleasant, of being liked by him to a certain degree, and a sort of *pleasure in the idea* of their being coupled in their friends' imaginations. (Emphasis mine, 139–40)

Emma does not picture Frank in her consciousness. She hears the sound of him, "Frank," "my son," "half-syllables" of his impending arrival. And she thinks him, "something in the name, in the idea of Mr. Frank Churchill." Emma imagines him as language—uttered and thought—but not pictured. Emma's attempt at picturing—the portrait of Harriet—is like her attempts at reading, lazy and inattentive. But her capacity to imagine ideas is vivid and completely attentive. As an idea, the nondepicted Frank is a semantic proposition that Emma holds in mind as "interesting," an idea about which she feels curiosity and one she intends to find pleasant in reality. Emma's imagining joins the idea of him to her, joins him to her in everyone's imaginations, and makes him in some subjunctive future the man she would marry, were she ever to marry. Emma's consciousness is by nature, I want to claim, like Austen's, one that constructs fancies based on ideas from names, from words. These primarily are the objects of Emma's mind, a mind that imagines in propositions first and experiences later. "A mind lively and at ease"—Emma's mind, Austen's mind—"can do with seeing nothing" if it is a mind that imagines in language, not in pictures.[6] And yet Austen describes this imagining not as a collection of thoughts but as "sensations." The passage moves to a new paragraph that begins, "With such sensations, Mr. Elton's civilities were dreadfully ill-timed" (140). How do Emma's imaginings work as sensations? Can words be sensations?

In his chapter "The Consciousness of Self," William James writes about the relation between sensation and idea this way:

> In attending to either an idea or a sensation belonging to a particular sense-sphere, the movement is the adjustment of the sense-organ, felt as it occurs. I cannot think in visual terms without feeling a fluctuating play of pressures, convergences, divergences, and accommodations in my eye-balls . . . My brain appears to me as if shot across with lines of direction, of which I have become conscious as my attention has shifted from one sense-organ to another, in passing to successive outer things, or in following trains of varying sense-ideas . . . *It would follow that our entire feeling of spiritual activity, or what commonly passes by that name[,] is really a feeling of bodily activities* whose exact nature is by most men overlooked. (Emphasis mine, I, 300–301)

For James there is no idea without the mind's sensation in one form or

---

6. In "Emma: The Shadow Novelist," Loraine Fletcher has caught in a thematic way the relation between Austen the novelist and Emma the story-imaginist. See as well David Lee Minter's "Aesthetic Vision and the World of *Emma*"; Stuart Tave's chapter "The Imagination of Emma Woodhouse," in his *Some Words of Jane Austen;* Miriam B. Mandel's "Fiction and Fiction-Making: *Emma*. For me, it is essential to understand the nature of Emma's imagining mind in relation to how Austen writes the nature of that mind, which is to say the relation of Austen's imagination to her depiction of self-consciousness itself.

another of it, no "spirit" or consciousness of self without a "feeling of
bodily activity" creating it. When considering what constitutes a subject of
discourse, what he calls a "conception," James asserts, "Each act of conception results from our attention singling out some one part of the mass of
matter for thought which the world presents, and holding fast to it, without confusion" (461–62). Perhaps the imagining mind moves between the
sensations it perceives to an attentional selective mind that conceives and
sculpts as it "images" its subject into being. Damasio writes this about the
brain's idea-image-making: "Events in the body are represented as ideas in
the mind. There are representational 'correspondences' and they go in one
direction—from body to mind . . . The mind is filled with images from
the flesh and images from the body's special sensory probes . . . Once you
form an idea of a certain object, you can form an idea of the idea, and
on . . . *The most basic kind of self is an idea*" (emphasis mine, *Descartes' Error*
212–15). For Damasio, therefore, all of our ideas are images of the brain's
representation of the body's experience as a living organism, affecting and
being affected by in the world. The idea of felt-experience, the idea of an
idea, the idea of a self, find their origin in the brain's image-processing of
the body's experience. That we experience at all, have ideas at all, come
from the "representational correspondence from body to mind." For James
and Damasio, therefore, all ideas must begin as sensations. What of reading
Emma? Do we "sense" Emma's imagined ideas? Are Emma's imaginings
James's "sense-ideas" and Damasio's image-ideas?

Elaine Scarry's *Dreaming by the Book* breaks open how the in-the-moment
experience of reading leads us to imagine sensations through repeated
linguistic patterns of the verbal arts, such as describing in words the presence of flashes of light against a background of darkness (what she calls
"radiant ignition") in order to coax out of the imagination an imagined
sensation of "vivacity." Scarry's text can be read as a response to Sartre's
understanding of language as that which by itself cannot produce images
except for when "dreaming over the book" in her descriptions of how
narrative language prompts from our imaginations the "as if" experience
of visual perception. She builds her argument from some of the most
tactile, material, and imagistic of authors—Flaubert, Emily Brontë, Tolstoy,
Hardy, Homer, Ovid. However, Austen does not call on the techniques or
patterns Scarry discerns to account for how language works to lead us to
imagine visual sensation: to "make pictures," "move pictures," or "repicture."
How are we to understand "handsome, clever, and rich" as the portrait
of a lady? Very deliberately in *Emma,* Austen makes portraits, but they
are almost without a physical trace. A parade of women come before our
reading eyes—twelve chapters of them before Mr. Elton's proposal, the first

major turn of plot—a parade of women who all reflect back through their mirroring presences how we are to "picture" Emma. Miss Taylor, Harriet, Miss Bates, Jane Fairfax, and later Augusta Hawkins all help us to *sense* Emma, but not because we can see them or her. The closest we come to such a visual record of seeing is Emma's incorrect portrait painting of Harriet, a picture that represents Emma's distorted vision of Harriet from the outside and from the inside. It is this inside space that most interests Austen, always, the space that constitutes what, as a writer, Austen represents and how—*character portraits*. I want to suggest that, in addition to the character portraits of other women who all stand in some relation to her, it's Emma's propositional imaginings themselves that create a representing self-consciousness that we sense—a *picture of Emma's mind*.

William James defines five characters of thought:

(1) Every thought tends to be part of personal consciousness.
(2) Within each personal consciousness thought is always changing.
(3) Within each personal consciousness, thought is sensibly continuous.
(4) It always appears to deal with objects independent of itself.
(5) It is interested in some parts of these objects to the exclusion of others, and welcomes or rejects—*chooses* from among them, in a word—all the while. (I, 225)

Emma's mind follows all five of James's characters of thought, which is to say, we know when we read *Emma* that we are in the presence of a personal consciousness. By my count fourteen of the fifty-five chapters of the novel begin from inside Emma's mind, while all the chapters (with the exception of Knightley's and Miss Taylor's conversation about Emma's nature in chapter 5) bring us repeatedly to the presence of Emma's consciousness through Austen's use of dramatized consciousness. Emma's moments of thinking, her natural tendency to imagine into being a world of ideas, her struggles to make sense of how the external world succeeds or fails to correspond to her imaginings of it create, I want to suggest, the presence of Emma's mind as a felt, reading sensation. As much as Austen's other women protagonists must each work to understand fully the nature of their thoughts and feelings in the theater of their own minds, it is Emma most of all who lives in a narrative state of self-imagining and self-reflection—there is very little to "distress or vex" that narrative state of inward turn. Reading Emma's propositions about the nature of the world—how she imagines the world—causes us to sense that we are in the presence of her mind.

The adventure of Frank, Harriet, and the gipsy children prompts Emma to name for herself, in this fine instance of dramatized consciousness, how she thinks, meaning Emma names the nature of her own mind and how it works.[7] Austen's discovery of how to narrate from outside and inside her protagonists' minds almost simultaneously, seamlessly, is critical to why we pay attention in part to how Emma defines her world as a reflection of how she imagines it. We read Austen's distance from Emma's ideas as we read Emma's ideas as if inside her mind, a double-voiced/double-minded discourse that allows both for ironic distance and self-reflective nearness. In what follows, Austen at once separates herself from Emma's mind—when she names Emma "she" and reports her thoughts in the past tense—and unites with Emma's mind—when Emma names herself and imagines in the present tense:

> Could a linguist, could a grammarian, could even a mathematician have seen what she did . . . without feeling that circumstances had been at work to make them peculiarly interesting to each other?—How much more must an *imaginist,* like herself, be on fire with *speculation* and *foresight!*—especially with such a ground-work of *anticipation* as her mind had already made. (Emphasis mine, 331)

Emma invents a word to define how her mind works—"imaginist." "Imaginist" is as close as Austen can come to defining "Emma." If the novel tells the story of what that means, which to say, defines how Emma knows herself to be this invented-imaginary word, "imaginist," Austen writes into being in the story of their relation—"Emma" and "imaginist"—a new understanding of being. "Cogito, ergo sum" for Emma means "I imagine, therefore I am." As an imaginist, Emma imagines and makes predictions about the future: she engages in "speculation," "foresight," and "anticipation"—all acts of seeing not what is before her but what might be in the future—these are her ideas as dreams and plots. Damasio calls this our capacity to "mind the future" (*Looking* 146).

Current research in the neuroscience of memory posits that brain-injured people with amnesia are cut off from both the past and the future, "marooned in the present, as helpless at imagining future experiences as

---

7. I use F. R. Leavis's term "dramatized consciousness" because for me it is a better name than "free indirect style" or "free indirect discourse" for Austen's technique for narrating her protagonists' minds. On the topic of who "discovered" this narrative technique and its different names, see Joseph Bray's "The Source of 'Dramatized Consciousness': Richardson, Austen, and Stylistic Influence." Bray's interest in origins prompts him to uncover the "first" naming of this technique, in 1912 by Charles Bally, who, in writing about French Modernism, names it "le style indirect libre." For further discussion of this adventure and the neologism at which it arrives, "imaginist," see Miriam B. Mandel in "Fiction and Fiction-Making: *Emma.*"

they are at retrieving old ones."[8] What this suggests is that when the hip-
pocampus—the neural seat of memory—is injured, a person's capacities
both to remember and to imagine are affected. If memory holds our sense
of the past, imagination, these scientists contend, holds our sense of the
future. And the neural networking of both, they claim, is almost identical.
In his chapter "The Perception of Time," William James writes about how
our relation to objects holds both memories of the past and imaginings
of the future this way: "A simple sensation is an abstraction, and all our
concrete states of mind are representations of objects with some kind of
complexity. Part of that complexity is *the echo of the objects just past,* and
in a less degree, perhaps *the foretaste of those just to arrive*" (emphasis mine,
II, 605). Austen constructs narrative worlds that tell time quite differently
from one another, in fact, that make the relation to time be part of the
story of what is imaginable or how a story is imaginable.[9] The bright sun-
niness of *Pride and Prejudice* has much to do with its predominantly day-lit
landscape of "now." For as long as Mrs. Bennett can hold on to thoughts
of the entailment does the novel imagine the future; likewise, for as long
as Darcy and Lizzy stay "lost" to each other or Lizzy reflects back on her
relation to Darcy and his letter does the novel imagine a past—which is to
say, perhaps the length of a chapter. *Pride and Prejudice* essentially imagines
"now"—life unfolding—unhindered for the most part by projection or
recollection except in the analytic moments of working-through, and tells
its story essentially in the present tense of dialogue or "scene."[10] To find its
way back to the present—to live again—*Persuasion* must imagine the possibility that there be a present tense to follow its crushing, unnatural end.
Set as the beginning of the novel, the end of the present must be recovered
from out of its ashes as the past. *Northanger Abbey* brings to its present the
temporal landscape of the Romance novels that inform how Catherine
"reads" what she experiences—Catherine's lived present tense reveals for
her the timescape of the Romances she reads superimposed on or in them.
As much as *The Mysteries of Udolpho* references the Middle Ages, it is the
"read Middle Ages," meaning a Romance of time, a time Catherine must
learn to distinguish from lived time. If Elinor and Marianne live in the
present tense and only know how to interpret what is before them in the
present, what the men in *Sense and Sensibility* bring to the women is the

    8. For a distillation of the current research on how amnesia reveals a brain-based relationship
between memory and imagination, see "Amnesiacs May Be Cut Off From Past and Future Alike"
by Benedict Carey in *The New York Times,* January 23, 2007, front page "Health and Fitness" section.
    9. For a more sustained analysis of Austen's imagining of time in her novels, see Julia Prewitt
Brown's article, "Jane Austen: In Search of Time Present."
    10. Genette's *Narrative Discourse* discussion of "scene" for me finds its great instance in *Pride and
Prejudice.*

past—their pasts—that which Elinor and Marianne must learn to recognize and interpret. More than that, when Edward and Willoughby each leaves the woman to whom he is attached, she, too, gains a past. *Sense and Sensibility* tells a story of how the woman comes to know and gain the past tense as part of her experience of being alive in time—something like the fall from the Edenic present into the knowledge of temporal experience, that which requires loss. Men, for Austen in *Sense and Sensibility,* are the creators and bestowers of loss. The past happens as story in *Mansfield Park* as well, but differently. Fanny is the keeper of the past, not Henry, not Edmund, not even Sir Thomas. She bears the past and calls it up in memory when the others would just as soon forget. This is why Fanny can be so hard to bear—like a historian, she forces the present to be known and understood always in relation to the remembered past by her, forgotten or repressed often by others. Fanny's rapturous recognition of the powers of the human mind focuses on how the mind exists in relation to time—as remembering and forgetting—a recognition that makes her, like Kant, at least for a moment, a philosopher of the categories of mind. Here's Fanny musing on the nature of how she experiences time in relation to how she experiences the shrubbery where she now sits with Mary Crawford:[11]

> "Every time I come into this shrubbery, I am more struck with its growth and beauty. Three years ago, this was nothing but a rough hedgerow along the upper side of the field, never thought of as anything, or capable of becoming anything; and now it is converted into a walk, and it would be difficult to say whether most valuable as a convenience or an ornament; and perhaps in another three years we may be forgetting—almost forgetting what it was before. How wonderful, how very wonderful the operations of time, and the changes of the human mind!" And following the latter train of thought, she soon afterwards added: "If any one faculty of our nature may be called *more* wonderful than the rest, I do think it is memory. There seems something more speakingly incomprehensible in the powers, the failures, the inequalities of memory, than in any other intelligences. The memory is sometimes so retentive, so serviceable, so obedient—at others, so bewildered and so weak—and at others again, so tyrannic, so beyond controul [*sic*]!—We are to be sure a miracle in every way—but our powers of recollecting and of forgetting, do seem peculiarly past finding out." (*Mansfield Park* 173–74)

11. I am indebted to Diana Birchall, fellow JASNA speaker and lifelong Austen scholar, for bringing this passage to my attention again.

Fanny understands that to recognize the difference between the past and the present, to recognize the evolutionary change of one time to another, one must have a memory. However insignificant the particular evolution of hedgerow to shrubbery to wall over the course of three years, seeing that development depends on the mind's remembering what something was, in order to appreciate what it now is, and what it will become. And however apt the shrubbery metonym is as a marker for Fanny's development over time, what is most remarkable about this passage is how it prompts Fanny to meditate on what her seeing of the shrubbery reveals—namely, what is most wonderful and most mysterious about the human mind—the workings of memory. *Mansfield Park* tells the story of what it means to remember—as the attention of mind—and what it means to forget—as the inattention of mind—and their consequences.

Emma's mind both creates meaning and predicts futures: she acts as author and augur. Emma's generation of frames about the nature of the objects before her and the nature of her self in relation to them are her indicative ideas of her world and her self. Emma's inventions of future frames are her subjunctive ideas. While constructed from the reflective past tense of Austen's authoring mind, *Emma* reflects the future tense of Emma's imagining-authoring mind. There are few novels written with an inscribed future tense: *Emma* is Austen's only future-tensed novel because it is her only novel that narrates how its heroine imagines *change*. Both forms of Emma's ideation-making—those that create meaning as author and those that predict the future as augur—define a self-consciousness that imagines narratives. The plots Emma imagines narrate change, but change she defines. The change comes not from the object affecting her, but rather from her imagining the object changed. This is why Emma's imagination so often gets it wrong: Emma's mental chamber stages scene after scene of changes imagined not from experience mixed with idea but from projected idea alone. This is what makes Emma's imagination both necessary to and insufficient as the whole of Emma's consciousness—that which distinguishes her imagining consciousness from the way Damasio imagines consciousness. Wayne Booth describes the novel's "insufficiency" of narrating consciousness when he compares *Emma* to *Persuasion:* "In *Emma* there are many breaks in the point of view, because Emma's beclouded mind cannot do the whole job" (250); and later, "Except for these few intrusions, and one in chapter 6, Anne's own mind is sufficient in *Persuasion,* but we can never rely completely on Emma" (253). What is wrong with Emma's narrating mind? The plot Emma's narrating mind imagines again and again is "the origin of all change"—marriage—which is a foreseeable future not seen, in the sense of actually lived in Austen's novels, only imagined. We can foresee the "perfect happiness" of the union of Knightley and Emma, but we do not see it because it's not the living of the "origin of all change" that interests Austen; instead it's its imagining—by Emma. For Emma to see this perfect happiness in the sense of imagining it, *she must change,* which means *the nature of her mind must change.*

4. "A SUBJECTION OF THE FANCY
TO THE UNDERSTANDING"

Stuart Tave's *Some Words of Jane Austen* remains one of the great collections of readings of Austen, teased out from his attention to a particular set of words or a word he discerns to be a significant verbal thread for understanding how each novel creates meaning. In "The Imagination of Emma Woodhouse," Tave, as do I, reads forward the importance of Emma's imagination—but to different ends. Tave writes of the thematics of Emma's imagination—as a fault of mind—as in, "The danger of a prevailing imagination . . . is that imagination reshapes the world, and the self, to the desires of mind . . . Turning from the difficult work of seeing and understanding what is before it and within it, and the exertion of acting upon that knowledge, the mind bends the world to its own wants" (208). When imagination is understood thematically like this, it opens the way for attention to moral failure. Austen links Emma's imagination to her lapses in ethical judgment—a stinginess of goodwill or an absence of tenderness—faults that come from having an imagination "unchecked" by experience. "The real evils of Emma's situation were the power of having too much her own way, and a disposition to think a little too well of herself" (37) is a statement at once about how Emma's situation in life and disposition of mind combine to create the "dangers" of Emma's narcissism. Tave's thematic reading of Emma's imagination as "failure of imagination" leads him to dwell on the difference between "fancy" and "real." "A prevailing imagination" leads not just to lapses in ethical judgment but also to epistemological confusion—Emma, for Tave, cannot discern the difference between the "imaginary" and the "true":

> The imaginist's failure of imagination is a loss of delicacy for others, a loss in recognition of the active principle which is not the self, an imposition of the self upon the shape of truth that is another. Mr. Knightley told her the truth and the truth mortifies. But most humiliating is the discovery of the imposition she has made upon her own truth of self. (237)

Reflecting Samuel Johnson's writings on the human condition and reading Austen as an admiring, concurring reader herself of Johnson, Tave understands Emma's lapses of character and distance from the truth to be the products of her prevailing imagination—prevailing because not tempered by reason—and the capacity to make good judgments that the judgment of reason brings. For Tave, what's at stake for Emma in knowing the difference between "the real" and "fancy" is knowing the truth.

Emma's limits of mind reveal the fundamental place this prevailing imagination holds in Emma's mind, in her having a mind. Emma's situation in life and disposition of mind free her not just to think a little too well of herself but, I would suggest, to be able to think of *herself at all,* and to be able to think of the *world at all.* Without an imagining mind, Emma would have no failures of self-understanding or of other-understanding because she would have no groundwork on which to build a conscious understanding of self and other. It is Emma's imagination that enables her to fail at times in her moral judgment or in her consideration because it is what creates the mental space for ethical evaluation and understanding. To imagine makes *possible,* is what it means to hold in mind consciously, an idea of self, of other, of world—and this is what I think the complex verbal narrative *Emma* brings to Damasio's wordless "simple narrative" of consciousness. Jean Piaget, the great psychologist of child development, writes in *The Principles of Genetic Epistemology,* "[A]ll knowledge involves an aspect of novel elaboration" and "creation of new material" (14). Not just the reflection of embodied *a priori* structures or just the product of empirical encounters with the world, the human mind for Piaget creates "knowledge as a continuous construction" (17). I read *Emma* as the portrait of a mind engaged in the continuous construction of knowledge and the creation of new material—this is the work of Emma's imagination.

But however necessary Emma's imagination is to the generation of knowledge, imagination alone is not sufficient to its understanding. Chapter 47 explodes with revelations in response to the sensation of a great shock: Harriet Smith loves Mr. Knightley and Harriet Smith believes that Mr. Knightley loves her in return. The object of Harriet's affections was never to be named—he is the unutterable. Emma's "Are you speaking of—Mr. Knightley?" (396) forces from out of Emma the realization that "Mr. Knightley must marry no one but herself!" (398). Strangely enough, Emma's *most* significant experience with an object in the world, external to herself, and not in the end refashionable according to Emma's fancy— Harriet—this "natural daughter of somebody"—prompts Emma to know and be able to name feelings, which she prior to this event could not do. Emma *sees* and *hears* and then withdraws from this actual, lived, *real*

encounter with an *object* to experience her self in a different way: "Emma's
eyes were instantly withdrawn; and she sat silently meditating, in a fixed
attitude for a few minutes. A few minutes were sufficient for making
her acquainted with her heart" (398). The feeling of what happens, the
shock that elicits the love, unmasks Emma's prior self-image and prompts
a new vision: "She saw it all with a clearness which had never blessed her
before . . . What blindness, what madness, had led her on!" (398). Emma
encounters her "extended consciousness." Damasio writes that "extended
consciousness provides the organism with an elaborate sense of self—an
identity and a person, you or me, no less—and places that person at a
point in individual historical time, richly aware of the lived past and of
the anticipated future, and keenly cognizant of the world beside it" (*The
Feeling* 16). Emma, at last cognizant of the world beside her, not of her
design, and of herself in relation to others over time, comes to know not
"the truth" but a shift in mind from a *self-consciousness informed by imagination* to an *extended consciousness informed by experience.*

I take chapter 47 not to be the dawning of "the truth." Emma has
imagined her idea of the truth in every chapter before chapter 47, has
even imagined how her truth-making as an "imaginist" has failed her.
Following what is for her the startling carriage scene with Mr. Elton,
Emma's dramatized consciousness recognizes with remarkable clarity, "She
had taken up the idea, she supposed, and made every thing bend to it"
(153). However, the moment with Elton is not enough to push her to a
new way of being. Elton, she imagines, had given her cause to imagine
her idea of him as attached to Harriet: "His manner, however, *must* have
been unmarked, wavering, dubious, or she could not have been so misled"
(emphasis mine, 153). More is needed than experiencing the shock of Elton's
proposal. Emma has not been subject to induced delusion—her mind has
not been captured by reading or listening to or believing other narratives
from without to be truer than her own internal reading from within of
what is true. Instead, Emma's sense of truth in chapter 47 expands and
extends and changes. With the remarkable shift in Emma's recognition of
her feelings for Mr. Knightley has come almost simultaneously the feeling
of *shame*—"what madness, what blindness has led her on!" Here is Emma's
mind lively, but *not* at ease. Here is what transforms the lively mind that can
do with seeing nothing and sees nothing that does not please to a mind
that sees something that is so beyond pleasing that the mind must work
hard to understand it and then imagine what to do to be at ease again. The
imaging becomes her past recollections of Harriet and Knightley together.
It then advances to become her present desire "[t]o understand, thoroughly
understand her own heart" (401), and the images to follow of her new and

future consciousness of what Mr. Knightley means to her, will mean to her, apparently always meant to her, without her knowing it. All this speaks to a coming into being of Emma's extended consciousness—a consciousness that calls up together images of the past, present, and future to create a fuller scene of understanding. And it as well speaks to what happens to Emma's mind when she grows conscious of love—feeling love, not just imagining the idea of love—a felt-experience that changes everything for Emma. This is what William James calls the "sensational tang" that marks the difference between *knowing* about "blue" and "pain" and *feeling* "blue" and "pain." For James, it is when we feel that we "make human knowledge of these matters real" (II, 7). Life, as she imagined it with a mind lively and at ease, opens for Emma into the unimaginable. Emma has to feel love, consciously, to know what is past knowing as an idea. What Amy Heckerling's Cher, the adapted 1995 Emma, says in disbelieving voice-over of this moment of revelation, "*I was totally clueless,*" Austen's Emma names coming to "knowledge of herself" (402).

Antonio Damasio's *Descartes' Error* is a behavioral neurologist's response to the ruling assumption that reason is the human brain's pathway to knowledge. Here is Damasio:

> I began writing this book to propose that reason may not be as pure as most of us think it or wish it were, that emotions and feelings may not be intruders in the bastion of reason at all: they may be enmeshed in its networks, for worse *and* for better . . . I suggest only that certain aspects of the process of emotion and feeling are indispensable for rationality. At their best, feelings point us in the proper direction, take us to the appropriate place in a decision-making space, where we may put the instruments of logic to good use. (xii–xiii)

"Emma the Imaginist" changes, expands, knows herself more fully because more attached to the world and how those attachments affect her, when she *feels.* Damasio's point, that we come to reason, come to judgment, come to knowledge on the back of emotion, is Emma's course. But it is a course that begins from her capacity to imagine ideas about herself and the world. What Mr. Knightley claims in chapter 5 Emma never could do, the *peripety* of chapter 47 compels her to do—Emma subjects her fancy to understanding. We can read "subjects" perhaps three ways—as makes subservient, as exposes to, and as what she lends to her subjectivity with the arrival of understanding. In this movement of mind, fancy has not met its end but instead has found its way to new company. Somewhere in the imagination's encounter with felt-experience and their negotiation with one another, Emma's self-consciousness expands toward knowledge. What Emma the character and *Emma* the novel suggest about the nature of mind is that the capacity to *imagine*—to do with seeing nothing and to see nothing that won't do—is *the core of our experience of self-consciousness*. It is the core of Emma's experience of self-consciousness until, from feeling shame to the recognition of her own limited powers of knowing, Emma subjects her imagination: "With insufferable vanity had she believed herself in the secret of everybody's feelings, with unpardonable arrogance proposed to arrange everybody's destiny" (402).

Why do we imagine? What role does fantasy play in consciousness? In Austen, more specifically, what is the relationship between self-consciousness and imagination? Perhaps what *Emma* teaches us is that that part of consciousness which imagines creates fantasies of change and rehearses responses to it, which means plays out the idea-visions of possible future scenarios and their understandings in mind and, too, their management. For an Austen heroine, however, the experience of control and management afforded by the imagination is always fleeting. Perhaps because she is "handsome, clever, and rich," perhaps because she most reflects the mind lively and at ease of Austen herself, Emma is allowed the longest streak of uninterrupted fantasizing of any of Austen's heroines—forty-seven chapters. The breaking in of "the object" to force its felt-experience, to change how the self imagines, must be wounding. How else is the narcissistic consciousness of a central protagonist's mind ever to know the existence of another as something other than as the extension of her own imagination and projection? This is why the gaining of knowledge is so painfully informed by shame in Austen.

"With the speed of an arrow" and the length of a novel, Emma changed by the breakthrough realization—that she must be first with Mr. Knightley—expands from self-conscious imaginist to a self made conscious by the wounding of experience to know *lack*—and what for all Austen's great heroines that knowing generates—*understanding*.

CHAPTER 2

"You Pierce My Soul"

Feeling Embodied and *Persuasion*

I can listen no longer in silence. I must speak to you by such means as are within my reach. You pierce my soul. I am half agony, half hope. Tell me not that I am too late, that such precious feelings are gone for ever. I offer myself to you again with a heart even more your own, than when you almost broke it eight and a half years ago. Dare not say that man forgets sooner than woman, that his love has an earlier death. I have loved none but you. Unjust I may have been, weak and resentful I have been, but never inconstant. You alone have brought me to Bath. For you alone I think and plan.—Have you not seen this? Can you have failed to have understood my wishes?—I had not waited even these ten days, could I have read your feelings, as I think you must have penetrated mine. I can hardly write. I am every instant hearing something that overpowers me. You sink your voice, but I can distinguish the tones of that voice, when they would be lost on others.—Too good, too excellent creature! You do us justice indeed. You do believe that there is true attachment and constancy among men. Believe it to be most fervent, most undeviating in

F. W.

I must go, uncertain of my fate; but I shall return hither, or follow your party, as soon as possible. A word, a look will be enough to decide whether I enter your father's house this evening or never.

—Jane Austen, *Persuasion*

1. THE REMARKABLE LETTER OF CHAPTER 23

For eight and a half years, Anne Elliot has longed for the words of Frederick Wentworth's letter, and we as *Persuasion*'s readers have waited for them as well—twenty chapters of waiting—since Anne's first murmuring of "*he*" at the close of chapter 3. However, I'd like to suggest that we've waited far longer for what this letter holds. If Jane Austen's novels all lead ineluctably to the return of "him" and the proposal (renewed or first offered), the heartfelt moment of declaration between the lovers before *Persuasion* seems in Austen's writing to be essentially nonrepresentational, though its idea can be alluded to as a shared ellipse between the lovers. We are given words after the proposal of when each realized that he or she loved, and how each feels now that the acknowledgment has been made. But Austen mostly drops a veil over the actual words of love first exchanged—the words of passion spoken in the moment, not recollected in the tranquility of a moment later from the position of the established "us."[1] Who then is this writer, Austen as Wentworth? Frederick Wentworth overhears Anne Elliot meditate out loud (apparently to Captain Harville) on what she has longed to tell Wentworth throughout the novel—of her attachment to him, disguised still in general terms as "the nature of a woman's attachment." And it calls forth from him not speech, but words written in the moment back to her—her call to his response becomes her longings met. Written in the

---

1. If Darcy's first declaration fails to incite anything like the passionate desire to attach and instead leads Lizzy to name him the "last man on earth" whom she'd marry, his second goes this far: "'You are too generous to trifle with me. If your feelings are still what they were last April, tell me so at once. My affections and wishes are unchanged, but one word from you will silence me on the subject forever'" (375). In *Northanger Abbey,* no words directly spoken are given: "She was assured of his affection; and that heart in return was solicited, which perhaps, they pretty equally knew was already entirely his own" (211). Likewise in *Sense and Sensibility,* the declaration is reported second hand with an added instruction about what it is as readers that we "need" receive as the "said": "This only need be said;—that when they all sat down to table at four o'clock, about three hours after his arrival, he had secured his lady, engaged her mother's consent, and was not only in the rapturous profession of the lover, but in the reality of reason and truth, one of the happiest of men" (306). Austen breaks into a narrative of explanation to account for how Edmund in *Mansfield Park* might move within the week from feeling heartbroken about giving up Mary Crawford to the recognition of his preference for Fanny Price. At the moment of declaration, we stand with Austen at a "subjunctive distance away" from their exchange: "His happiness in knowing himself to have been so long the beloved of such a heart, must have been great enough to warrant any strength of language in which he could cloathe it to her or to himself; it must have been a delightful happiness!" And then Austen tells of Fanny's feelings in response—that which cannot be represented: "But there was happiness elsewhere which no description can reach. Let no one presume to give the feelings of a young woman on receiving the assurance of that affection of which she has scarcely allowed herself to entertain a hope" (455). Knightley manages in his Knightley way to be the most direct and commanding in his address, but the forwardness is really a call for her to speak immediately, which might relieve him of speaking at all: "'My dearest Emma,' said he, 'for dearest you will always be, whatever the event of this hour's conversation, my dearest, most beloved Emma—tell me at once. Say "No," if it is to be said.'—She could really say nothing.—'You are silent! at present I ask no more.'" But then he asks for more: "'At present I ask only to hear your voice, once to hear your voice.'" Emma continues to meet his inability to speak his love with her own. And then Austen interrupts Emma's silent run of thoughts with "What did she say?—Just what she *ought,* of course. A lady always does.—She said enough to show there need not be despair—and to invite him to say more himself" (emphasis mine, 417–18). We do not know what Emma said. However, if *Emma* is driven by a desire to narrate what a "man ought to be" and what a "woman ought to be," here words of the heart, or a desire to narrate what "they ought to be," is strikingly absent.

present tense, this letter, built around the imperative "must," insists on the emergence of these words that must be said because something must be represented. These words body forth as this letter—this representation of what Wentworth feels now—asserts he has always felt. There is no time to lose, no time for reflection, no time for the separation of felt-experience from thought-experience. And for Austen, I want to assert, there is no time to lose. Austen probably knows by the time of the letter's final composition in 1816 that she is dying. She is forty years old.[2] If ever there is a moment for Austen to feel pressed by her losing ground with life and able by her maturity in life to write a language of love, the writing of *Persuasion* is that moment. What can be more pressing than the present tense when death stands near it, still in the future but almost itself the present? Saying it "now," what one knows now, becomes everything.[3] And the now is language that travels between Austen/Wentworth's body that feels and Austen/Wentworth's consciousness that feels, and that constructs between them a meeting place in the space of metaphor. "'I can listen no longer in silence. I must speak to you by such means as are within my reach'" make the "I" be ears that must act by finding voice in a hand that holds a pen. The "I" becomes a "soul" because it is pierced by "you"—body becomes consciousness in the presence of the beloved other ("you"), but only through a metaphor of physical penetration ("pierce"). "I" pierced by you is a being split in two between two half feelings, agony and hope. "I" therefore is now composed of two feelings, or agony and hope now share equally in being "I." Feelings are personified when a body/consciousness is said to be them ("Half hope, half agony am I") and a body/consciousness is made affect when feelings are said to be "I" ("I am half agony, half hope"). The predicate nominative construction tells us that this metaphor holds in both directions: "I am half agony, half hope" and "Half hope, half agony am I" and that what it holds are feelings embodied.

This chapter grows out of my desire to try to account for the letter of

2. Linda Raphael in *Narrative Skepticism* writes, "In the summer of 1815, when Austen began work on *Persuasion*, she was finding her illness, Addison's disease, 'so baffling and elusive that she knew it might be incurable'" (31). Claire Tomalin, in *Jane Austen: A Life*, complicates the diagnosis by wondering if it really was Addison's disease. Austen's illness distinguished itself from the usual course of Addison's disease in that her skin color was described by her niece Caroline to be "pale" as opposed to tan; she suffered from fevers and was not said to suffer from sudden faintness and collapse on standing. Because of these differences, Tomalin with the help of her contemporary Dr. Eric Beck suggests: "One possibility is that she suffered from a lymphoma such as Hodgkin's disease—a form of cancer—which would lead to recurrent fevers and progressive weakening, leading to death" (282). Austen was born December 16, 1775, and died July 18, 1817, at the age of forty-one.

3. Tomalin's account of Austen's composing of chapters 23 and 24 (as written, discarded, rewritten) coupled with her descriptions of Austen's physical pain during the time of their revised composition in the summer of 1816 supports my sense of Austen's urgency. See Claire Tomalin's *Jane Austen: A Life*, in particular her own chapter 23, 252–64.

chapter 23. It is so unlike any other letter in Austen's writing in the sustained depth of its embodied language of feeling. Frederick Wentworth's words represent the deepest feelings of attachment in the moment, something Austen for the most part does not represent in her work but does write in *Persuasion,* and they represent the feeling of attachment in the moment as embodied. At issue for me is, how does this letter work both to mirror and to be the culminating expression of the novel and the writing career that it concludes?

2. THE FEELING OF KNOWING

From 1796 to 1797, twenty years prior to her writing of *Persuasion,* Austen at age twenty-one writes this about the twenty-one-year-old Elizabeth Bennet: "Elizabeth, agitated and confused, rather *knew* that she was happy, than *felt* herself to be so" (*Pride and Prejudice* 381). What does it mean that Elizabeth Bennet has knowledge of her emotional happiness but not the feeling of it? As Lizzy makes her way toward what Austen will define as "rational happiness" by the end of *Pride and Prejudice,* what stands between her knowing happiness and feeling it, I would assert, is her body, and perhaps as well the youthful Jane Austen's body. Elizabeth questions, doubts, judges, ponders, examines, and concludes—quickly—always quickly. True to her quickness, most of all, she is a wit. She and Darcy meet regularly in energetic conversation in which their words bring their minds, as it were, "face to face." Darcy comes to know her mental capacities as he comes to see her "fine dark eyes," the most distinguishing somatic marker of Lizzy's presence, whose beauty is rendered mental when he defines them as "intelligent" (70). Elizabeth's being moves. Like her "quickness" of mind, she walks by "crossing field after field at a quick pace, jumping over stiles and springing over puddles with impatient activity" (79), but in an almost formless way. Essentially unbounded and undefined, her movement or activity is not deeply housed in a body. We don't experience her body's contours pressing upon us as her readers or hold some kind of whole sense of her as a physical being: instead, we imagine her at moments with some separate, distinguished physical particularity. While, with the exception of these few references to eyes and movement, we don't much feel Elizabeth's physical presence in the text, we do feel her thinking presence. The bounty of Lizzy's words, her meditations on language, the rational delight she takes in which nouns to choose to define experience, give her a mental presence that creates a container for quickness and motion, until her mental alacrity comes to be arrested after she collides with the physical presence of Darcy's letter. Forced to slow down, even stop, her thoughts move from "Till this moment I never knew myself" to in the end a description of Elizabeth as a primarily mental state that frames her feelings of confusion: "Elizabeth, agitated, confused, rather *knew* that she was happy, than *felt* herself to be so."

William James in his chapter "Emotions" from *The Principles of Psychology* makes necessary the link between emotions and their physical enactment.[4] He writes: "A purely disembodied human emotion is a nonentity . . . for *us,* emotion dissociated from all bodily feeling is inconceivable . . . whatever moods, affections, and passions I have are in truth constituted by, and made up of, those bodily changes which we ordinarily call their expression or consequence" (II, 452). For James, we feel an emotion because our body feels itself change in the emotion's expression. Lizzy's absent access to her feeling of happiness happens because of, I want to assert, its disembodiment. Feeling happiness is for her a "nonentity." If "fine dark eyes," as the outermost manifestation of brain, feed an intelligent mind within observations for it to judge in *Pride and Prejudice* without much by way of a containing body to hold the process of representation, what results is few instances of the feeling of knowing—with one great exception. Lizzy has a body when she feels shame—she feels what it is to know that. Unlike "fine dark eyes" and quick motion, Elizabeth's other chief physical attribute—her blushes—are a somatic marker of how she feels. Her body marks shame when Darcy is witness to her family's social failures: her body glows the red her consciousness feels. Lizzy's embodied knowledge of the feeling of shame is shared by Austen's women protagonists. Blushes and tears are how the bodies of Austen's heroines express at times the feeling of knowing shame. Shame works in Austen's writing as the first feeling on the way to an expanded consciousness begun from the demand for separation from others. In knowing feelings of humiliation, Catherine Morland expelled from Northanger Abbey returns home alone an "ordinary" heroine, Marianne Dashwood finally breaks from Willoughby and conceives of a later, second attachment, Fanny Price "experiences and expresses real feeling" often as silence or as a negation of who or what surrounds her (Marshall 87), and, as I discuss in chapter 1, Emma Woodhouse moves from her extraordinary tears of mortification, to her exiling of Harriet, to her imagining the loss of Knightley and what that might mean. As much as the blush is a response to the social, its feeling state—shame—prompts Lizzy to turn away from the

---

4. As I note in the introduction, James's theory of emotion is often referred to as the "James-Lange theory" because of the near-simultaneous publication of their ideas, Professor Lange's as a scientific pamphlet in 1885 (which James cites and about which makes comments in *The Principles*) and James's as an article in *Mind* in 1884.

object that causes her to feel the emotion, an act which makes her a body that separates from others. Darwin writes of this in his chapter on "Blushing" from *The Expression of the Emotions in Man and Animals:* "Under a keen sense of shame there is a strong desire for concealment. We turn away the whole body, more especially the face, which we endeavor in some manner to hide. An ashamed person can hardly endure to meet the gaze of those present, so that he almost invariably casts down his eyes or looks askant" (320–21). In Lizzy's moments of shame, she invariably turns her eyes away from Darcy's, even divides herself physically from him.[5] Elizabeth, I want to suggest, feels shame, has (in her blushes) an embodied consciousness of shame and feels the accompanying desire to separate from its object, but she does not yet feel happiness and its accompanying embodied feeling of attachment to its object. How Lizzy can *know* happiness that she does not yet *feel* works as a metaphor for what James calls "the vital point of my whole theory, which is this: If we fancy some strong emotion, and then try to abstract from our consciousness of it all the feelings of its bodily symptoms, we find we have nothing left behind, no 'mind-stuff' out of which the emotion can be constituted, and that a cold and neutral state of intellectual perception is all that remains" (II, 451).

How differently does Anne Elliot experience happiness: "No, it was not regret which made Anne's heart beat in spite of herself, and brought the colour into her cheeks when she thought of Captain Wentworth unshackled and free. She had some feelings which she was ashamed to investigate. They were too much like joy, senseless joy!" (178). The rational mind is put away or at least overtaken ("ashamed to investigate"; "senseless"); Anne feels something "like joy," which is "senseless joy" in her very present body—the heart that beats "in spite of herself" and the color brought to her cheeks. Austen describes in *Persuasion* what William James first suggests and Anto-

---

5. I am deliberately focused on Lizzy's blush of shame because it marks her emerging consciousness in separation from its object, as opposed to the blush of aggression or eros that urges a consciousness toward its object in some form of attachment. I have chosen this focus because I take it to be the case that Austen's predominant account of embodied feeling before *Persuasion* is her representation of shame. If feeling happiness requires knowing the feeling of "desired-object-attachment," Lizzy's knowledge of the feeling of shame (and separation from its object) will not take her there. Mary Ann O'Farrell's wonderful account of the blush in Austen treats the blush not just as a marker of separation—the mortification that divides—but as the social sign of embarrassment that leads to a recovery of the erotic body in a world of manners. She writes: "Embarrassment's colloquial relation 'mortification' describes with punning aptitude the process by which the social body draws repeatedly to its surface its own blood . . . Jane Austen discovers pleasures in the ability of embarrassment's pangs to recover a sense of the body in manners" (26–27). See Mary Ann O'Farrell's *Telling Complexions: The Nineteenth-Century English Novel and the Blush,* especially chapters 1 and 2. See as well Anita G. Gorman's "Blushing and Blanching: The Body as Index of Emotion" in *The Body in Illness and Health: Themes and Images in Jane Austen* (127–62), which takes up the blush across Austen's works in its many guises as "embarrassment, shame, self-consciousness, anger, and passion."

nio Damasio now builds on to posit how we come to consciousness—in "the feeling of knowing." Damasio hypothesizes: "We become conscious when our organisms [our particular beings] internally construct and internally exhibit a specific kind of wordless knowledge—that our organism has been changed by an object—and when such knowledge occurs along with the salient internal exhibit of an object. The simplest form in which this knowledge emerges is the feeling of knowing" (*The Feeling* 168–70). Coming to consciousness, Damasio imagines, depends on our capacity fundamentally to do three things: represent ourselves as organisms to ourselves, represent an object to ourselves, and re-represent how being in relation to the object changes ourselves, all of which we do in wordless narratives that are feelings as mental images (images here mean all forms of sensorimotor representation—not just visual). Damasio's and William James's ideas on emotion and "the feeling of knowing" help open our eyes to how Austen writes the representation of self-consciousness in *Persuasion*—as embodied feelings.

3. NO BODY

A radical shift in language and, therefore, in representation occurs as we move inside the world of *Persuasion* from that of *Pride and Prejudice*. Loss— unbearable yet borne—and recovery—wondrous yet never felt without still knowing the loss that came before it—live embodied as felt-language in *Persuasion*. If Elizabeth Bennet's body remains mostly out of focus and so too does her language of feeling (except in her consciousness of shame), Anne Elliot's body is the object by which all is known because felt in the language of emotion of *Persuasion*. At first it seems that this—a body—is what Anne is without. She is, we are told again and again, a woman without "bloom":

> A few years before, Anne Elliot had been a very pretty girl, but her bloom had vanished early; and as even in its height, her father had found little to admire in her, (so totally different were her delicate features and mild dark eyes from his own); there could be *nothing in them now* that she was faded and thin, to excite his esteem. (Emphasis mine, 37)

As an object before Sir Walter's representing consciousness, Anne does nothing to "excite his esteem"—her bloomless body does not bring him to emotion, which reduces her to a nonpresence for him. Austen tells us this when she writes,

> Anne, with an elegance of mind and sweetness of character, which must
> have placed her high with any people of real understanding, was *nobody*
> with either father or sister: her word had *no weight;* her convenience was
> always to give way;—she was only Anne. (Emphasis mine, 37)

Anne with "no weight," as disembodied to them, erases Anne as a mental
image for her remaining family. She has no words that can enter Elizabeth
and Sir Walter and so she gives way because she has no other way to be
with them. To be "only Anne" means for Anne not to be to them. Anne
Elliot is not held in her family's consciousness.

Damasio's model focuses on how the self comes to consciousness in the
representations generated by the organism of self, object, and self changed
by object. But what of the representations by another of oneself as his or
her object? Isn't having oneself be represented by another as an object who
changes the representer's consciousness necessary to the emergence and
maintenance of one's own feeling of being known and knowable, as well as
knowing? For Anne to be a nonobject to Sir Walter and Elizabeth, for her
not to be contained in their consciousnesses, works to subtract from her
feeling of knowing. While to have bloom suggests a "state of great beauty"
and works as a metaphor for sexual ripeness,[6] at its core I want to suggest
in *Persuasion* it means for a woman to be *perceivable*—redness can be seen,
whiteness cannot. Having "bloom" makes a woman visible because marked
in red as desirable, admirable, sexual, while being "faded" makes her invisible because marked in white as bloodless, sexually erased. Anne needs to
feel perceived as present to support her own feeling of knowing herself to
be present. And she needs to feel seen in bloom to feel conscious of her
sexuality, beauty, embodiment as a woman of twenty-seven.

Anne knew once, and then briefly again, what it was to be held as an
admired object in another's mind:

> She knew that when she played she was giving pleasure only to herself;
> but this was no new sensation: excepting one short period in her life,
> she had never since the age of fourteen, never since the loss of her dear
> mother, known the happiness of being listened to, or encouraged by any
> just appreciation or real taste. (73)

In the loss of her mother, Anne lost the sensation of being held in her
mother's consciousness, which meant the sensation of feeling her own

---

6. See Anita Gorman on Austen's use of the word "bloom" in "Blushing and Blanching: The
Body as the Index of Emotion" in *The Body in Illness and Health* (156, 158).

presence as an object worthy to be held as "listened to" and "encouraged" by an equally worthy mind of "just appreciation" and "real taste." She lost the feeling of having another make space for her inside and admire her. As well, Anne lost the chief object of her own representing mind and the chief object that had most deeply defined Anne's own relational re-representation of herself as changing in response to the presence of her mother. Such a physical/emotional loss finds itself with a kind of fairy-tale horror repeated in her attachment to Frederick Wentworth at nineteen—he holds her in his consciousness; he is the object of her consciousness. And what each holds in mind is something like "perfection": "They were gradually acquainted, and when acquainted, rapidly and deeply in love. It would be difficult to say which had seen highest perfection in the other, or which had been the happiest" (55). Persuaded to give him up, Anne relinquishes the sensation of being held in his mind and too the capacity to be fully conscious. The object that prompts her to feel her own being as present and loved, as well as his, is gone, and no substitute is possible: "No one had ever come within Kellynch circle, who could bear a resemblance with Frederick Wentworth, as he stood in her memory. No second attachment" (57).

With no second object of attachment, Anne's consciousness or feeling of knowing "retrenches." And all this before the novel begins. The novel's present, where we enter, is years after Frederick's departure and after the process of Anne's "retrenchment of being" have begun. Lady Russell's capacity to see Anne still and hold her in esteem offers Anne's being some internal room in which to reside as herself. But Lady Russell's holding in mind is itself a retrenched one. While she resembles her mother, she is a poor substitute. Lady Russell is never mentioned in the passage defining Anne's pleasures of being listened to by others of just appreciation: "[E]xcepting one short period in her life . . . never since the loss of her dear mother [had she] known the happiness of being listened to, or encouraged by any just appreciation or real taste" (73). Her as-if motherly persuasion (spawned by her inability to really listen?) brings Anne misery: Lady Russell initiates Anne's loss of Wentworth, the "one short period in her life" of happiness. If then Lady Russell gives Anne a space of being seen, what Anne sees reflected back is what she has lost, her mother and her lover. And if Anne's memory of Wentworth—her emotional memory of their relational past—enables her still to have him and herself, it is a having in memory only.[7] The pressure of Wentworth as a living object represented in her consciousness becomes a memory of an attachment worn down by time. Austen writes of Anne

---

7. For a fine discussion of emotional memory as the "felt residue of the relational past," see Donna Orange's *Emotional Understanding: Studies in Psychoanalytic Epistemology* (105–24).

at the start of the novel, after more than seven years of separation from him interrupted by no live encounter: "[T]ime had softened down much, perhaps nearly all of peculiar attachment to him" (57). Apparently Anne does not fully know how much of that "peculiar attachment to him" she still feels.

The outward signs of Anne's consciousness are hidden or at least in retreat: the surface of her body of faded bloom shows feeling withdrawn; her language has collapsed into just a few uttered phrases set next to vast stretches of pause, separated from the flow of narrative with phrases such as "Here Anne spoke" (49), or "After the little pause" (51), or "After waiting another moment" (52). The felt-quality of loss throughout the opening is what we experience as what outwardly remains of Anne registered through her body—faded, thin, quiet—traces of a consciousness that has lost its relational objects.

4. SENSATION

But the horrible fairy tale of loss repeats itself with a difference—he is not dead. Frederick Wentworth returns from war very much alive. And with his return, Austen narrates a remarkable account of how coming back to consciousness, full consciousness, from such loss is possible. What has remained inwardly in Anne of her being—her invisible trace of the feeling of knowing—is understanding. Silently, Anne registers his presence to herself, wonders what he feels about their meeting now that he is but a half mile away, feels their having no conversation together now when once there was so much, catches a glance of his eye and curl of his lip and so sees what others miss of his real response to a moment, and most of all lets herself take in "that he could not forgive her" (113). Damasio's nonverbal narratives of representation of consciousness-making are here the nonverbal encounters between Anne and Frederick that create a space between them. George Butte calls this the space of "intersubjectivity" in Austen where "groups of selves, of perceiving identities [are set] into motion together in a new dance of subjects, of consciousnesses. The energies of this dance build from tensions, as it were negotiations, among these consciousnesses that are present (partially) to each other, in body, gaze, or language as self and Other."[8] As Wentworth gathers a community of women about him in flirtatious chatter, the two silently take each other in. His bodily presence

---

8. George Butte (57). Considering how consciousness in Austen is intersubjective, Butte presents a graceful treatment of her texts in intersubjective relation to Merleau-Ponty's phenomenology in "Shame or Espousal? *Emma* and the New Intersubjectivity of Anxiety in Austen" (54–65).

and the sound of him in relation to others prompt back into being her understanding created from their past—that part of her representation of him as an object begins to return. But it is a representation gathered from the past and from observing him from afar. Being conscious of what she feels in relation to him now, in her body, is what Anne cannot yet do because an embodied Anne is barely present—until his touch brings her physical relief and begins to bring back the sensation of her presence in the present:

> [S]he found herself in the state of being released from him; some one was taking him from her, though he had bent down her head so much, that his sturdy little hands were unfastened from around her neck, and he was resolutely borne away, before she knew that Captain Wentworth had done it.
>
> Her sensations on the discovery made her perfectly speechless. She could not even thank him . . . His kindness in stepping forward to her relief—the manner—the silence in which it had passed . . . produced such a confusion of varying, but very painful agitation, as she could not recover from. (103)

And:

> Captain Wentworth, without saying a word, turned to her, and quietly obliged her to be assisted into the carriage.
>
> Yes,—he had done it. She was in the carriage, and felt that he had placed her there, that his will and hands had done it, that she owed it to his perception of her fatigue, and his resolution to give her rest. She was very much affected by the view of his disposition towards her which all these things made apparent. This little circumstance seemed the completion of all that had gone before. She understood him. He could not forgive her,—but he could not be unfeeling. Though condemning her for the past, and considering it with high and unjust resentment, though perfectly care-less of her, and though becoming attached to another, still he could not see her suffer, without the desire of giving her relief. It was a remainder of former sentiment; it was an impulse of pure, though unacknowledged friendship; it was proof of his own warm and amiable heart, which she could not contemplate without emotions so compounded of pleasure and pain, that she knew not which prevailed. (113)

Wentworth's wordless "kindness in stepping forward to her relief" and his "desire of giving relief" are about his silent noticing of Anne's suffering—

little Walter about her neck, fatigue from walking too long. He engages in something like what Daniel Stern calls "affect attunement,"[9] which I reframe here as "embodied attunement": Wentworth expresses the feeling of a shared affect/physical state without imitating its exact expression. In his noticing of her body's pain and sharing in it, she has again a perceivable body to him, not a body in bloom, but a body in pain. He acts in attunement to what he imagines of her body's sensations. And in the touch of his hands on her skin, she has a physical feeling of absence—a burden lifted, fatigue removed—and of presence—his hands on her neck, his hands helping her into the carriage—accompanied by an emotional feeling created in tandem with the physical of "painful agitation" and "emotions so compounded of pleasure and pain that she knew not which prevailed." Wentworth makes her his object of wordless representation. And, in response to his attunement to her, touches Anne's body. Relieved to discover through the touch of his hands on her that she has a body—that she can feel physical relief—in coming to consciousness of her body not in pain and brushed into momentary contact with his body, emotional pain and pleasure come again into being as the feeling of knowing, however confusing that knowledge might be. Physical pain, physical pleasure are felt by Anne as emotional pain, emotional pleasure. The object of her consciousness—Wentworth—again affects her body, agitates her mind, creates new feelings that she re-represents to herself. Wentworth's touch brings her to somatic knowledge conscious of itself, of who she was, of who she is. Anne's relief is to awaken to full being.

Awakening to being, for Anne Elliot, has everything to do with returning to a set of original sensations that first defined being. In his chapter "Sensation," William James asks, "Where, then, do we feel the objects of our original sensations to be?" And replies:

> For the places thus first sensibly known are elements of the child's space-world which remain with him all his life; and by memory and later experiences he learns a vast number of things *about* those places which at first he did not know. But to the end of time certain places of the world remain defined for him as the places *where those sensations were;* and his only possible answer to the question *where anything is* will be to say "there," and to name some sensation or other like those first ones, which shall identify the spot. (Emphasis mine, II, 35)

We can imagine Anne's mother to be the object of her original sensation

---

9. For a full account of "affect attunement," see "The Sense of a Subjective Self: II. Affect Attunement" in Daniel Stern's *The Interpersonal World of the Infant: A View from Psychoanalysis and Developmental Psychology* (138–61).

who called her to being in the prenarrative of Anne's feeling her mother's presence. However, the text makes it be otherwise: "'[A] few months more, and *he,* perhaps will be walking here'" (54). The poignancy and mystery of the italicized *he* that concludes chapter 3 finds its source in how the narrative uncovers how *he* is Anne's "there," or "where those sensations were" that grant her a "space-world." The irreplacibility of Wentworth for Anne as the object of representation has something to do with how he carries "there" to Anne, and with how in her sensation of him she comes to know herself relationally, as the feeling of knowing what it means to be "here." Anne here is Anne in bloom—visible, alive, embodied.

Anne's second spring of youth and beauty is somehow missed by Frederick. If he has felt her presence since his return, he hasn't seen her return from "altered beyond his knowledge" (85) to "something like Anne Elliot again" (125). Seeing Anne again requires that she be seen first by another man so that Wentworth's eyes can follow as the "again." But more than that, his new seeing of her, which is an old seeing of her, seems to require an out of body or to another body shift as Wentworth's eyes go from the gentleman's to Anne's. Turning from him becomes returning to her. Here is the her he returns to:

> She was looking remarkably well; her very regular, very pretty features, having the bloom and freshness of youth restored by the fine wind which had been blowing on her complexion, and by the animation of eye which it had also produced. It was evident that the gentleman, (completely a gentleman in manner) admired her exceedingly. Captain Wentworth looked round at her instantly in a way which showed his noticing of it. He gave her a momentary glance,—a glance of brightness which seemed to say, "That man is struck with you,—and even I at this moment, see something like Anne Elliot again." (125)

Blown back to life, touched from without to become animated within, Anne is again visible, admired, in bloom. She becomes in this momentary glance of brightness the object toward which Wentworth's consciousness (re)turns. If the first half of the novel—"half agony"—has been about the return of Anne's being as fully conscious because fully embodied and Wentworth as the relational object that enables that representation, the second half—"half hope"—is its mirrored reflection. With Anne now present as here, in bloom, Wentworth surrenders to an uncontrolled shift in consciousness toward her as the chief object of his representation of longing. The surrender is given an assist by the glance of the gentleman's eye, which functions like the dawning of an aspect.[10] When Frederick sees the stranger admire her, his own seeing shifts from seeing her "altered beyond his knowledge" to altered back to his knowledge. She is something like Anne Elliot again. But the shift requires more than seeing the object again—it demands being in relation for a full re-representation to occur.

Louisa's fall makes her body fall away from Wentworth. Her falling-away body clears the space from Louisa's prior blocking presence from which Frederick now can call and Anne now can answer. "'Is there no one to help me?'" (130). These are the words of Frederick vulnerable, Frederick needing, Frederick open. Anne fills in the open space. The "no one" becomes her presence as an embodied presence of mind, commanding in words what Wentworth has lost consciousness of, namely what to do, in the falling away of Louisa and in the opening of himself. In his drawing a blank, he becomes vulnerable to Anne again because he has space for her to enter him again as his relational object. No more does he defend himself against her "power," as he had at the outset of the text, when Austen takes us inside the only instance of his consciousness displayed in something like Anne's dramatized consciousness, though cast more as summary: "He had been most warmly attached to her, and had never seen a woman since whom he thought her equal; but, except from some natural curiosity, he had no desire of meeting her again. Her power with him was gone forever" (86). His consciousness shifts to allow in her power with him. If Anne a moment after first meeting Frederick again finds that to "retentive feelings eight years may be little more than nothing" (85), Frederick must witness another's seeing of Anne and another's blow to the head (having sense knocked in) to recognize by sight and then insight his own enduring attachment.[11] Anne's attachment to him is called up immediately in her as somatic knowledge—what Donna Orange in *Emotional Understanding* describes as "the way experience encodes itself in our whole being as memory" (111). Anne's feeling of attachment is encoded memory "remembered" by the sight of him. It will take his touch for the attachment to be embodied in her again literally as his hands

10. I'm drawing here on Wittgenstein's idea from *The Philosophical Investigations* of the "dawning of an aspect" (193–94e). To illustrate how the dawning of an aspect differentiates itself from "continuous seeing," Wittgenstein looks at Jastrow's drawing of the "duck-rabbit." When the object is seen continuously as a rabbit or as a duck, but not as one and then the other, then the observer engages in "continuous seeing." However, when the duck or the rabbit is seen, where before the other was not seen, then the observer experiences the "dawning of an aspect." If Wentworth engages in a continuous seeing of Anne as "altered beyond his knowledge," seeing her admired in the gentleman's glance prompts in him the "dawning of an aspect"—a new seeing of her.

11. Alan Richardson's fine "Of Heartache and Head Injury: Minds, Brains, and the Subject of Persuasion" in his *British Romanticism and the Science of Mind* and "Of Heartache and Head Injury: Reading Minds in Persuasion" address Louisa's "blow to the head" in relation to the neuroscience of Austen's day and what the fall and change it produces in Louisa's character reveal about Austen's writing of the embodied mind.

attached to her, freeing her emotions to know themselves as attached to him. For Frederick, the attachment lives in him as the "unthought known," Christopher Bollas's phrase for the tacit or inarticulate knowledge that we know but for which we have no words, "the more than we can say that we know."[12] Wentworth makes evident his unthought known attachment to Anne when he lets Louisa drop. John Wiltshire writes of the moment this way: "He is not feeling and responding as she is feeling: their missing each other's hands at 'the fatal moment' is a sign that he cannot 'attach himself' to her which he already unconsciously knows" (188).[13] His hands have already "caught" Anne twice by relieving her of little Walter and handing her into the carriage—these are other moments of his unthought known attachment to Anne. Once his unthought known has been transformed into the "thought known," Wentworth articulates how his attachment had lived in him as the "unthought known" when he tells Anne, following their mutual reacknowledgment of their attachment to each other when at last linked arm in arm, "that he had been constant unconsciously, nay unintentionally; that he had meant to forget her, and believed it to be done" (244).

When Anne delivers her "true attachment and constancy" of women speech to Captain Harville and the overhearing Frederick, she explains how it is that Frederick might have come to lose consciousness of his attachment. A man needs an "object," she claims, for his attachment to live on, present to him as the woman who loves him and who lives for him. Wentworth had lost his "object," and with this loss had gone consciousness of his attachment. With the return of his relational object, Frederick can again know himself in *conscious articulation* of his attachment. Yet the articulation of the attachment as Frederick's "final" coming to consciousness of his feelings happens in relation to another, before himself. Like the other gentleman's glance and the wrong lover's blow to the head, Frederick comes to articulate his attachment to Anne only after his encounter with an object outside of himself that mirrors his position or enables him to encounter himself through his identification with the object. Frederick finds the words to express to Anne not his own but Benwick's attachment to Fanny Harville: "'A man like him, in his situation! With a heart pierced, wounded, almost broken! Fanny Harville was a very superior creature; and

---

12. About the idea of "the unthought known," see the literary-psychoanalyst Christopher Bollas's work on object relations in *The Shadow of the Object: Psychoanalysis of the Unthought Known;* the philosophical-psychoanalyst Donna Orange's discussion of unconscious encoded emotional memory in *Emotional Understanding* (107–11); and the philosopher Michael Polanyi's work on "the ineffable" in *Personal Knowledge: Towards a Post-Critical Philosophy.*

13. No more does Wentworth mistake Louisa's brash pigheadedness for firmness of mind—her infirmity of mind to follow the second failed catch makes this change in understanding impossible to miss. Louisa's head, it turns out, does not resemble the firmness of a nut.

his attachment to her was indeed attachment. A man does not recover from such a devotion of the heart to such a woman!—He ought not—he does not'" (192). In conceiving first of Benwick's attachment, Frederick is trying on the words that he will come to attach to himself, "A heart pierced, wounded, almost broken!" rehearse, "You pierce my soul . . . a heart even more your own than when you almost broke it . . . ." From uttering words about another's devotion from which there is no recovery, Frederick can articulate the words about himself as a re-representation in writing—as a letter.

5. "I AM HALF AGONY, HALF HOPE"

Frederick comes to consciousness of his feelings from the outside in—he perceives objects external to himself, conceives of them as themselves, and then uses them as mirrors to reflect back to him himself. The movement from perception to conception to identification draws forward his own emotions, buried within. Unlike Anne, Frederick never lost his bloom, his sense of self as fully embodied. Whereas when they first meet after the years of separation he thinks her "altered beyond his knowledge," she thinks, "No; the years which had destroyed her youth and bloom had only given him a *more glowing, manly, open look,* in no respect lessening his personal advantages. She had seen the same Frederick Wentworth" (emphasis mine, 86). Wentworth returns to her "openly" in his body, his somatic being all aglow, but not openly in his feelings. And if Anne, in the moment she lays eyes on him again, returns to feel the charge of her former feelings, she does so at first in an almost disembodied way. For Anne to recover her body—feel herself in her body—and for Frederick to acknowledge that from such an attachment there is no recovery—feel himself in his feelings—each must recover the lost relational object that enables them to experience happiness again, as an embodied feeling of attachment. In her most poignant speech of the novel, Anne claims a woman's heart needs no object to continue to feel her devotion, even "when existence or when hope is gone" (238). While Anne may not need the "the object" present to remember *the idea* of her devotion to Frederick, the course of Austen's *Persuasion* reveals how she does need him to be present to bring back to full consciousness *the feeling* of her devotion to him in the present, to feel fully herself again, to experience the feeling of knowing again—that Anne is alive and in love.

What Anne Elliot and Frederick Wentworth feel from before the opening pages of *Persuasion* is loss. And it is the feeling of loss that transforms to "senseless joy" when each experiences the other's physical and emotional return that leads to self-consciousness—of the pain of being alive and the wonder of return bound to "always the hope of more"—in feeling embodied together again. For Jane Austen, to represent such deep feelings of attachment as she is dying meant, I'm imagining, her own coming to a new self-consciousness of feeling—half agony, half hope.

PART II
George Eliot and Other-Consciousness

CHAPTER 3

"A Voice Like Music"

The Problem of Other Minds and *Middlemarch*

The breach from one mind to another is perhaps the greatest breach in
nature.

—William James, *The Principles of Psychology*

1. THE REAL PROBLEM OF OTHER MINDS

George Eliot meditates on the nature of consciousness throughout her
works of fiction with the insistence of a philosopher who cannot end the
meditation. What does it mean to know? How does one know? What can
one know? These are the questions that structure Eliot's epistemological
search, while her narratives embody their working-through. As works of
biographical fiction, the novels named for characters (*Adam Bede, Silas
Marner, Daniel Deronda, Romola, Felix Holt*) are primarily about the search
for knowledge as a means of coming to self-knowledge. *Middlemarch,* in
its representation of a community in the middle—the middle class of a
mid-nineteenth-century English province—shifts the ground of the inves-
tigation, however, from "what do *I* know?" to "what do I know of *you*?"[1]
Descartes' fall into radical skepticism and his ascent out of it through the
claim of self-cognition enables him to assert first that he knows his mind,

---

1. Alan Palmer's fine "Intermental Thought in the Novel: The *Middlemarch* Mind" explores
how Eliot writes the community mind—the "intermental mind"—of *Middlemarch* by asking who
constitutes this collective mind, how the rhetorical presence of this intersubjective mind works, what
the judgments are of this intermental mind, and why Eliot writes a community mind—to what end
are its effects on the central lives of its individual characters?

then his body, then God, then others and the world. Descartes knows that others exist, but not *how* they exist as themselves, in their own minds, or even if they have minds. What might it mean to know or feel the mind of another? What does it mean that we cannot? I take these to be the central questions to follow on the heels of Descartes' skepticism, the questions philosophers group together as "the problem of other minds." Stanley Cavell in "Knowing and Acknowledging" defines the problem of other minds this way: "What is this 'knowing a person'? What does it mean to say, 'I know he is in pain,' and how does that differ from saying, 'I know I am in pain?'" (253–54). And: "The skeptic comes up with his scary conclusion—that we can't know what another person is feeling because we can't have the same feeling, feel his pain, feel it the way he feels it—and we are shocked; we must refute him, he would make it impossible ever to be attended to in the right way" (246–47). While we can't really seriously doubt existence—that part of Descartes' radical skepticism no longer stirs much anxiety—we continue, I think, to take seriously the post-Cartesian discovery that we can't experience the mind of another, and so can't know what it means to be another or to experience the world as another does or to know, in particular, another's pain. And however disturbing that discovery leaves us, the accompanying recognition—"If I can't experience as does another his or her mind, then neither can another experience my mind as I do and so another cannot know me or my pain as I do"—leaves us with the shock and sorrow that we may then never be, as Cavell puts it, "attended to in the right way." To recognize the problem of other minds means to recognize that we may never know another or be known as we do ourselves. It means to acknowledge that that which enables us to know—the mind—may be that which keeps us from knowledge of and by others. It means we are divided by our minds.

But why? Must we be? Explaining the phenomenon physiologically, at the space where body and mind meet, Antonio Damasio writes in *The Feeling of What Happens:*

> Life is carried out inside a boundary that defines a body. Life and the life urge exist inside a boundary, the selectively permeable wall that separates the internal environment from the external environment. The idea of the organism revolves around the existence of that boundary . . . I believe that minds and consciousness, when they eventually appeared in evolution, were first and foremost about life and the life urge within a boundary. To a great extent they still are. (137)

For Eliot, the problem of other minds is not just a philosophical question, nor is it just about adopting a skeptical mood. Choosing to describe the experience of minds as narrative, not to define the nature of mind as philosophical argument, means representing consciousness as alive and par-ticular and separate—held to a boundary—embodied. For George Eliot, the problem of other minds is a real problem of representation in *Middlemarch*.

The opening to chapter 17 of *Adam Bede* heralds what will be an ongo-ing concern throughout her writing career and so, too, will be of ongoing concern to her readers, namely Eliot's stated project: how to "give a faithful account of men and things as they have mirrored themselves in my mind" (177). As her readers, we turn and return to this bit of text because of its clothed mantle of intent—how the character Rector of Broxton fictionally figures the means for Eliot to write the real:

> "This Rector of Broxton is little better than a pagan!" I hear one of my lady readers exclaim, "How much more edifying it would have been if you had made him give Arthur some truly spiritual advice. You might have put into his mouth the most beautiful things—quite as good as reading a sermon."
>
> Certainly, I could, my fair critic, if I were a clever novelist, not obliged to creep servilely after nature and fact, but able to represent things as they never have been and never will be. Then, of course, my characters would be entirely of my own choosing, and I could select the most unexceptionable type of clergyman, and put my own admirable opinions into his mouth on all occasions. But you must have perceived long ago that I have no such lofty vocation, and that I aspire to give no more than a faithful account of men and things as they have mirrored themselves in my mind. The mirror is doubtless defective; the outlines will sometimes be disturbed; the reflec-tion faint or confused; but I feel as much bound to tell you, as precisely as I can, what that reflection is, as if I were in the witness-box narrating my experience on oath. (177)

To give a "faithful account of men and things" can occur only through the penetration by Eliot's mind of the natures of those men and things. Here, she asserts, this happens through reflection. Eliot turns her mirroring mind toward the object of study, the character Rector of Broxton—what constitutes "him," which reflects itself back to her mind as what she knows of "men and things," which she then reports as faithfully as she can in the voice of the first-person narrator, "as if I were in the witness-box nar-rating my own experience on oath." The mirror, while "defective[,] the outlines . . . sometimes . . . disturbed[,] the reflection faint or confused," is what Eliot is bound to tell, is all she can tell, as if it is her own first-person experience. But it is not her own experience—the boundary of her body, her mind, her being as the implied author divides her from other men and things. If Eliot's desire is to write "a faithful account of men and things," what she acknowledges is that she cannot, except as defective, disturbed, faint, confused interactions between the world without and a mirroring mind within. Eliot's realism, therefore, is her acknowledgment of skepticism.[2] However, her ongoing yearning to discover how we might know another and be known, and how she might make such a discovery transparent, reveals what I take to be the deepest longing of her writing: to transcend the terrors of separateness—one body from another, one mind from another, one human being from another.[3] William James describes the great source of terror to infancy as solitude, the source that accounts for the infant's "expression of dismay—the neverfailing cry—on waking up and finding himself alone" (II, 418). I read George Eliot's novels as adult expressions of dismay—the "neverfailing cry" of a consciousness waking up to the solitude that accompanies feeling unknown. For George Eliot to seek an answer to the problem of other minds reveals the problem of her own mind: can she transcend her own skepticism?

"By virtue of my interaction with him, I now understand myself differently"; or, "Because of that exchange with her, I now imagine myself this way as opposed to that"—these are the moves of a shifting self-consciousness in which Eliot's characters so often engage. They are about the gaining of self-knowledge through encountering another. As J. Hillis Miller writes, "By far the most important 'events,' for George Eliot's characters, are encounters

---

2. Linda Raphael, in her work *Narrative Skepticism: Moral Agency and Representations of Consciousness in Fiction,* writes about the relation between Eliot's realism and skepticism. We share an interest in Eliot's reflections on what as narrator she can and cannot know, can and cannot say in her novel. I'm grateful to Raphael for her careful research, her understanding of character and how we as readers respond to character, and her philosophically driven consideration of how skepticism and narrative meet. While not defining the condition as "skeptical," J. Hillis Miller writes about the self as unknowable to the other and writes about the other as unknowable to the self in *Middlemarch:* "If what each person at bottom is, even for himself or herself at certain traumatic moments, is an unknown and unknowable alterity, the roar on the other side of silence, then one person cannot in principle know another. The other person is a cluster of signs held together as a fictitious order by the force of the other's ego, projected unwittingly or unwittingly therefrom, and then misread by me on the basis of my own egoistic structuring of myself and my surroundings" ("The Roar on the Other Side of Silence: Otherness in *Middlemarch, EDDA* 3 [1995], 242). This essay appears in revised form in Miller's *Others.*

3. Tom Sperlinger's finely attuned "'The Sensitive Author': George Eliot" discusses Eliot's portrayals of sympathy through her own vulnerability to criticism. He writes: "Sympathy allows Eliot's characters to support one another, which shuts out the glare in their own self" (259). And wonders: "Why is solitude, being left with oneself, so terrifying? In *Middlemarch,* even when characters are alone, they are protected by the novel. The interconnectedness of different lives means that no loneliness is absolute" (268). Sperlinger concludes that while for some the presence of Eliot's "personal need" in her novels overshadows their own experience as readers, for others "Eliot is, for the same reason, a curiously intimate presence . . . [R]eaders of many kinds still find they can bring to her novels their urgent concerns, questions, needs, and terrors" (272).

with those clusters of signs that are other people" ("The Roar" 238). Perhaps the greatest instance in Eliot's writing of how a character comes to know herself because of exchanges with another occurs in *Daniel Deronda:* Gwendolen Harleth's self-consciousness depends on her repeated interactions with Deronda. Without their dialectic exchanges, in which he questions her about her sense of self and she responds with an increasing sense of uncertainty and possibility, one wonders whether Gwendolen would ever engage in the pursuit of self-knowledge. *Middlemarch* at times depends on the brush with another, but differently. Here the engagement becomes an application of the other onto and even into the self, so that Eliot imagines the possibility of the self knowing another mind, however briefly, as feeling the presence of the other residing within. All who come into contact with Bulstrode in Book Seven feel the encounter as a form of contagion from which they must cleanse themselves; Rosamond, by virtue of her momentary, shocked recognition of Dorothea's nobility becomes, for a moment, noble herself; Fred comes to stop expecting luck to see him through, stops expecting the world to support him, in coming to understand what it means to be the "fair brother" who is Farebrother; Ladislaw knows what it is to be the "perfect crystal" in his feeling of devotion to Dorothea, which is a response to his experience of Dorothea as the "perfect crystal." To imagine the boundary between minds as porous so that moments of mind-to-mind entrance, encounter, and exchange can occur requires a *porousness* of the body—the boundary that keeps mind from mind.

2. SOUND

The wearing of another's consciousness seems at first to be a representation of visual experience in *Middlemarch;* Eliot's use of the microscope as an organizing object and metaphor of the first part of the novel apparently asserts this. However, what is known by sight, even enhanced by the microscope or telescope, proves invariably to be a faulty means of making the other's mind present. Eliot acknowledges the flawed results of knowing another through mirrored reflection in the opening paragraphs of chapter 17 that I cited from *Adam Bede.* While she asserts here that all attempts to mirror the other back to herself will be defective (because they will be subjective and therefore limited to her consciousness, a consciousness separate from the mirrored one), I take it to be significant that her words to define this process throughout the passage are only visual: "mirror," "reflect," "outline." For Eliot, what is seen most of all reflects back the one who sees. In the way that Lydgate looks through the lens of a microscope in hopes of seeing his preconceived idea of the "primitive tissue," Eliot focuses the lens of a metaphoric microscope on scenes of provincial life in a minute analysis of its moments with an eye toward gaining access to an objective vision or greater consciousness of life.[4] Both investigations are motivated by previsions of a desired end. Throughout *Middlemarch,* however, Eliot questions how far her desire to see things for "what they are" can go, even with looking to detail with microscopic attention. She perpetually wonders: Do any of us see another for who he or she really is? What does it mean that a particular pair of eyes, connected to a particular consciousness, is doing the seeing and analysis? What Eliot suggests is that we see not with greater objectivity but with an intensified subjectivity:

> Even with a microscope directed on a water-drop we find ourselves making interpretations which turn out to be rather coarse; for whereas under a weak lens you may seem to see a creature exhibiting an active voracity into which other smaller creatures actively play as if they were so many animated tax pennies, a stronger lens reveals to you certain tiniest hairlets which make vortices for these victims while the swallower waits passively at his receipt of custom. In this way, metaphorically speaking, a strong lens applied to Mrs. Cadwallader's matchmaking will show a play of minute causes producing what may be called thought and speech vortices to bring her the food she needed. (59–60)

Seeing through a microscope is difficult, even faulty. However, what one sees are the causes and motivations that drive the self. Mrs. Cadwallader needs to make a match; therefore, she thinks and speaks in such a way that she will get what she desires—a match motivated by her. For Eliot, looking to "see" the consciousness of another as a means of knowing another

4. Other writers on Eliot's realism focus much of their attention on how Eliot uses visual forms of writing to define her realism, as in Gillian Beer's analysis of Eliot's use of visual metaphor/imagery to discuss invisible ideas: "The imagery of transcendence, of the invisible world, is one which George Eliot shares. The microscope and the telescope, by making realisable the plurality of worlds, scales, and existences beyond the reach of our particular sense organisation were a powerful antidote to that form of positivism which refused to acknowledge possibilities beyond the present and apparent world" in *Darwin's Plots* (141–42); or George Levine's assertion about *Middlemarch* that "That novel seems, encyclopedically, to participate, in a vast range of intellectual activity. But George Eliot does attempt to make that activity ultimately consonant with the scientific vision. Her preoccupation throughout the novel with the problem of perception, for example, belongs in the whole tradition of Victorian concern with what it means to 'see,'" in *The Realistic Imagination* (257); and Barbara Hardy in her attention to the "surfaces" of *Middlemarch* essentially analyzes Eliot's use of visual detail, as in, "When Dorothea feels the impact of the red hangings in St. Peter's 'like a disease of the retina,' an image which is clearly related to major themes, situations and other images, it is essential that we recognize the pressure of the surface: this sight, this physical impact," in *Particularities: Readings in George Eliot* (40–41).

means seeing the other through the lens of the self. Seeing involves a negotiation between image and its analysis, an analysis based on the seer's past knowledge or experiences or desires. To see the other means always to know a "negotiated" other, or reflection of the self.

What accounts in *Middlemarch* for the almost magical possibility of the movement of one mind to and even into another is sound.[5] Characters that are alive in the moment to what they hear are most vulnerable to or most powerfully able to meet the mind of another. Eliot uses the *metaphors* of voice, deafness, musicality, and attunement to sound as the rhetorical space where the idea of the problem of other minds is staged. However, it is in her physical descriptions of how characters hear or make sounds, are deaf or are silent that she works through how one consciousness comes to know or not know another as a *physical solution* to the problem of other minds. Eliot makes the interaction between minds physical, where each remains separate at the boundary of his or her body, but where both meet through how one body emits sound and another body receives it in aural sensation. The sensation of sound carries with it the possibility for Eliot of experiencing the other's mind as that received sensation, not transformed through the self but potentially transforming of the self.

Eliot's contemporary Hermann Helmholtz, the great scientist of the physiology of perception and one of the founders of modern psychology, in

5. Beryl Gray's pioneering study *George Eliot and Music* (1989) sets itself apart from the critical tradition that has made its primary focus "the awareness of Eliot's need to make us see" in her attention to Eliot's auditory imagination (ix). Gray and I share in the perception that it is through sound that Eliot writes her ethic of empathy. Gray says it this way: "The extent to which sound permeates and animates the novels has failed to permeate our understanding of them, and we have remained therefore partly deaf to that which George Eliot would have her own art 'teach.' For the ability to listen—to be stirred by the tones and modulations of the human voice, and to discern and respond to all forms of natural and humanly wrought harmony—invariably symbolises George Eliot's most cherished moral virtue: the capacity for human sympathy. The degree to which a character possesses this ability is the infallible guide to our judgement" (x). Delia da Sousa Correa's *George Eliot, Music and Victorian Culture* (2003) joins Gray's analysis as the only other book-length study that explores how, as Eliot says about herself, she wrote "'as a person with an ear and a mind susceptible to the direct and indirect influences of music'" (2). Da Sousa Correa's work distinguishes itself from Gray's in its attention to how Victorian culture trained Eliot's ear and mind in its susceptibility. Da Sousa Correa connects Eliot's musical allusions to the scientific discourse and discourse on women's relation to music of Eliot's day. She as well brings notions of German idealism to her reading of the presence of the "uncanny" and alludes to Eliot's interest in Helmholtz's work on sympathetic vibration. John Picker makes Helmholtz a central figure in his *Victorian Soundscapes,* particularly with regard to how he reads *Daniel Deronda.* Peter Capuano in "The Objective Aural-Relative in *Middlemarch*" explores Eliot's understanding of music through her translation of and interest in Arthur Schopenhauer's *Die Welt als Wille und Vorsetllung,* an understanding of an "aural reality," revealed in Schopenhauer's discussion of the relation of Will to music: "Music never expresses the phenomenon, but only the inner nature, the in-itself of all phenomena, the will itself . . . [T]he object of perception . . . contain[s] particulars only as the first forms abstracted from perception, as it were, the separated shell of things; thus they are, strictly speaking *abstracta;* music, on the other hand, gives the inmost kernel which precedes all forms, of the heart of things" (924).

his 1863 work *On the Sensations of Tone as a Physiological Basis for the Theory of Music,* writes about sensation, and in particular the sensation of sound, in groundbreaking ways that bridge the physiology of sound with the psychology of its experience, ways that continue to inform sound theory, ways that drew Eliot to him. Reading Helmholtz on music and visiting him in Freiburg with Lewes to observe a demonstration of his work, Eliot found a source for her understanding of sound in her attention to Helmholtz's work on the sensation of tone.[6] Helmholtz writes:

> Sensations result from the action of an external stimulus on the sensitive apparatus of our nerves. Sensations differ in kind, partly with the organ of sense excited, and partly with the nature of the stimulus employed. Each organ of sense produces peculiar sensations, which cannot be excited by means of any other; the eye gives sensation of light, the ear sensations of sound, the skin sensations of touch. Even when the sunbeams which excite in the eye sensations of light impinge on the skin and excite its nerves, they are felt only as heat, not as light. In the same way the vibration of elastic bodies heard by the ear, can also be felt by the skin, but in that case produce only a whirring sensation, not sound. The sensation of sound is therefore a species of reaction against external stimulus, peculiar to the ear, and excitable in no other organ in the body, and is completely distinct from the sensation of any other sense. (7)

The sensation of sound occurs because of the interaction between ear and external stimulus, or because of the way sound waves vibrate against the basilar membrane. Modern researchers of the physiology of sound, such as Mark Jude Tramo, confirm Helmholtz's pioneering studies; Tramo writes in "Music of the Hemispheres," "Residing in the cochlea of our inner ear is the basilar membrane. This membrane behaves like guitar strings of varying thickness, enabling groups of sensory receptors (hair cells) along its length to be activated in response to sounds of specific frequencies. The pattern of hair cell excitation is as orderly as the arrangement of keys on a piano, with equal steps along the chromatic scale mapped as equal distances along the basilar membrane" (55). In order for there to be sound, there must be atmospheric vibration, and in order for there to be sound heard, there must be a corresponding activation or vibration of the sensory receptors in the ear. An outside stimulus corresponds to a particular receptor in the

---

6. Eliot notes in her journal that she and Lewes visited Helmholtz in Freiburg in 1868 to observe a demonstration of his tuning forks. Writing in a journal entry of February 24, 1869, Eliot reveals that she was reading "Helmholtz on Music." Eliot published *Middlemarch* in 1871–72. For more biographical notes on Eliot's attentions to Helmholtz, see da Sousa Correa, 34.

body to make a particular sensation. Helmholtz's work on the physiology of perception, in particular his treatises on music and optics, explores how the correspondences between a physical stimulus and the body work to create sensation and perception.

Eliot draws on the idea of the interaction of external stimulus (sound wave) to physical organ (ear) as a means of working through how one consciousness meets or misses another. For Eliot, the ear is the porous space of the body, the boundary through which the voice, the messenger of the mind, can travel. Functioning as metaphors to represent open- or closed-mindedness and as literal embodiments, an "open ear" is the physical boundary that makes possible the entrance of the mind-sound of others into another's consciousness, and "a closed ear" is the physical closing that makes a consciousness deaf to the mind-sound of others. As William James writes, "Almost the entire difference lies in the fact that the bodily sounding-board, vibrating in one case, is mute in the other" (II, 471). Casaubon, Rosamond, Bulstrode are almost deaf to any voice but their own. For them the "problem of other minds" remains a problem because of their inability to understand or, worse still, acknowledge the very existence of another mind—they cannot allow in an external stimulus. This happens because all three live inside self-narratives that preclude the possibility of their being alive to the presence of others and what they might experience if they could hear their difference. Bulstrode holds tight to the threads of his present-day story of piety to keep the sins of the past at bay; Casaubon clings to an ongoing narrative about the importance of his work to keep from meeting his fear that it amounts to nothing and to keep from knowing his own puny, faulty heart. Rosamond lives inside a preconceived romance in which she maps out the course of her life as heroine, manages everyone, and need never change her mind because of her certain belief in her narrative. Narcissists, all three know themselves to be the candle at the center of the other metaphoric mirror—the pier-glass of chapter 27. Whereas Eliot attempts to mirror other men and things in her mind, the narcissist imagines himself to be the sun, the center, the light around which all others gather to mirror back to the sun its reflection: "Your pier-glass or extensive surface of polished steel made to be rubbed by a housemaid, will be multitudinously scratched in all directions; but place now against it a lighted candle as a centre of illumination, and lo! the scratches will seem to arrange themselves in a fine series of concentric circles round that little sun" (264). All three candles/egoisms understand the random scratches to tell with certainty the narratives they cling to, until the narratives fail. It's not that Rosamond, Casaubon, or Bulstrode is physically deaf or cannot make sound. All three hear and speak, but with such determination

to hear and to shape their sounds in a certain way that they do not hear
other ways or other sounds that do not correspond to their preconcep-
tions of or desires for a certain sound. Nor do the sounds they make ever
erupt into displays of spontaneity; instead, they use their voices as a form
of control. Artful, measured, Bulstrode always speaks in "undertones" and
uses his voice to point to others' errors (128); Casaubon pontificates in like
cadences to the imagined sounds of a Pascal, Locke, or Milton, and desires
that Dorothea be an "elegant-minded canary-bird" singing her uncritical
awe of him (200); and Rosamond speaks always with the self-control taught
her at Mrs. Lemon's finishing school and is the model of a "finished" Mrs.
Lemon's girl (96).

There seems to be no center to Rosamond other than her mirror: "She
was by nature an actress of parts that entered into her *physique:* she even acted
her own character, and so well, that she did not know it to be precisely her
own" (117). If Rosamond is by nature mimetic—an imitation—she displays
that most thoroughly in her relation to sound. Rosamond is known to be
the "best musician in Middlemarch" (117). Her piano instruction happened
at the hands of a Master Kapellmeister. Eliot writes:

> Rosamond, with the executant's instinct, had seized his manner of playing,
> and gave forth his large rendering of noble music with the precision of an
> echo. It was almost startling, heard for the first time. A hidden soul seemed
> to be flowing forth from Rosamond's fingers; and so indeed it was, since
> souls live on in perpetual echoes, and to all fine expression there goes
> somewhere an originating activity, if it be only that of an interpreter . . .
>
> Her singing was less remarkable, but also well trained, and sweet to
> hear as a chime perfectly in tune . . .—she only wanted to know what her
> audience liked. (161)

Rosamond can hear with uncanny clarity the music of Kapellmeister—so
much so that her piano performances live as his echo. Likewise, her voice
reflects a chime perfectly in tune. Rosamond is an embodied, desired record-
ing: she plays back the sounds of the world that she knows are well liked.
Almost soulless, Rosamond's is a well-liked copy, an interpretation. What
she cannot do, however, is listen to what is generally not pleasing; nor can
she make sounds as herself, not in imitation of others. The experience of
intersubjectivity—knowing another and being known by another—depends
on the acknowledgment of separate and mutual presence, or experiencing
one's own separate presence in simultaneity with the other's separate, co-
presence. There are no separate others for Rosamond to hear, finally, because
Rosamond has no separate soul yet of her own to hear—only echoes.

Lydgate, upon first hearing her play, imagines Rosamond to be "something exceptional," imagines her playing to reflect her own soul, realizes over time, through their marriage, that what he imagined is not so. In his mounting despair, Lydgate comes to understand that it is Rosamond's impenetrability, her iron resistance to hearing his difficult words, his hard reasons, his unpleasant pleas—her incapacity, finally, to be moved by him—that is the yoke that undoes him. He wonders, "What place was there in her mind for a remonstrance to lodge in?" (666). Rosamond can neither hear his critique of her nor hear his own despair. She does not house models of those sounds and so cannot make their echoes. Until Rosamond's brief encounter with Dorothea, we learn that there is no place, no room in her mind for Lydgate's troubled consciousness because she has not yet desired to master through imitation its type—the sounds of pain.

3. SYMPATHETIC VIBRATION

By contrast, when Dorothea muses about Will Ladislaw, after she learns of the codicil to the will and feels its effect—her "sudden strange yearning of heart towards Will Ladislaw" (490)—she realizes, "he was a creature who entered into every one's feelings, and could take the pressure of their thought instead of urging his own with iron resistance" (496). Will does what the skeptic claims he cannot—enter into "every one's feelings," as their feelings, without forcing his own. Because Will is always present to the array of stimuli that surround him, his openness makes him vibrate with an immediate responsiveness to what enters him. His eyes see, but his porous, open ears prompt a deeper sensation, make a deeper corresponding vibration. Will gets it wrong when he meets Dorothea—her words about his pictures, her attachment to Casaubon—"[He] had made up his mind that she must be an unpleasant girl" (80). Mind and eye mix. Will cannot yet encounter Dorothea, but catches her sound. We learn for the first time in the novel of Dorothea's voice, something no one until Will has heard: "But what a voice! It was like the voice of a soul that had once lived in an Aeolian harp" (80). And later when Will observes Dorothea as a tearful statue in Rome, leaning into her hand, he can, like his friend the painter Naumann, appreciate her for the moment as a living painting. However, it is Dorothea, the living woman, to whom he is most responsive. Will asks Naumann, "'This woman whom you have just seen . . . how would you paint her voice, pray? But her voice is much diviner than anything you have seen of her'" (191). Will feels her aliveness through his encounter with her voice—how it enters him, stirs him, vibrates within him.

Helmholtz differentiates music from noise when he asserts that noise makes "rapid irregular, but distinctly perceptible alternations of various kinds of sounds, which crop up fitfully . . . On the other hand, a musical tone strikes the ear as a perfectly undisturbed, uniform sound which remains unaltered as long as it exists, and it presents no alternation of various kinds of constituents" (7–8). If Dorothea's voice is like music, we can imagine an undisturbed, uniform sound that remains unaltered as long as it exists. However, we can't hear her voice—just that it is like an Aeolian harp, angels, the *Messiah:* "'She speaks in such plain words, and a voice like music. Bless me! it reminds me of bits in the *Messiah*—"and straightway there appeared a multitude of the heavenly host, praising God and saying"; it has a tone with it that satisfies your ears'" (552), Caleb Garth rhapsodizes. Her "voice like music" holds for Caleb the deepest of emotional experiences. Yet, how are we, as Eliot's readers unable to hear Dorothea, to understand this? Susanne Langer, the modern philosopher of aesthetics, who makes the relation between music and emotion her great topic, links feeling to form:

> Music is not the cause or cure of feelings, but their logical expression. (*Philosophy in a New Key* 218)

> The tonal structures we call "music" bear a close logical similarity to the forms of human feeling—forms of growth and attenuation, flowing and stowing, conflict and resolution, speed, arrest, terrific excitement, calm, or subtle activation and dreamy lapses—not joy and sorrow perhaps, but the poignancy of either and both—the greatness and brevity and eternal passing of everything vitally felt. Such is the pattern, or logical form, of sentience; and the pattern of music is that same form worked out in pure, measured sound and silence. Music is a tonal analogue of emotive life. (*Feeling and Form* 27)

Hearing Dorothea's sounds perhaps feels for both Caleb and Will as if they are being touched by something divine because her music is the tonal analogue of feeling blessed. For Martha Nussbaum music feels more like a dream that carries us not to the divine but to the most vulnerable, feeling parts of ourselves—

> Music can bypass habit, use, and intellectualizing, in such a way that its symbolic structures seem to pierce like a painful ray of light directly into the most vulnerable parts of the personality. Lacking the narrative and objectual structures to which we are accustomed in language, it frequently has an affinity with the amorphous, archaic, and extremely powerful emo-

tional materials of childhood. And it gives them a sharpening, an expressive precision, what Mahler calls crystallization, that they did not have when covered over by thoughts, in their still-archaic form. One enters the "dark world," in which language and daily structures of time and causality no longer reign supreme; and one finds the music giving form to the dim shapes of that darkness. Another way of expressing the point is that music seems to elude our self-protective devices, our techniques of manipulation and control, in such a way that it seems to write directly into our blood. (*Upheavals of Thought* 269)

In the way that a dream can penetrate so deeply and disorient so fully, music for Nussbaum has the power to carry us back to the darkness of the amorphous, the archaic—to infancy—to being again a bundle of defenseless, unknowing feelings in the dark world of utter vulnerability. The authors of "The Music of Nature and the Nature of Music," like Langer and Nussbaum, acknowledge that we find meaning and emotion in music. To understand that relation, these contemporary scientists do not suggest analogues but instead turn to the brain of our preverbal past: "Such an impenetrable vagueness about this most basic of human creations seems to signal that the roots of music lie closer to our lizard brain than to our more reasoning cortex, that music has a more ancient origin even than human language" (Gray et al. 54). Hearing the music of Dorothea perhaps feels divine, perhaps feels like a dream, perhaps feels archaic because of how it strikes the ancient, preverbal emotional chords of the "lizard brain" of those who can hear her. William James describes how when we listen to the human voice perform one of the verbal arts or when we listen to music, we feel our bodies respond, which we experience as our emotional response: "In listening to poetry, drama, or heroic narrative we are often surprised at the cutaneous shiver which like a sudden wave flows over us, and at the heart-swelling and the lachrymal effusion that unexpectedly catches us at intervals. In listening to music the same is even more strikingly true" (II, 457).[7] Dorothea's voice does not create chills in all who

7. Damasio helps explain James's recognition of the pleasurable response of the emotional body to voiced art and music in *Looking for Spinoza:* "There is an intimate and telling three-way connection between certain kinds of music, feelings of either great sorrow or great joy, and the body sensations we describe as 'chills' or 'shivers' or 'thrills.' For curious reasons, certain musical instruments, particularly the human voice, and certain musical compositions, evoke emotive states that include a host of skin responses such as making the hair stand on end, producing shudders, and blanching the skin. Perhaps nothing is more illustrative for our purposes than evidence from a study conducted by Anne Blood and Robert Zatorre. They wanted to study neural correlates of pleasurable states caused by listening to music capable of evoking chills and shivers down the spine. The investigators found those correlates in the somatosensing regions of the insula and anterior cingulate, which were significantly engaged by musically thrilling pieces. Moreover, the investigators

hear her. Eliot uses Dorothea's voice to distinguish one soul's quality and breadth from another. To feel the thrilling quality of Dorothea's sound marks her hearer as one with a like quality and breadth of emotion: Caleb feels a shiver like that which he feels listening to the *Messiah;* Will feels her resonating through him like the Aeolian harp; Lydgate feels her sound as a soul-piercing cry made part of his somatic memory. "Our good depends on the quality and breadth of our emotion" (469), Eliot writes. These are the men in *Middlemarch* whose good is akin to Dorothea's.

However, Eliot wants us not just to imagine what it sounds and feels like to hear Dorothea: she wants us to wonder what it means for a mind to hold music—what it means for words and music to meet—as a *poetry of being.* As Dorothea's readers, we are closest to her sounds when we hear the plainness and directness of Dorothea's language, mostly from her exchanges with Will about art or the good, as in:

> "I have a belief of my own, and it comforts me."
>
> "What is that?" said Will, rather jealous of the belief.
>
> "That by desiring what is perfectly good, even when we don't quite know what it is and cannot do what we would, we are part of the divine power against evil—widening the skirts of light and making the struggle with darkness narrower."
>
> "That is a beautiful mysticism—it is a—"
>
> "Please not to call it by any name," said Dorothea, putting out her hands entreatingly. "You will say it is Persian, or something else geographical. It is my life. I have found it out, and cannot part with it." (392)

Dorothea's simple words—"perfectly good"; "It is my life"; "I have found it out, and cannot part with it"—are her belief, her life, what she has experienced, what keeps her alive. They are the verbal expression of her deepest self. She refuses Will's desire to move toward the complexity of a learned language to analogize her belief or to place her words in some intellectual context: Dorothea literally pushes the intellectualizing process away with her hands. Dorothea's nature compares with Eliot's description in "Liszt, Wagner, and Weimar" of the great artists and musicians who are inspired not through their intellects, but for whom "the symbol rushes in

---

correlated the intensity of the activation with the reported thrill value of the pieces (which individual participants hand-picked) and not the mere presence of music" (102–3). Damasio draws on the research of Jaak Panksepp, "The Emotional Sources of Chills Induced by Music," *Music Perception* 13 (1995): 171–207, and Anne Blood and Robert Zatorre, "Intensely Pleasurable Responses to Music Correlate with Activity in Brain Regions Implicated in Reward and Emotion," *Proceedings of the National Academy of Sciences* 98 (2001): 11818–23.

on their imagination before their slower reflection has seized any abstract idea embodied in it" (88–89). The "symbol" for Eliot is involuntary and comes from a place of inspiration and passion, not from an idea. We can read Dorothea's simple sentences and understand that her words are the traces of her soul brought forward from within carried through her sounds—the mixed media of her soul's expression. Her words mean her feelings, as her voice makes their sounds. The music of Dorothea, therefore, is her being—simple, direct, unalterably intent on pursuing her truth—"a poem," Will calls her.

Strangely, perhaps, Caleb can hear Dorothea and be moved by her in the way that he is moved by the sounds of business. What for Helmholtz is the noise of industry, for Caleb is a symphony: "The echoes of the great hammer where roof or keel were a-making, the signal shouts of the workmen, the roar of the furnace, the thunder and plash of the engine, were a sublime music to him" (250). Caleb knows what it means to feel stirred by the stimuli of the labor that supports the social body: alive to its presence, he carries its sound within him as music. Labor for Caleb is consciousness of the social body. His attunement to the music of labor and its beneficent effects lead him to an idea: if he can bring consciousness of the social body to Fred's consciousness, then he will make a man of Fred. Eliot writes of the moment when the idea stirs inside Caleb in the way that Helmholtz writes of the idea of sympathetic vibration:

Deep in the petrous bone out of which the internal ear is hollowed lies a peculiar organ, the cochlea or snail shell—a cavity filled with water, and so called from its resemblance to the shell of a common garden snail. This spiral passage is divided throughout its length into three sections, upper, middle, lower, by two membranes stretched in the middle of its height. The Marchese Corti discovered some very remarkable formations in the middle section. They consist of innumerable plates, microscopically small, arranged orderly side by side, like the keys of a piano. They are connected at one end with the fibres of the auditory nerve, and at the other with the stretched membrane . . . [figure 1]

   In the so-called vestibulum, also where the nerves expand upon little membranous bags swimming in water, elastic appendages, similar to stiff hairs have been lately discovered at the ends of the nerves. The anatomical arrangement of these appendages leaves scarcely any room to doubt that they are set into sympathetic vibration by the waves of sound which are conducted through the ear. Now if we venture to conjecture—it is at present only a conjecture, but after careful consideration I am led to think

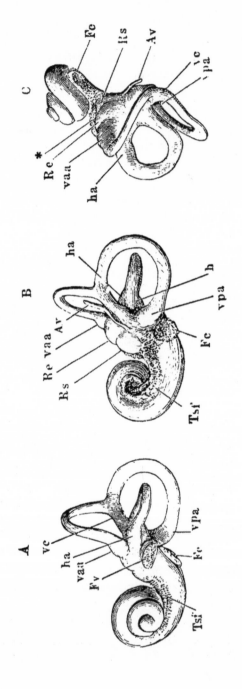

FIGURE 1 *Original description of figure*: A, left labyrinth from without. B, right labyrinth from within. C, left labyrinth from above. Fc, fenestra cochleae or round window. Fv, fenestra vestibŭli, or oval window. Re, recessus ellipticus. Rs, recessus sphaerĭcus. h, horizontal semicircular canal. ha, ampulla of the same. vaa, ampulla of the front vertical semicircular canal. vpa, ampulla of the back vertical semicircular canal. vc, common limb of the two vertical semicircular canals. Av, cast of the aquaeductus vestĭbŭli. Tsf, tractus spirālis forămĭnōsus. *Cast of the little canals which debouch on the pyrāmis vestĭbŭli

SOURCE: *On the Sensations of Tone as a Physiological Basis for the Theory of Music*, Herman L. F. Helmholtz, translated by Alexander J. Ellis (New York: Dover Publications, Inc., 1954), p. 136.

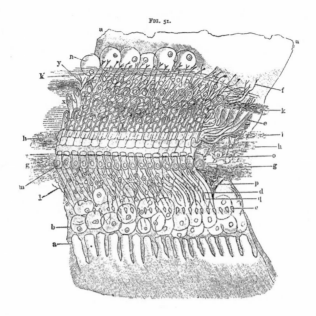

FIG. 51.

FIGURE 2
SOURCE: *On the Sensations of Tone as a Physiological Basis for the Theory of Music,* Herman L. F. Helmholtz, translated by Alexander J. Ellis (New York: Dover Publications, Inc., 1954), p. 141.

it very probable—that every appendage is tuned to a certain tone like the strings of a piano, then the recent experiment with a piano shows you that when (and only when) that tone is sounded the corresponding hair-like appendage may vibrate, and the corresponding nerve-fibre experience a sensation, so that the presence of each single tone in the midst of a whole confusion of tones must be indicated by the corresponding sensation. (Helmholz 136, 141) [figure 2]

Helmholtz observed that when a sonorous body is struck and its sound waves are carried to a corresponding receptor (a stringed musical instrument or the hair cells of the cochlea), vibrations are induced in the receptor and a like sound and harmonics are made. He called this sympathetic vibration or resonance.[8] Eliot writes: "I am not sure that certain fibres in Mr. Garth's mind had not resumed their old vibration towards the very

8. See *On the Sensations of Tone,* chapter 3, "Analysis of Musical Tones by Sympathetic Resonance," 36–49, and "On the Physiological Causes of Harmony in Music," 42–44.

end which now revealed itself to Fred" (561). One can almost imagine Caleb's mind vibrating in response to an idea that is likewise vibrating in Fred's mind. Eliot is interested in the moments of attunement that occur between minds—the scene with the railway workers becomes an idea for Fred's labor, which functions like the sound waves of a sonorous body carried from Garth's mind to Fred's corresponding and hence sympathetic mind. She uses Helmholtz's idea of the sympathetic vibration of sound to create a physiologic ground for mental attunement—what it means to be on the same "mental track"—a metaphor made real. The idea is yet to be spoken, but Fred vibrates in response to Caleb, in his like, corresponding presence.

But even more than a metaphor made real, sympathetic resonance embodies empathy—makes it possible—because it gives empathy a *physiology* for Eliot in *Middlemarch*. From the voicing of one's pain to its reception by another and resonance back, the embodiment of empathy happens for Eliot in the sound waves that travel across body boundaries potentially carrying from mind to mind. Damasio offers a neurologic account of embodied empathy through what are known as mirror neurons: "Those neurons can represent, in an individual's brain, the movements that very brain sees in another individual, and produce signals toward sensorimotor structures so that the corresponding movements are either 'previewed,' in simulation mode, or actually executed. These neurons are present in the frontal cortex of monkeys and humans, and are known as 'mirror neurons'" (*Looking* 115). The movement from taking in another's pain by hearing its account or seeing it causes the body to feel a mirrored pain in response because the mirror neurons represent its presence and the body executes its experience in an "as-if" way—Damasio's notion of the "as-if-body-loop." The mirror neurons and the as-if-body-loop make empathy possible—the pain of one felt in the body of another as if one's own pain. "Mirroring" as a holding and reflecting back of the object prompts the association of a visual signaling back and forth. Damasio writes of "the movements that very brain sees in an individual's brain"; William James writes that "the sight of suffering or danger to others is a direct exciter of interest, and an immediate stimulus, if no complication hinders, to acts of relief" (II, 410). But sight is only one form of its image-making/sensory enactment. For Eliot "mirroring" means *resonating,* a resonance prompted not by seeing another's pain, but by hearing it and vibrating back in sympathy. "The mirror is doubtless defective; the outlines will sometimes be disturbed; the reflection faint or confused; but I feel as much bound to tell you, as precisely as I can, what that reflection is, as if I were in the witness-box narrating my experience on oath." However defective, disturbed, faint, or

confused the process of reflective mirroring is for Eliot—because of its
nature as a looking-at experience—resonating in sympathetic vibration is
for Eliot not defective, not disturbed, faint, or confused. To resonate with
means to know the other, to be one with the other—at least for that
moment of resonance.

Lydgate hears Dorothea's cry about the dying Casaubon:

> "Oh, you are a wise man, are you not? You know all about life and death.
> Advise me. Think what I can do. He has been labouring all his life and
> looking forward. He minds about nothing else. And I mind about nothing
> else"—
>
> For years after Lydgate remembered the impression produced in him
> by this involuntary appeal—this cry from soul to soul, without other con-
> sciousness than their moving with kindred natures in the same embroiled
> medium, the same troublous fitfully illuminated life. (289–90)

The sound of Dorothea's pain enters Lydgate; it is impressed inside him;
Lydgate and Dorothea as corresponding sonorous bodies become "kindred
natures"; their minds meet in sympathetic resonance. Dorothea's sounds
continue to stay in Lydgate and resound later in his memory as "wondering impressions," as part of his somatic memory. Inside him, months later
he hears, "Advise me—think what I can do," and from the sound waves
outside he hears in response to his plea to Rosamond to help him in
their times of growing financial hardship and in his moment of mounting
despair, "What can I do, Tertius?" (593–94). The conditions must be right
for sympathetic resonance to occur—a corresponding sonorous body must
be present to vibrate to the emitted sound waves—something like what
Eliot means by having like "complexions of the soul." Lydgate cannot keep
himself from Dorothea's pain; he takes her in not by choice but because as
a corresponding sonorous body, he hears and then holds her cries within.
The movement of sound waves from Dorothea to Lydgate starts to free
her mind of pain's hold because of this re-embodiment of her pain in
him—her mind met and held by his mind. Rosamond, by contrast, cannot
open herself to Lydgate's pain. She does not choose, as Eliot puts it, this
complete missing of his "mental track"—she just does. Not a corresponding
sonorous body to Lydgate and so unable to hear him, Rosamond cannot
hold him within and resonate back. Without this sonorous resonance, the
boundary between Rosamond and Lydgate hardens and their minds divide.

Lydgate's pain is dropped. It falls back into the silence of Lydgate's mind
after the waves of sound find nowhere else to vibrate. Unheard and unheld
by another, Lydgate's silenced pain expands to fill his mind, to silence his

other voices, and to shake his sense of worth, until the appearance of a
corresponding sonorous body in Book Eight. Dorothea returns to share
in the emission and vibration of Lydgate's sound—now his cry from soul
to soul:

> "Not because there is no one to believe in you?" said Dorothea, pouring
> out her words in clearness from a full heart. "I know the unhappy mistakes
> about you. I knew them from the first moment to be mistakes. You have
> never done anything vile. You would not do anything dishonourable."
>
> It was the first assurance of belief in him that had fallen on Lydgate's
> ears. He drew a deep breath, and said "Thank you." He could say no more:
> it was something very new and strange in his life that these few words of
> trust from a woman should be so much to him.
>
> "I beseech you to tell me how everything was," said Dorothea fear-
> lessly. "I am sure that the truth would clear you."
>
> . . . He sat down again, and felt that he was recovering his old self in
> the consciousness that he was with one who believed in it . . .
>
> Dorothea's voice, as she made this childlike picture of what she would
> do, might have been almost taken as proof that she could do it effec-
> tively . . . he gave himself up, for the first time in his life, to the exquisite
> sense of leaning entirely on a generous sympathy, without any check of
> proud reserve. And he told her everything. (762–63)

Lydgate can come to consciousness of himself again because he is held by
Dorothea's belief in him, belief that she knows his consciousness still to
be his. Her knowledge of him is given to him through her words, which
enter him, resonate, and create a spaciousness for him to meet himself
again. And he meets himself through his words, which he offers both to
Dorothea and to himself. While Lydgate may have rehearsed the story
in his head, the utterance makes Lydgate's story concrete. He can give
the story to Dorothea for her to hold; as it is spoken out loud to her,
Lydgate can hear the story for himself; and he can feel the return of his
being somewhere between the waves of sounds they share. The Aeolian
harp has strings tuned in unison, on which the wind produces varying
harmonics over the same fundamental tone. I read it as a metaphor for
the body "mirrored" in sound in an as-if-body-loop exchange that occurs
between Lydgate and Dorothea—his pain held in her, her belief given back
to him—resonating between their voices and their hearing. Dorothea's
voice, this sound first heard by Will to be "like the voice of a soul that
had once lived in an Aeolian harp" (80), now invites Lydgate's voice, the
wind. So her belief in him—the fundamental tone—meets his story—the

varying harmonics. Lydgate can hear the sounds of his own consciousness for himself because they have been prompted to expression and held in the steady supportive tone of Dorothea's belief in him, as the strings that resonate in response to the wind of his voice. Dorothea's presence enables Lydgate to know himself again because he can hear himself again through her hearing sympathetic resonance.

In the way that Lydgate has no choice but to feel himself impressed by Dorothea's pain because of their "kindred natures," Dorothea has no choice but to feel Lydgate's pain. However, Dorothea's experience of resonance with Lydgate leads to a moral act. Dorothea offers herself to Lydgate, first as his hearer and then as his advocate. Most of all what she gives him in that space of offering is her belief in him. Lydgate's belief in himself has been hurt by the weight of carrying his pain alone and in silence; Dorothea's voiced belief in him reanimates its sounds within him, gives him the chance to know the sounds of belief again within and for himself. For Eliot, if sympathetic resonance makes feeling empathy a real possibility, choosing to judge and to act from that feeling endows empathy with the potential for moral judgment and moral action, what I take Eliot to mean by "the good."

4. BEING AND RESONANCE

Whereas Will "warbles" at the piano or lies on the rug and hums when in the company of Rosamond, when in the presence of Dorothea, Will feels no such easy pleasure of expression. He knows moments of intimate expression he's never before experienced, moments of fiery emotional outpouring, and moments in which he turns to stone. With the imposition of silence between corresponding souls, where the possibility for sympathetic resonance is withheld, comes the sensation of "two creatures slowly turning to marble in each other's presence" (543). The codicil imposes Casaubon's living death between them—it takes the form of silence. Eliot writes, "[E]ach was looking at the other, and consciousness was overflowed by something that suppressed utterance" (630–31). The aliveness that Dorothea and Will discover between them happens when they talk. For the lovers, not to speak means that what constitutes their aliveness, how they make their sounds together, is dampened. What remains is for them to be killed by the passion that cannot be uttered—the silence turns them to stone—or leads them to stage multiple partings in hopes that a sound will at last escape that starts the resonating cycle. In irritated response to Dorothea's "Please remember me," Will's "As if I were not in danger of forgetting everything else" (634) frees Dorothea's consciousness. It's as if the entrance of his words inside her causes her to become larger: "At that moment the parting was easy to bear: the first sense of loving and being loved excluded sorrow. It was if some hard icy pressure had melted, and her consciousness had room to expand; her past was come back to her with larger interpretation" (635). Will's speech—the entrance of his love inside her—melts the hard icy pressure (Casaubon's dead hand and not yet knowing Will's heart) that had squeezed Dorothea's consciousness into something smaller. The sound waves that carry the verbal expressions of his love don't just enter her consciousness, but transform it, expand it, and make her feel herself to be more. The silence between Will and Dorothea, two corresponding souls, is broken. Will's words and sounds enter Dorothea and, in sympathetic vibration, her consciousness breaks open to know a new freedom of feeling and being—a lover.[9]

Other minds remain for the realist, as for the skeptic, unknowable—another person's pain cannot be felt as he or she would feel it. In *Middlemarch,* there is no getting away from other minds. "[A]ny one watching keenly the stealthy convergence of human lots, sees a slow preparation of effects from one life on another" (95). For George Eliot, it is the human lot to converge—one human life affects others and one human life is affected by others. Any suffering or joy in *Middlemarch* reveals that preparation of effects from one life to another—a burst into expanded consciousness and the joy of feeling alive, or just a burst and the sorrow of feeling broken—trace in *Middlemarch* how a mind comes to know and feel known by another and expands, or fails to do so and breaks. Pain is just one part of a person's consciousness that may go unknown or unfelt by another, or that may resonate with another when a corresponding mind appears to hear the pain and bears it in mind and resonates back.

---

9. Catherine Gallagher pays needed critical attention to Dorothea's "strange yearning" toward Will Ladislaw for its erotic nature, for how it makes Dorothea not transcendent but immanent, embodied because sexual in her fine "George Eliot: Immanent Victorian," 71–72. Perhaps less erotic but equally embodied because surgical, in much the same way that Will's words melt the hard icy pressure inside Dorothea, when Dorothea goes to Rosamond to speak on behalf of Lydgate, Eliot writes of the effects of the entrance of Dorothea's tones inside even the immoveable imitation that is Rosamond as a bursting—though "as if a wound within her had been probed." Momentarily, she even makes Rosamond feel what it is to be a corresponding sonorous body to Dorothea—

> Dorothea, completely swayed by the feeling that she was uttering, forgot everything but that she was speaking from out of the heart of her own trial to Rosamond's. The emotion had wrought itself more and more into her utterance, till the tones might have gone into one's very marrow, like a low cry from some suffering creature in the darkness. And she had unconsciously laid her hand again on the little hand that she had pressed before.
> Rosamond, with an overmastering pang, as if a wound within her had been probed, burst into hysterical crying. . . . (795)

For Eliot, imagining and bearing another's pain is possible only if one has the capacity to imagine and bear one's own. "We should be very patient with each other, I think" (82) is an understanding Dorothea must learn over the course of the novel to feel for herself.

"Consciousness begins as the feeling of what happens when we see or hear or touch," writes Antonio Damasio (*The Feeling* 26). To be aware of one another, to know one another, to enter into and affect one another happens in *Middlemarch* when characters *hear* others as themselves.

CHAPTER 4

"Beloved Ideas Made Flesh"

The Embodied Mind and *Daniel Deronda*

1. GEORGE ELIOT'S EMBODIED MIND

I only know that I saw my wish outside of me.

—*Daniel Deronda,* George Eliot

Wanting her readers to know as she knows Hetty Sorrel's beauty—that which she calls a "springtide beauty"—George Eliot acknowledges in *Adam Bede* that that desire cannot be met:

> I might mention all the divine charms of a bright spring day, but if you had never in your life utterly forgotten yourself in straining your eyes after the mounting lark, or in wandering through the still lanes when the fresh-opened blossoms fill them with sacred, silent beauty like that of fretted aisles, where would be the use of my descriptive catalog? *I could never make you know what I meant by a bright spring day.* (Emphasis mine, 128)

What Eliot addresses is the possible failure of metaphor to make or be an object of shared understanding: if we have never felt about spring's beauty the way Eliot has, how are we her readers ever to know in the way that Eliot knows what it is meant to embody, namely the far more abstract and unknowable beauty of her creation Hetty? Though we share in the knowledge of spring, even in spring's beauty, we cannot know that we have experienced or felt that beauty in the same way; though we read Eliot's writing, and have minds to imagine what her words mean, we cannot know that we know what Eliot means.

The ache we hear in Eliot's voice about the possible failure of the metaphor "springtide beauty" to make present to us Hetty's beauty concludes in an expression of Eliot's powerlessness to bring us into her mind: "I could never make you know what I meant by a bright spring day." Her questioning of the efficacy of metaphor in *Adam Bede* contributes, I think, to her vision of mind as separate—not wholly enclosed because mirroring of others—yet generally limited to the experience of self-enclosure. As I discuss in chapter 3, not only does *Adam Bede* express Eliot's doubts about her powers as author to know other "men and things" except as reflections of her mind, but in this moment she as well doubts that her readers can know how she means those reflections. Metaphor, the mirroring medium of representation of the verbal arts, she tells us, fails.

But no such resignation about the limits of metaphor to make understanding between minds possible weighs down the pages of *Daniel Deronda*. In moments of profound shifts of recognition brought on by one mind making its way into another, startling uses of metaphor—metaphors that literally "bite"—fill the pages of *Deronda* with an insistence that makes visible the fundamental role metaphor plays in the rhetorical architecture of the novel. What I'm imagining is that sometime between Eliot's writing of *Adam Bede* and *Daniel Deronda*, Eliot's doubts about the possibility of mind meeting mind transform into hopes. In the way that sound makes possible a physical space for minds to mingle in *Middlemarch,* metaphor—the medium of Eliot's art—makes possible a space of imagining for minds to meet in *Daniel Deronda.* Perhaps this has something to do with her own shifting of consciousness from philosopher who writes ideas as arguments about the nature of being to novelist who embodies ideas as representations of being—from philosopher who writes arguments to artist who represents in metaphor.

Eliot reveals her shifting acknowledgment of the powers and uses of metaphor as a reflection both of the powers and limits of mind and of the sheer pervasiveness of metaphorical thinking in *Middlemarch* and *The Mill on the Floss.* Casaubon, who imagines a future of "that matrimonial garden" and trades in his bachelorhood for that metaphor, comes not to experience that garden. Eliot writes of the power of metaphor to influence Casaubon's fatal choice as an example of how we all fall prey to metaphor's control of our minds and so, too, of our actions: "[F]or we, all of us, grave or light, get our thoughts entangled in metaphors, and act fatally on the strength of them" (85). In *The Mill on the Floss,* when considering the failures of Tom to grasp Latin and his tutor Mr. Stelling to grasp that Tom's mind is unique, Eliot wonders about how metaphor can both represent and fail to represent another mind. For Mr. Stelling, Tom's mind, in its inability to grasp "etymology and demonstrations," must be "ploughed and harrowed":

> [I]t was his favourite metaphor, that the classics and geometry constituted that culture of the mind which prepared it for the reception of the subsequent crop. I say nothing against Mr. Stelling's theory: if we are to have one regimen for all minds his seems to me as good as any other. I only know it turned out uncomfortably for Tom Tulliver as if he had been plied with cheese in order to remedy a gastric weakness which prevented him from digesting it. (147)

To have a "favourite metaphor" for *all* minds assumes all minds can be represented in one way because they are the same, which is to say, because they are the same reflection of the author's mind. To act on that favorite metaphor by treating the other mind as the metaphor defines a model of human interaction—"I know you to be my metaphor of you, as its embodiment, and I behave toward you as that metaphor"—Tom Tulliver is to be ploughed and harrowed. But Tom doesn't do well as Stelling's metaphor of him. "It turns out uncomfortably for him," Eliot writes, and then represents his mental discomfort with the gastric simile "as if he had been plied with cheese in order to remedy a gastric weakness which prevented him from digesting it." Stelling for Eliot models how we each depend on favorite metaphors; how the holding of that favorite metaphor determines how we know, imagine, and treat another; how difficult it is to change those metaphors when they don't work; and how perhaps even more difficult it is to try to particularize metaphors of mind to represent how we understand the particularity of one another's minds. To follow Stelling's metaphor with a simile of her own reveals Eliot's recognition that her own capacity to render Tom's mind, as his author, depends on metaphor. Even in her recognition of the limits of metaphor to say what something is, Eliot cannot transcend her own metaphorical thinking. But the turn to metaphor does not mean in *The Mill on the Floss* the incapacity to know what another knows for Eliot, but rather makes evident how one knows and how one conveys one's knowledge. Eliot continues:

> It is astonishing what a different result one gets by changing the metaphor! Once call the brain an intellectual stomach, and one's ingenious conception of the classics and geometry as ploughs and harrows seems to settle nothing. But then, it is open to some one else to follow great authorities and call the mind a sheet of white paper or a mirror, in which case one's knowledge of the digestive process becomes quite irrelevant. . . . O Aristotle! if you had

had the advantage of being "the freshest modern" instead of the greatest ancient, would you not have mingled your praise of metaphorical speech as a sign of high intelligence, with a lamentation that intelligence so rarely shows itself in speech without metaphor,—*that we can so seldom declare what a thing is, except by saying it is something else?* (Emphasis mine, 147)

"!" and "astonishing" make rare appearances in *The Mill on the Floss*. Their presences invite us to feel astonished by what they modify: the powers of metaphor. Change the metaphor and our understanding of mind radically alters. The mind as *tabula rasa,* the mind as mirror, the mind as intellectual stomach—each representation is a conception of mind, each creates another way of knowing what it means to be human. What greater power of language is imaginable? Eliot "astonished" tells us of the world-making capacity of metaphor. But then, Eliot "lamenting" tells us that that world-making speech has limits: "[W]e can so seldom declare what a thing is, except by saying it is something else." In her apostrophe to Aristotle, Eliot understands Aristotle's praise of metaphor in *Poetics* to be an ancient conception of metaphor's powers. Here's Aristotle: "It is a great thing to make use of . . . double words and rare words . . . but by far the great thing is the use of metaphor. That alone cannot be learned; it is a token of genius. *For the right use of metaphor means an eye for resemblances*" (emphasis mine, *Fragmenta* XXII, 16). Eliot's recognition that there is no "right" use of metaphor, just different uses, and that an "eye for resemblances" acknowledges an ability to say merely what something is "like" or "not," not what it is, is for Eliot the modern sense of metaphor's powers, which means its limits. Thomas Nagel, the philosopher of mind, helps make sense of Eliot's modern recognition of how difficult it is to say what something "is":

I believe it is precisely this apparent clarity of the word "is" that is deceptive. Usually when we are told that *X* is *Y* we know *how* it is supposed to be true, but that depends on a conceptual or theoretical background and is not conveyed by the "is" alone. We know both how "X" and "Y" refer, and the kinds of things to which they refer, and we have a rough idea how the two referential paths might converge on a single thing, be it an object, a person, a process, an event, or whatever. But when the two terms of the identification are very disparate it may not be so clear how it could be true. We may not even have a rough idea of how the two referential paths could converge, or what kinds of things they may converge on, and a theoretical framework may have to be supplied to enable us to understand this. Without the framework, an air of mysticism surrounds the identification. ("What?" 6)

For Nagel, to say "is" is to say X is Y—which is to say something is something else. And for the most part this works because we get a "rough idea" of how the referential paths of two like things might converge because of their shared conceptual framework. So the best we can do is follow in a rough way how path X similar to path Y meet, or how something is something else in this frame of similarity. However, when the paths or what stands on opposite sides of the "is" lacks a shared conceptual framework to help us understand how or where they meet, then we don't know where we are because we can't frame how X is Y. Like Nagel, Eliot recognizes in *The Mill on the Floss* that our speech by nature is metaphoric—that the best we can do is say something is something else. And that we use conceptual frames to help us understand what our metaphors mean. The shared conceptual frame of "objects that can be filled" enables us to understand how X, the mind, is Y, a blank page or mirror or intellectual stomach. Yet Eliot still laments that metaphoric speech means in the words of the linguist George Lakoff and the philosopher Mark Johnson "understanding and experiencing one kind of thing in terms of another" (*Metaphors* 5).

The Mill on the Floss displays how the particular natures of character minds reveal themselves partially through those characters' similes for Maggie. We understand her mother's conventionality in the metaphors of its destruction or alterity that she chooses for Maggie: "like a wild thing"; "gypsy"; "like a small Medusa with her snakes cropped." We understand the social ordering of Tom's mind in his metaphors of Maggie's domestication: "[S]hetland pony" and "sky terrier," and its failure: "like a young lioness." Philip's romantic model of understanding leads him to name Maggie a "princess turned into an animal," while her father's passionate nature names her his "little wench." Maggie's understanding of her own mind reveals itself in her self-metaphor as one who "fashioned the world afresh in her thoughts"—as an author. But the author cannot say what she seeks to author. It is a "something" that seems to defy the X is Y. Eliot the narrator writes Maggie's mind first as an extended, almost nonconcretized metaphor and then as almost without metaphor:

> Maggie was a creature full of eager passionate longings for all that was beautiful and glad . . . with a blind, unconscious yearning for *something* that would link together the wonderful impressions of this mysterious life and give her soul a sense of home in it. (Emphasis mine, 247–48)

And later:

> She thought it was part of the hardship of her life that there was laid upon

her the burthen of larger wants than others seemed to feel, that she had to endure this wide hopeless yearning for that *something, whatever it was,* that was greatest and best on earth. (Emphasis mine, 300)

Maggie's search for the "something" is for me Eliot's search for the X of X—that which is beyond metaphor, that which we can know not as something else but as itself, and not just any something but that which is "greatest and best on earth." Maggie's desire is to reach beyond metaphor to "the thing itself"; Maggie's experience is to reach it by half: "[S]he felt the half-remote presence of a world of love and beauty and delight, made up of vague, mingled images from all the poetry and romance she had ever read, or had ever woven in her dreamy reveries" (400). Significantly, Maggie moves halfway into the world of love, beauty, and delight when she hears Stephen sing. If Eliot comes in *Middlemarch* to imagine sound as the fundamental means through which one mind can know another, *The Mill on the Floss* makes sound the promise of such knowledge, such experience unfulfilled. But it is not whole. In her rejection of Stephen, Maggie remembers "longing after perfect goodness" (497). Loving Stephen when Lucy and Philip must suffer from it makes her love of Stephen not the "something," and essentially ends the possibility of its discovery. Tom reunited with Maggie in death may constitute an end, but it does not constitute an answer to the search. Eliot's emerging acceptance of metaphor as a pathway toward understanding other minds does not seem to alter her rejection of metaphor as a means of knowing and of expressing "what the something is" in *The Mill on the Floss.* Rather, it is an expression of a seeming inexpressibility, the unknowable because unnamable X.

The work of George Lakoff and Mark Johnson, who bring current research in cognitive science to their revisionary account of the mind/body problem, helps uncover why, from a cognitive perspective, Eliot might have grown naturally less skeptical of metaphor's capacity to move minds closer together, even if metaphor doesn't yield the X of X. In *Philosophy in the Flesh,* Lakoff and Johnson make three basic claims: "The mind is inherently embodied. Thought is mostly unconscious. Abstract concepts are largely metaphorical" (3). They write:

> Our subjective mental life is enormous in scope and richness. We make subjective judgments about such abstract things as importance, similarity, difficulty, morality, and we have subjective experiences of desire, affection, intimacy and achievement. Yet, as rich as these experiences are, much of the way we conceptualize them, reason about them, and visualize them comes from other domains of experience. These other domains are mostly

sensorimotor domains, as when we conceptualize understanding an idea (subjective experience) in terms of *grasping an object* (sensorimotor experience) and failing to understand an idea as having it go *right by us* or *over our heads.* The cognitive mechanism for such conceptualizations is conceptual metaphor, which allows us to use the physical logic of grasping to reason about understanding. (Emphasis mine, 45)

They continue:

> Our brains are structured so as to project activation patterns from sensorimotor areas to higher cortical areas. These constitute what we have called primary metaphors. Projections of this kind allow us to conceptualize abstract concepts on the basis of inferential patterns used in sensorimotor processes that are directly tied to the body. (77)

Understanding the structuring of our conscious and unconscious thought as reflective of how the brain uses patterns of sensorimotor processing to conceptualize abstractions helps us in turn to understand why when we want to express a thought or feeling we do so as an *object* or through *physical orientation* or through a *language of containment.* If the mind is embodied, then the mind must rely on how the body experiences being to structure how conscious and unconscious thought and feeling manifest themselves. As William James writes, "All our inward images tend invincibly to attach themselves to something sensible, so as to gain corporeity and life. Words serve this purpose, gestures serve it, stones, straws, chalk-marks, anything will do. As soon as anyone [*sic*] of these things stands for the idea, the latter seems more real" (II, 305). The relation of the brain's processing of the body's physical experience to the mind's processing of abstract thought meet in metaphor. We need objects and their signifying presence in language—*nouns*—and containers and orienters and what they add in their signifying presence—*prepositions*—to help to think and feel what is abstract precisely because abstraction has no material presence or orientation or containers to "grasp"—"to gain corporeity and life." This is the work of metaphor.

If we acknowledge that abstract thoughts are largely metaphorical, then *Adam Bede* and *The Mill on the Floss,* like *Daniel Deronda,* must depend on metaphor for much of their telling. But I want to suggest that Eliot has a different relation to her use of metaphor in *Deronda,* that she has put it to work not just as an unconscious reflection of her embodied mind, or even as a conscious analysis of how minds conceive of other minds as forms of self-reflection, but as a conscious artistic choice for how to display moments of meeting, mingling, and metamorphosis of mind between her characters, her readers, and herself. My assertion is this: minds meet in *Daniel Deronda* as their metaphors for themselves and one another. Lakoff and Johnson suggest something of how this might be possible when they write in *Metaphors We Live By:*

> Understanding our experiences in terms of objects and substances allows us to pick out parts of our experience and treat them as discrete entities or substances of a uniform kind. Once we can identify our experiences as entities or substances, we can refer to them, categorize them, group them, and quantify them—and, by this means, reason about them. (25)

To understand our feelings and thoughts in terms of objects makes it possible to subject them to objective analysis—to reference, categorization, grouping, quantification—in essence, to empirical understanding. How much easier to grasp one's own mental abstraction when it is embodied, and, when the mental abstraction is another's, how much more possible. But is being able to reason together about a concretized abstraction enough to bring us to a shared understanding or knowledge of it—to a *meeting of minds?*

At some moment in my study of *Deronda,* I became so overwhelmed by the presence of Eliot's metaphors or metaphorlike constructions that I found myself doing what Lakoff and Johnson suggest our minds do to make sense of a mental experience: I began to keep records of them and to group them into the categories of a cognitive map I call "Modes of Shift." I set to work on this map to help me recognize and keep track of Eliot's metaphors, to understand what Eliot means by their presence in *Daniel Deronda,* and to analyze why these expressions feel so overwhelming. While technically not all metaphors, all of the following instances of linguistic modal shift borrow from metaphor's metamorphosing magic to transform one being into another, or to claim equivalence between beings, so that "this" is "that." Here is the outline of that cognitive map:

MODES OF SHIFT

I. *Words Become Animate Objects*
   a. "The words had nestled their venomous life within her, and stirred continually the vision of the scene at the whispering stones" (424).
   b. "They both stood silent for a minute, as if some third presence had arrested them,—for Deronda, too, was under the sense of pressure which is apt to come when our winged words seem

to be hovering around us" (452).

   c. "The words were like the touch of a miraculous hand to Gwendolen. Mingled emotions streamed through her frame with the strength that seemed the beginning of a new existence" (769).

II. *Internal Life (Wishes, Dreams, Feelings, Consciousness) Becomes Solid Objects*

   a. "Could there be a slenderer, more insignificant thread in human history than this consciousness of a girl, busy with her small inferences of the way in which she could make her life pleasant?" (124).

   b. "There was a gust—he was struck—I know nothing—I only know that I saw my wish outside me" (696).

   c. "This sort of passion had nested in the sweet-natured, strong Rex, and he had made his mind up to its companionship, as if it had been an object supremely dear, stricken dumb and helpless, and turning all the future into a shadow of the past" (711).

III. *Inanimate Objects Become Animated with Words*

   a. "Within all the sealed paper coverings was a box, but within the box there was a jewel-case; and she felt no doubt she had the diamonds. But on opening the case, in the same instant that she saw their gleam she saw a letter lying above them . . . It was as if an adder had lain on them . . . and as she opened the bit of thin paper, it shook with the trembling of her hands. But it was legible as print, and thrust its words upon her.

      'These diamonds, which were once given with ardent love to Lydia Glasher, she passes on to you . . . I am the grave in which your chance of happiness is buried as well as mine'" (358).

   b. "Gwendolen had said to herself that she would never wear those diamonds: they had horrible words clinging and crawling about them, as from some bad dream, whose images lingered on the perturbed sense" (426).

IV. *Objects Reappear as the Same Form, but Different*

   a. The Dead Head of the portrait revealed from out of its casing becomes Grandcourt's Dead Face.

   b. The Key to the portrait's casing becomes the Key to the boudoir that holds the knife.

V. *Desires Become People*

   a. "Reverently let it be said of this mature spiritual need that it was akin to the boy's and girl's picturing of the future beloved; but the stirrings of such young desire are feeble compared with the passionate current of an ideal life straining to embody itself" (474).

Becomes:

"He was struck by the appearance of Deronda, and it is perhaps comprehensible now why Mordecai's glance took on a sudden eager interest as he looked at the new-comer: he saw a face and frame which seemed to him to realise the long-conceived type" (479).

   b. Gwendolen's desire to "master" and Grandcourt the master appears.
   c. Hope is Deronda: "So pregnant is the divine hope of moral recovery with the energy that fulfills it. So potent in us is the infused action of another soul before which we bow in complete love. But the new existence seemed inseparable from Deronda: the hope seemed to make his presence permanent" (769).

VI. *People Become Objects*
   a. The chest becomes Deronda's grandfather.
   b. The diamonds are Lydia—and more generally "a woman's life" (152).

VII. *Objects Change Meaning*
   The Necklace:
   a. The necklace *pawned:* "They [the three turquoises] had belonged to a chain once her father's; but she had never known her father; and the necklace was in all respects the ornament she could most conveniently part with" (19).
   b. The necklace *rescued:* "It was Deronda; he must have seen her go into the shop; he must have gone in immediately after, and repurchased the necklace. He had taken an unpardonable liberty, and had dared to place her in a thoroughly hateful position . . . he was entangling her in helpless humiliation" (20).
   c. The necklace as *memorial:* "When Gwendolen was dressing, she longed, in remembrance of Leubronne, to put on the old turquoise necklace for her ornament . . . Determined to wear the memorial necklace somehow, she wound it thrice around her wrist and made a bracelet of it" (440).
   d. The necklace as *understanding:* "I suppose there is some understanding between you and Deronda about that thing on your wrist. If you have anything to say to him, say it. But don't carry on a telegraphing which other people are not supposed to see" (446).

VIII. The Meaning of One Thing Becomes the Meaning of Another Thing
    a. The meaning of gambling—"Your win is another's loss"—
       Becomes:
       "I ought not to have married . . . I broke my promise . . . I
       wanted to make my gain out of another's loss—you remem-
       ber?—it was like roulette—and the money burnt into me . . . It
       was as if I had prayed that another should lose and I win. And
       I had won" (692).
  IX. One Kind of Physical Action Becomes Another
    a. "Deronda felt the look as if she had been stretching her arms
       towards him from a forsaken shore" (769).
   X. One Mode of Experience Becomes Another
    a. Gwendolen's emotional pain is physical pain:
       LYDIA: "The wrong you have done me will be your curse"
       (448).
       GWENDOLEN: "Why did you put your fangs into me and not
       him?" (448).

These expressions suggest sometimes a form of equivalence between unlike entities, sometimes a yoking together of qualities that is unexpected (something like Coleridge's idea of "Fancy" or Donne's of conceit), sometimes a transformation from "this" into "that." But *always* they define a mental experience that is embodied: the physical presence of the transforming or transformed object lends weight and mass to the internal experience both to grant its occurrence in space and time and to turn it from being a subjective internal event to an intersubjectively available external event. And *always* they define an experience that is about bringing together—so that a feeling state of holding gets enacted that refuses to allow separation. These moments happen during instances of shifting recognition, and are never easy. One mind presses upon another with its claims, its presence, and the receiving mind responds in refusal or in acceptance. These negotiations of consciousness-mingling occur almost always in *Daniel Deronda* as a felt-metaphoric exchange. In perhaps the most poignant moment of one mind seeking attachment to another, Daniel offers himself to the Alcharisi: "'Mother! Take us all into your heart . . . Take my affection.' . . . 'I reject nothing, but I have nothing to give,' she released his hand and sank back on her cushions. Deronda turned pale with what *seems always more of a sensation than an emotion—the pain of repulsed tenderness*" (emphasis mine, 634). "Take us all into your heart. Take my affection"—the metaphor of being held in the mother's heart as the embodied plea for emotional attachment physically finds its enactment in held hands, until they are dropped—the plea refused.

Deronda's response, what he feels—"the pain of repulsed tenderness"—is for Eliot only knowable as emotional-sensation/sensational-emotion because sensation and emotion here cannot be separated. Eliot never stands back in *Daniel Deronda* to wonder whether we can know what she means by these metaphors; instead, she writes us into the feeling states of her characters' minds and her mind by embodying their emotional power and presence as forms of physical power and presence—feeling states made intersubjectively available "out there" and held in attachment between our minds "in here."

George Eliot's recognition of human understanding as bound always to the reality-making consciousness of a particular mind forces her to embrace what she can know—her own mind. Set in motion, her ideas move across world-representing pages, embodied in characters that mirror for us Eliot's mind. And we can see reflections of Eliot's mind because of what she has given us to imagine:

> . . . commonplace, perhaps half-repulsive objects which are really the beloved ideas made flesh. Here undoubtedly lies the chief poetic energy:—in the force of imagination that pierces or exalts solid fact, instead of floating among cloud-pictures. (381)

Eliot's embrace and harnessing of the "chief poetic energy"—"the force of the imagination that pierces or exalts fact"—leads her to dwell in and see through the commonplace, object world to "beloved ideas made flesh." This for me is the first in a series of astonishing turns that Eliot makes in *Daniel Deronda:* the physical world, she asserts, holds the metaphysical—ideas embodied as flesh. Eliot's translations of Spinoza's major philosophic texts, *Tractatus theologico-politicus* in 1849 and the *Ethics* in 1854, must have contributed to how Eliot came to consider the embodiment of ideas. In much the same way that Damasio describes his own intellectual odyssey in *Looking for Spinoza* from reading Spinoza as an adolescent and saving on a strip of paper some words by Spinoza on the notion of the self, to reading him again as an adult neurologist and discovering their convergence of thinking on the relation of mind and body, I'm imagining that the thinking Eliot did about Spinoza's ideas while translating his works prior to her emergence as a novelist finds its way into how she comes to imagine the nature of being.[1] To spend the hours of intense focus and study necessary to bring Spinoza's work to life in English from the Latin meant not just that Eliot was thinking about his ideas day after day, but that his thinking mattered

---

1. Linda Raphael in *Narrative Skepticism* makes note of Eliot's probable turn to Spinoza's thinking, citing Susan James's discussion of Spinoza in her *Passion and Action: The Emotions in Seventeenth Century Philosophy,* when Raphael considers the "bodily nature of Dorothea's pain" (79).

to her enough to merit devoting those years to it. Damasio returns like a refrain to a proposition from the *Ethics* II: "The human mind is the very idea or knowledge of the human body" (*Ethics* II, Proposition XIX, 101).[2] For Eliot metaphor is that refrain. Metaphor works in *Daniel Deronda* as a verbal trace or presence of its truth—ideas and word pictures are bound together, one holds the other, depends on the other to be. To dwell deeply in metaphor means to feel/know the inseparability of body/mind, physical/ metaphysical. However, for the mind to make and inhabit its metaphors and the metaphors of others requires that "chief poetic energy"—imagination. Through the force of imagination that sees through or raises up facts, Eliot claims, we come to our beloved ideas, not by wandering in the clouds. *Imagine the facts to understand the ideas.* But what does it mean to imagine the facts? Aren't facts what we accept? And what ideas do the facts hold?

2. IMAGINING THE UNIMAGINABLE

> It had been Gwendolen's habit to think of the persons around her as stale books, too familiar to be interesting. Deronda had lit up her attention with a sense of novelty: not by words only, but by *imagined facts,* his influence had entered into the current of that self-suspicion and self-blame which awakens a new consciousness.
>
> —*Daniel Deronda,* George Eliot (emphasis mine)

Imagine asking the question "What is a Jew?" And then imagine saying the sentence "I am a Jew, and am glad of it." This movement—from imagining the other to imagining the other as another self or as oneself—is the final and most pressing rhetorical act of imagining other minds that George Eliot prompts us to undertake in *Daniel Deronda.* But it comes to us as the culmination of a long series of such prompts that take us as their readers from imagining a person, a thought, a feeling "out there" to imagining being that person, thinking that thought, feeling that feeling "in here." Here's a sample of such moments in *Deronda:* "*Imagine* him in such a scene: a boy of thirteen, stretched prone on the grass where it was in shadow, his curly head propped on his arms over a book" (emphasis mine, 164). And: "*Imagine* her—it is always good to *imagine* a human creature in whom bodily loveliness seems as properly one with the entire being as the bodily loveliness of those wondrous transparent orbs of life that we find in the sea—*imagine* her with her dark hair brushed from her temples, but yet showing tiny rings there which had cunningly found their own way

2. See, as well, Proposition XIII on this idea.

back, the mass of it hanging behind just to the nape of the little neck in curly fibres" (emphasis mine, 372). And: "*Imagine*—we all of us can—the pathetic stamp of consumption with its brilliancy of glance to which the sharply defined structure of features reminding one of a forsaken temple, give already a far-off look as of one getting unwillingly out of reach; and *imagine* it on a Jewish face" (emphasis mine, 495).[3] Elaine Scarry's *Dreaming by the Book* is a remarkable account of how the language of novels can bring its readers to imagine that what is not present is present. Novels call on their readers to imagine all the time, indeed to imagine everything. With the exception of brief, infrequent addresses to the "Reader" or postmodern narratives constructed in the second person, they do so mostly implicitly. However, *Deronda* does so as an imperative and as a refrain throughout its eight hundred pages. Hearing the pressing return of Eliot's "imagine command," we must wonder, why is Eliot so deeply invested in the self-conscious call to imagine, to bring us to repeated consciousness that we are imagining in *Daniel Deronda*?

The opening of *Deronda* does not begin, "Imagine a man, arrested by the sight of a woman, and lost in wondering, 'Was she beautiful or not beautiful?'" Instead, in her epigraph to the first chapter, Eliot tells us that to begin anything—from science to poetry—we must have "the make-believe of a beginning," meaning we must imagine the beginning of time or a time. Eliot claims from her opening words that *we experience by imagining,* and that we do so without for the most part consciously knowing it. As Eliot's readers, we don't know that that is what we are being framed to do at what stands as the imaginary beginning of *Deronda,* "Was she beautiful or not beautiful?" (7). We begin as we expect to begin, by unconsciously becoming present through the descriptions of words to an imaginary world. As *Deronda* evolves from the opening, however, Eliot

3. Here are other such moments: "*Imagine* a rambling, patchy house, the best part built of grey stone, and red-tiled, a round tower jutting at one of the corners, the mellow darkness of its conical roof surmounted by a weather-cock making an agreeable object either amidst the gleams and greenth of summer or the low-hanging clouds and snowy branches of winter" (emphasis mine, 339). And: "*Imagine* the difference in rate of emotion between this woman whom the years had worn to a more conscious dependence and sharper eagerness, and this man whom they were dulling into a more neutral obstinacy" (emphasis mine, 345). And: "*Imagine* the conflict in a mind like Deronda's, given not only to feel strongly, but to question actively, on the evening after that interview with Mordecai . . . it had stirred Deronda so deeply, that with the usual reaction of his intellect he began to examine the grounds of his emotion, and consider how far he must resist its guidance" (emphasis mine, 509). And: "*Imagine* the difference in Deronda's state of mind when he left England and when he returned to it. He had set out for Genoa in total uncertainty how far the actual bent of his wishes and affections would be encouraged . . . He came back with something like a discovered charter warranting the inherited right that his ambition had begun to yearn for: he came back with what was better than freedom—with a duteous bond which his experience had been preparing him *to accept gladly*" (emphasis mine, 744).

becomes increasingly insistent that we attend to what we are actually doing. It stops being enough that we accept unreflectingly the narrative's transmission of being. In actively attending to what we imagine, we are being urged by Eliot to move from "that world, those people" described by Eliot to "this world, this people" imagined and taken in as or through ourselves. I would assert that Eliot calls upon us not just to "imagine otherness" but to feel knowingly what it means to imagine another in the sense of being another, or in the sense of another being oneself. And she does so to portray how it is possible for a consciousness to metamorphose from one way of being to being another: by imagining being another in *Daniel Deronda,* one becomes (an)other.

Early in the novel, Eliot stages Gwendolen and Deronda in a push-and-pull struggle, in which each feels at once drawn to and repelled by the other. Feeling arrested by the presence of the other in the sense of drawn to and coerced by are the feeling states of "unrest" Eliot defines throughout the novel. Deronda's question "Was she beautiful or not?" leads him to "[W]hy was the effect that of unrest rather than of undisturbed charm? Why was the wish to look again felt as coercion and not as a longing in which the whole being consents?" (7). And a few pages later, Eliot writes of Gwendolen, "[H]er eyes met Deronda's, and instead of averting them as she would have desired to do, she was unpleasantly conscious that they were arrested—how long?" (10). Feeling drawn to the other against one's will, while not pleasant, is necessary in the world of *Deronda.* There seems to be no choice for these characters: this is a book about the moment when, as the philosopher and animal trainer Vicki Hearne calls it, attention must be paid to "the simple and astounding knowledge that others exist" (xvi), the moment when the other must be noticed, to the point of "taking the other in." And it is a book about how taking the other in occurs through the imagination, and what follows from it. Barbara Hardy describes imagination in Eliot as the performance of imaginative actions: her characters "image, generalize, relate, harmonize, unify, sympathize, invent, and make" (181). For Hardy, Eliot sets imagination in motion through forms of imaging, synthesis, and invention. And William James in his chapter "Imagination" writes, "Fantasy, or Imagination, are the names given to the faculty of reproducing copies of originals once felt" (II, 44). Whether a cognitive act of visual synthesis or some form of reproduction of the once felt, imagining in both descriptions requires a movement between the experienced "out there" and the remaking/re-experiencing of it "in here." My sense in *Deronda* is that Eliot's interest is to prompt us to imagine what it means to imagine another so deeply that the experience of the other once felt becomes "reproduced" in ways that feel as if self and other now live internally together. Such a shift from being a solitary indweller to indwelling as a synthetic multiple being through Eliot's radical account of imagining the other constitutes the basis in *Deronda* of transformation in consciousness, even metamorphosis.

At the moment of Gwendolen's reception of the abstract of Grandcourt's will, Eliot writes a phrase between two dashes that hold what Eliot calls the "whole" of Gwendolen's being: "Her whole being—pride, longing for rebellion, dreams of freedom, remorseful conscience, dread of fresh visitation—all made one want to know what the paper contained" (601). However complex the relation of Gwendolen's narcissism to her feelings of dread and impulse, Gwendolen has a knowability about her as a set of qualities that we, along with Deronda, can imagine about her without being told by Eliot, "Imagine her." Gwendolen is the only major figure of the novel who does *not* receive that rhetorical imperative. Instead, what Eliot does with the figure of Gwendolen is ask the implicit questions, which become worked through as the "British half" of the novel: How could a narcissist imagine another as other from the self? When would that happen? And what might result from such an imagining? Once we leave the "make-believe of a beginning" that is the beginning of *Daniel Deronda* and travel through the opening fourteen chapters of the novel, we learn that Gwendolen's first encounter with Deronda at Leubronne is the beginning of her imagining another. Appropriately, it is a visual experience: she sees his scrutinizing eyes find fault with her. The image that he seems to reflect back to her of herself, as someone "less" than himself, is at once an image that she cannot bear and that nonetheless she feels coerced to see. By imagining how Deronda imagines her, Gwendolen starts to reimagine herself—through his eyes. Daniel Stern, the infant psychiatrist, in *Diary of a Baby* writes about the mutual gaze between the three-and-one-half-month old infant "Joey" and his mother:

> Mutual gaze provides the structure for these interactions. Gazing back and forth, rather than talking back and forth, is the action. During this epoch, mutual gaze is the central event that everything else, like expressions of joy, turns or is built on. And mutual gaze is an intense experience.
>
> Babies act as if the eyes were indeed windows to the soul. After seven weeks of age, they treat the eyes as the geographic center of the person . . .
>
> The eyes are central for Joey and for us all. Looking at eyes that are looking back at you is something else again. First, you "feel" the mental life of the other person. Second, mutual gaze is extremely arousing. Adults will remain locked in silent mutual gaze—with no words spoken—for only seconds at a time unless they are falling in love, or are about to make

love or to fight. Mutual gaze without speaking can be almost intolerable.
(49–50)

Stern captures the intensity of the feelings of arousal that arise between
Gwendolen and Deronda again and again in their moments of mutual gaze,
feelings of attraction, and threat and danger. For infants as young as Joey,
to feel the power of his eyes to attract another to him and to feel the
presence of the other gazing upon him—so much so as to make the eyes
the "geographic center of the face"—helps explain why Gwendolen and
Deronda feel the contact between their eyes to hold such force. They are
each held in the geographic center of the other, that which houses "the
mental life of the other person," that which gazing upon makes one "'feel'
the mental life of the other person." Before encountering Deronda's eyes,
Gwendolen's eyes met with admiration, which enabled her perpetually to
imagine herself admirably. His scrutiny enters her and prompts her to know
self-scrutiny. This is a new form of knowing for Gwendolen—for it brings
her to "self-suspicion" and "self-blame," feelings carried into Gwendolen
through the "imagined facts" she comes to hold about Deronda, feelings
that awaken "a new consciousness."[4] As Gwendolen imagines facts, her
ideas about herself change. Elaine Scarry's idea of the "mental retina," like
Stern's work on mutual gaze, helps concretize how the eye-to-eye seeing
between Deronda and Gwendolen creates within Gwendolen both the space
and the images for a shift in consciousness. First, about the retina, or eye
that perceives, Scarry writes in terms like Stern's: "Eyes are, according to
neurobiologists, the direct outcropping of the brain: not content to receive
messages by mediation, the brain has moved out to the surface of the skull
in order to rub against the world directly (no wonder it is overwhelming
to look into a person's eyes; one beholds directly the moist tissue of the
person's brain)" (*Dreaming* 68). Thinking about the eye as the brain exter-
nalized, Scarry goes on to define the process by which the eye imagines

4. Gwendolen's narcissism as an "absence of self" seeking perpetually to find herself through
others' admiring encounters with her finds its most explicit description in "What she unwillingly
recognised, and would have been glad for others to be unaware of, was that liability of hers to fits
of spiritual dread, though this fountain of awe within her had not found its way into connection
with the religion taught her or with any human relations. She was ashamed and frightened, as at
what might happen again, in remembering her tremor on suddenly feeling herself alone, when for
example she was walking without companionship and there came some rapid change in the light.
Solitude in any wide scene impressed her with an undefined feeling of immeasurable existence aloof
from her, in the midst of which she was helplessly incapable of asserting herself. The little astronomy
taught at school used sometimes to set her imagination at work in a way that made her tremble: but
always when someone joined her she recovered her indifference to the vastness in which she seemed
an exile; she found again her usual world in which her will was of some avail . . . With human ears
and eyes about her, she had always hitherto recovered her confidence, and felt the possibility of
winning empire" (63–64).

as the "mental retina," or "worktable and vertical floor on top of which vivid images come into being" (275). For Scarry the readerly mental retina becomes engaged when read images from the written text enter our brains and become recomposed there—imagined as if perceived by the mental retina. What I'm imagining is that Gwendolen's "reading" of Deronda's eye on her eye engages her mental retina and then becomes recomposed as Deronda's image of her reimagined as her own. For the mental retina to see differently—to imagine—means for the mind to change, feels like the awakening of a new consciousness.

Klesmer's dismissal of Gwendolen's musical talent functions chronologically (we learn after the novel's beginning), as the first instance of another's scrutiny.[5] His searing critique, however, does not enter or undo her in the same way as do Deronda's eyes. While Klesmer's words prompt Gwendolen to relinquish the dream of becoming a lyrical actress, she is not drawn to imagine Klesmer in the sense of "take him in," to imagine him to reside within her. Klesmer does not engage her mental retina—he is an *accepted,* not an imagined, fact. This has something to do with how visual an imagination Gwendolen has and with how Deronda's visual scrutiny is offered literally through his eyes meeting hers. But as well it has to do with why Gwendolen feels compelled to imagine the otherness of Deronda and not Klesmer. Gwedolen's choice can be understood as an *aesthetic act.* The psychoanalyst Christopher Bollas defines the aesthetic moment as

> [a] spell that holds self and other in symmetry and solitude, time crystallizes into space, providing a rendez-vous of self and other (text, composition, painting) that actualizes deep rapport between subject and object. The aesthetic moment constitutes this deep rapport between subject and object and provides the person with a generative illusion of fitting with an object, evoking an existential memory . . . Such moments feel familiar, uncanny, sacred, reverential, and outside cognitive coherence. ("Aesthetic Moment" 40)

Gwendolen has an aesthetic moment with Deronda. As his eyes take her in, her eyes become his eyes. She imagines what it is to see herself as he sees her. If Gwendolen at first takes herself to be Deronda's object—as if the aesthetic moment is his—the text actually writes the aesthetic moment as

---

5. Asked by Gwendolen to comment on her singing, Klesmer replies: "It is a form of melody which expresses a puerile state of culture—a dandling, canting, see-saw kind of stuff—the passion and thought of people without any breadth of horizon. There is a sort of self-satisfied folly about every phrase of such melody; no cries of deep mysterious passion—no conflict—no sense of the universal. It makes men small to listen to it" (49). I will return to this response later on in the chapter.

hers. She is the subject engaged unconsciously in "transformational object seeking": finding the object Deronda prompts Gwendolen to experience herself as Deronda does, or how she imagines his subjective experience of her becomes her transformed experience of her own subjectivity. I understand Gwendolen's experience of Deronda and then Deronda's/Mordecai's experience of each other as forms of transformational object-seeking in which the longed-for return to something of the mother/infant dyad—the earliest experience of knowing what it is to feel merged with and separate from another—finds itself replicated as an existential memory, uncanny, outside cognitive coherence. There is *something* about this object, Deronda, and his scrutinizing eyes and his capacious sympathy (his own vast powers of imagining another, which is to say, his absent mother) that compels Gwendolen to try to take in *something* of both qualities as her own self-scrutiny and imagining of another, *something* that leads her to feel a deep rapport between subject and object or the "generative illusion of fitting" with him, *something* that leads her to exalt and pierce him to imagined fact. If Gwendolen's deepest dread is of attachment, in seeking out this object Deronda, what she risks is feeling her way to and through that dread, followed by the possible loss of the object to which she comes to feel attached.

With Gwendolen having used the rescued necklace as a telegraph to signal her understanding of Deronda's gesture and her responsiveness to his offering of rescue, her transformational object-seeking leads her to pursue Deronda's presence and ask for his words to help her in the wearing of her yoke of wrongdoing (the rescued necklace carries to her the feeling state of that yoke). His three imperatives—"Turn your fear into a safeguard. Keep your dread fixed on the idea of increasing that remorse which is so bitter to you. . . . Try to take hold of your sensibility, and use it as if it were a faculty like vision" (452)—become the mantra Gwendolen will repeat to herself throughout the next four hundred pages. Gwendolen's holding to Deronda's words functions like a holding to a vision of him mixed with a vision of a possible her, awakening to a new self-idea or consciousness from that imagined intermingling. In mid-metamorphosis, Gwendolen writes to the departing Deronda at the novel's close, "I have remembered your words—that I may live to be one of the best of women, who make others glad that they were born. I do not yet see how that can be, but you know better than I. If it ever comes true, it will be because you helped me" (810). Gwendolen's subjunctive mood reflects the evolving indeterminacy of her story and of her consciousness at once devastated by his departure and still transforming from her object-seeking imagining of him.

Eliot's refusal to write of Gwendolen Harleth, "Imagine her," has something to do with the ease with which Eliot imagines we are able and desire to accept her as a fact—this British, upper-class, Church-of-England, striking, young, marriageable woman. We accept her because she is "one of us." Eliot imagines Gwendolen not as the one whom we must struggle to imagine, but rather as the one who in her narcissism (which is to say our British narcissism) must struggle to imagine another, different from herself. She models for us "our" British struggle to imagine facts—that which we feel to be other to us—which plays itself out more globally as Deronda's struggle to imagine a Jew. Eliot's larger design in *Daniel Deronda,* to make Jews imaginable to her British reader, makes the Jews of the novel the object of the imagine command—the "them." We, along with Deronda, are being commanded to imagine Mordecai and Mirah, to move with Deronda from taking them to be so foreign that they are unacceptable and unimaginable, to holding them to and into our breasts in Eliot's imagining of some larger, more global vision of what constitutes "us."

Deronda's desire to know something about Judaism in order to understand more deeply Mordecai and Mirah resembles Thomas Nagel's description of how we come to consider the consciousness of a different organism—"The fact that an organism has consciousness at all means, basically, that there is something it is like to be *that* organism . . . i.e., something it is like *for* that organism" ("What?" 435)—something it is like for *them,* but not for Deronda. As Deronda is drawn to know more of them, and repelled by being mistaken for one of them, his imagining of "the Jew" comes to play itself out as the most radical metamorphosis of consciousness of the book. The wonder of Mirah[6] and his attraction to the lost awaken in Deronda what Eliot calls "a new interest—this passing from the supposition that *we* hold the right opinions on a subject we are careless about, to a sudden care for it, and a sense that *our* opinions were ignorance" (emphasis mine, 363). Deronda's changes in interest from feeling careless to suddenly feeling care, from imagining his opinion was right to recognizing his opinion was ignorant, that opinion which Eliot describes as "ours." William James writes about how an idea enters us to become a reality, or how we choose to let it be reality when before it was not, this way:

> When an idea *stings* us in a certain way, makes as it were a certain electric connection with our self, we believe that it *is* a reality. When it stings us in another way, makes another connection with our Self, we say *let it be* a reality . . . The "quality of reality" which these moods attach to things is

6. Mirah, meaning to wonder at, shares the same root—"mira"—with miracle.

not like other qualities. It is a relation to our life. It means *our* adoption
of the things, *our* caring for them, *our* standing by them. (Emphasis mine,
II, 568–69)

Deronda is stung in a "let it be a reality" way—not yet that the Jew "is"
his reality, but rather that his adoption, caring for, and standing by the Jew
is becoming a chosen reality. And Eliot's language of imperative and of
shifting pronoun reference works a linguistic metamorphosis that begins to
transform Deronda's narrative of imaginative discovery to be ours as well.

The opening push-pull between Gwendolen and Deronda is replicated
between Deronda and the Jews—drawn to and repelled by—these are
Deronda's "original feelings" in response to these first encounters. We
stand with Deronda as he wanders into these experiences and feelings.
But Deronda's vast powers of sympathy, which he exercises to the point
of negative capability, distinguish him from us: how are we to imagine
the state of "half-speculative, half-involuntary identification of himself
with the objects he was looking at, thinking how far it might be possible habitually to shift his centre till his own personality would be no
less outside him than the landscape" (189)? Eliot has told us already that
Deronda is a "rarer" sort of man who "sees [his] own frustrated claim
as one among myriad, the inexorable sorrow takes the form of a fellowship and makes the imagination tender" (175). Deronda's depth of
sorrow in not knowing whether Sir Hugo is his father and in having
never known his mother, except "straining to discern something in that
early twilight, [he] had a dim sense of having been kissed very much,
and surrounded by thin, cloudy, scented drapery, till his fingers caught
in something hard, which hurt him, and he began to cry" (165),[7] leads
him to identify with the injured and to move into their sorrow with
his capacity to imagine it with great tenderness. And we come to learn
of his particular longing to make his sympathy partial and focused—to
be in essence a "positive capability"—meaning "an organic part of social
life, instead of roaming in it like a yearning disembodied spirit, stirred
with a vague social passion, but without fixed local habitation to render

7. Eliot's description of Daniel as an unsleeping beauty, who by the past sensation of kisses,
scented drapery, and a pinprick holds to the essential memory of his life—that of his absent mother
as an extension of the sensations of his body—resonates with William James's discussion of how an
infant comes to have a meaning called "body." Here's James: "By his body, then the child later means
simply *that place where* the pain from the pin, and a lot of other sensations like it, were or are felt. It
is no more true to say that he locates that pain in his body, than to say that he locates his body in
that pain. Both are true: that pain is part of what he *means by the word body*" (II, 35). Deronda has
a body, a "self," because of those early, seemingly precognitive sensations of his body touching and
being touched by his mother. She is his memory of those sensations, which means *she* is to him his
sensations.

fellowship real" (365). Deronda's capacity to turn his personality "inside out" to hold a whole landscape, his tenderness of imagination, and his desire to find a "somewhere" to focus his sympathy make him a being who cannot be fit between two dashes as can Gwendolen. He imagines his way *outside* the dashes, to the words that come before and after, to the worlds the words represent.

But still, Eliot asks us to imagine him. More than any other character, Deronda is not a fact to accept. Daniel Deronda, the title of the novel and the name of the character, is the object and subject of Eliot's imperative "imagine command." As Deronda's imagination comes to imagine a copy of Mordecai into his soul from the original once felt, the metamorphosis is not one of changing, as it is for Gwendolen as she tries to imagine Deronda's scrutiny and capacity to be "better," nor is it of stretching as it is for us, as we try to imagine being as capacious as Deronda in his sympathizing imagination. Instead, it is a metamorphosis of fixing, choosing, and locating the tenderness of imagination here and not there.[8] Transformational object-seeking is all that Deronda has ever known—it is his consciousness. Miraculously, *the object is found*—Daniel meets his mother—the Alcharisi. Equally miraculous, *the transformation is fixed* when Daniel makes his choice—Mordecai and not Gwendolen. Deronda chooses "the chosen people," and says of his choice, "I am glad of it," repeatedly, to the Alcharisi, to Sir Hugo, to Hans, to Mordecai, to Mirah, and finally to Gwendolen. To three in that group Deronda offers his affectionate sympathy; the others he abandons. If the Alcharisi rejects his offer by claiming he cannot imagine what it is to be she (and is the only figure throughout the text to do so), Mirah accepts his offered hand and Mordecai fills his offered soul through a metamorphosing process of transfiguration figured by Eliot as a form of mutual adoption between Mordecai as "mother" and Deronda as "son." Both men have sought their transformational object (Mordecai by waiting on a bridge for five years and Deronda by being Moses floating down the Thames since the age of thirteen) and have found the sought object in each other.[9]

8. After Deronda returns from Genoa and goes "home" to visit Sir Hugo and Lady Mallinger, Eliot writes of Deronda's and Gwendolen's metamorphosis: "Deronda walked about this room, which he had for years known by heart, with a strange sense of metamorphosis in his own life. The familiar objects around him, from Lady Mallinger's gently smiling portrait to the also human and urbane faces of the lions on the pilasters of the chimney-piece, seemed almost to belong to a previous state of existence which he was revisiting in memory only, not in reality; so deep and transforming had been the impressions he had lately experienced, so new were the conditions under which he found himself in the house he had been accustomed to think of as a home—standing with his hat in his hand awaiting the entrance of a young creature whose life had been also undergoing a transformation—a tragic transformation towards a wavering result, in which he felt with apprehensiveness that his own action was still bound up" (766).

9. First Mordecai offers the adoption to Deronda: "You will be my life: it will be planted

These then are the ideas of the imagined facts: Gwendolen feels a new consciousness awaken within in her imagining of Deronda; Deronda feels his consciousness come to definition in his imagining of Mordecai. And if Eliot's imperative imagine command leads the reader to shift from imagining Deronda's imagining "What is a Jew?" to the reader's imagining "What is a Jew?," it prompts an even more radical shift in consciousness. If we have taken that command to heart so that in imagining another we become (an) other, Deronda's response, "'I am a Jew, and am glad of it,'" becomes ours as well. William James's "let it be a reality" becomes for Deronda, becomes for us, a reality.

If the accepted fact of the other necessarily divides one mind from another, the imagined fact of the other opens a space of transport to carry one mind to another, to make one mind feel not only knowable to another but subject to metamorphosis by virtue of that imagining. "Minds are temporary existences," writes William James (I, 199). The fluctuations and movements of mind in *Daniel Deronda* happen when minds imagine other minds. But to be able to imagine another, one must have something to imagine. Making an object of a thought or feeling gives a mind something to imagine. For Eliot to imagine Judaism as held in Mordecai's soul makes it possible for Mordecai to imagine transferring it to be held in Deronda's soul. For Deronda to imagine that Gwendolen's holding of his words—"'This sorrow, which has cut down to the root, has come to you while you are so young—try to think of it, not as a spoiling of your life, but as a preparation for it. Let it be a preparation—'" (769)—can lay the groundwork for the making of a new consciousness and makes it possible for Gwendolen to imagine that Deronda has become part of her new consciousness and is therefore inseparable from her—their inseparability sealed with "hope."

Daniel Deronda imagines how it's possible for a consciousness to undergo radical change by meeting and mingling with another mind, even to achieve a kind of inseparability between souls—that metaphysical metamorphosis. But the imperative to imagine does not end there. Eliot's own longing to know and not feel separated from "the something . . . that was greatest

---

afresh; it will grow. You shall take the inheritance; it has been gathering for ages. The generations are crowding on my narrow life as a bridge: what has been and what is to be are meeting there; and the bridge is breaking. But I have found you. You have come in time. You will take the inheritance which the base son refuses because of the tombs which the plough and harrow may not pass over or the gold-seeker disturb; you will take the sacred inheritance of the Jew" (500). And then Deronda accepts Mordecai's offer: "It is through your inspiration that I have discerned what may be my life's task. It is you who have given shape to what, I believe, was an inherited yearning—the effect of brooding, passionate thoughts in many ancestors" (750).

and best on earth" leads her to what is perhaps the most astonishing act of imagination of *Daniel Deronda*—to write that "something."

3. ETERNAL SOUNDS

Shema yisra'el adonay eloheynu adonay ehad.
Baruh shem kevod malhuto le'olam va'ed.
Hear, Israel: THE ETERNAL is our God,
The ETERNAL ONE alone!
Blessed be the name and glory of God's realm, forever!

—Deuteronomy 6:4

Divided between the British plot and the Jewish plot, *Daniel Deronda* describes not just individual minds and their refusals and struggles to imagine themselves and one another, it as well describes the almost simultaneous, almost nonintersecting presences of whole, different cultural consciousnesses, embodied perhaps most starkly in their different "facts" of time. The British plot of the novel embodies an evolutionary time that is secular, forward-looking, linear, and built on causal sequence. The worldly desires of Gwendolen and Grandcourt, Lydia Glasher and Sir Hugo—desires about name, property, and inheritance—propel the narrative forward and demonstrate how cause leads to effect. It is, therefore, a story of social history as progressive change. While the outcome is not fixed (it is neither determined nor static), the time of the British plot in its very openness seems to demand that its players compete to shape its evolution. This competitive narrative of survival struggles with yet can never escape its own underlying understanding—one person's gain means another's loss. The British figures of the text each want to determine the future before someone else does. Their wishes and wills come to fruition as embodied, visible ends: Sir Hugo sees his wish to secure Diplow Hall come true; Grandcourt's will sees to it that without Gwendolen's producing an heir, Lydia Glasher's son inherits his name and property; and Gwendolen sees her wish outside herself—Grandcourt's dead head. The settling of property, a name, a head are spatial visualizations of the arrival of the future—struggled over as a battle of wills, but settled; yet, it is a future worn out, even finished. Grandcourt's descent into the water marks the descent of man as evolution ended; and Gwendolen's sentiments "I shall live, I shall be better" remain in the hazy stillness of the unrealized subjunctive.

If the British plot makes visible an evolutionary time that moves forward to the future and then seems to collapse from fatigue and overuse upon its arrival, the Jews of *Daniel Deronda* embody past human history.[10] When Deronda first looks at Mordecai, what he sees is "A man in threadbare clothing, whose age was difficult to guess—from the dead yellowish flatness of the flesh, something like an old ivory carving" (385). But as Deronda continues to look, the "old ivory carving's" indeterminate age transforms by a thought "glanced through Deronda": "precisely such a physiognomy as that might possibly have been seen in a prophet of Exile, or in some New Hebrew poet of medieval time" (386). Mordecai appears to Deronda's meditative eye to be ancient or perhaps medieval. And then Eliot asks us with her imagine command to join Deronda in his visual meditation on Mordecai as an embodiment of the past. Eliot writes: "Imagine—we all of us can—the pathetic stamp of consumption with its brilliancy of glance to which the sharply defined structure of features reminding one of a forsaken temple, give already a far-off look as of one getting unwillingly out of reach" (495). We, all of us, apparently have seen this Jew, because that's what the Jewish face does: holds in its physiognomy the forsaken temple of King David. Mordecai's face—this old ivory carving, ancient prophet, medieval poet, forsaken temple—carries the past into the present by functioning as a visual spatialization of times and civilizations that are no more. He is a barely walking contradiction to Darwin's theory of natural selection—a human artifact. Not adapted, not transformed, the Jew as Mordecai lives in the present moment as the past.

But as much as the visual presences of the British and Jews of *Deronda* work to reveal a future-driven model of evolutionary time and a past-bound model of non- or anti-evolutionary time, their sound presences take us outside this binary account of time and human history to a place altogether different. Yet again, Eliot asks us to imagine what sound makes possible that sight cannot. With the exception of Catherine Arrowpoint's talent as a pianist (a talent that receives no attention in the novel after her marriage to Klesmer), no English figure has a relation to sound that is worthy of note. Gwendolen's desire to hear Klesmer comment on her singing leads him to reply: "It is a form of melody which expresses a puerile state of culture—a dandling, canting, see-saw kind of stuff—the passion and thought of people without any breadth of horizon. There is a sort of self-satisfied folly about every phrase of such melody; no cries of deep mysterious passion—no conflict—no sense of the universal. It makes men small to listen to it" (49). The breadthless horizon of Gwendolen's passionless voice is not improved upon by any of her English peers. Gwendolen's small sound

---

10. For extended studies of Eliot's relationship to Judaism and Jewish thought, its uses and representations in her works, see the writings of William Baker, in particular, *George Eliot and Judaism;* and Saleel Nurbhai and K. M. Newton's *George Eliot, Judaism and the Novels.*

becomes over the course of the novel an absence of English musical sound. It is here—in sound—that the binary Englishman/Jew is dropped because the British side of that structure falls away into nonpresence.

Klesmer, Mirah, and the Alcharisi, each a great musician, are all Jews. Klesmer's imperious magic at the piano "seemed to send a nerve-thrill through ivory key and wooden hammer, and compel the strings to make quivering lingering speech for him" (49–50); Mirah's purity of voice "had that essential of perfect singing, the making one oblivious of art or manner, and only possessing one with the song. It was the sort of voice that gives the impression of being meant like a bird's wooing for an audience near and beloved" (372); and the Alcharisi was the greatest lyric actress of her day. One of the ways Eliot hints early on at Deronda's birthright is by revealing his musical gifts: "Daniel had not only one of those thrilling boy voices which seem to bring an idyllic heaven and earth before our eyes, but a fine musical instinct, and had early made out accompaniments for himself on piano, while he sang from memory" (168).[11] Such a voice must in the world of *Daniel Deronda* be a Jew. But why?

The music that makes "an idyllic heaven and earth" or that "gives the impression of a bird wooing an audience near and beloved" would seem to offer the possibility of "breadth of horizon," "of the universal," of some way of experiencing beyond the future-driven or past-bound forms of being-in-time by virtue of their vastness or distinct beauty—"the something." But after Eliot opens our ears to the power of aesthetic sound, to its soul-opening capacities, she abandons secular music. Klesmer essentially disappears from the novel halfway through, and the musical careers on stage of Mirah and the Alcharisi become narrative points to summarize. Eliot moves us slowly, almost imperceptibly, from scenes in which we are to imagine hearing great Jewish musical artists perform to hearing ordinary religious Jews pray. And she does this, I want to assert, to lead us with open ears from one space into the other: so that it is possible for us, like Deronda, to hear these unknown Hebrew sounds that we don't understand, and not resist them; so that we, like Deronda, can *imagine this fact,* which means here to experience what it is to feel *moved* as if by some mystical force. Writing on the "*aleph-beth*" (the Hebrew alphabet) as understood in the Kabbalah, Rabbis Ginsburgh, Trugman, and Wisnefsky claim: "The spiritual force of the word is its power to arouse—'move'—the emotions of man, in the secret world of Formation. While sight may 'attract,' hear-

---

11. Gwendolen compares the richness of Deronda's voice to the emptiness of Grandcourt's: "His [Deronda's] voice, heard now for the first time, was to Grandcourt's toneless drawl, which had been in her ears every day, as the deep notes of a violoncello to the broken discourse of poultry and other lazy gentry in the afternoon sunshine" (331).

ing 'moves'" (emphasis mine, 13). Hearing Mirah sing the Hebrew words of the prayers literally moves Deronda into a synagogue in Frankfurt and then arouses his soul. The essential experience for Deronda and for us as his readers happens as hearing and feeling sound—as *entrance*—

> [T]he chant of the *Chazan's* or Reader's grand wide-ranging voice, its passage from monotony to sudden cries, the outburst of sweet boys' voices from the little quire, the devotional swaying of men's bodies backwards and forwards, the very commonness of the building and shabbiness of the scene where a national faith, which had penetrated the thinking of half the world, and moulded the splendid forms of that world's religion, was finding a remote, obscure echo—all blent for him as one expression of a binding history, tragic, yet glorious. He wondered at the strength of his own feeling; it seemed beyond occasion—what one might imagine to be a divine influx in the darkness, before there was any vision to interpret. (367–68)

Like the vision of Mordecai that conjures up some distant past, the sounds of the Chazan, choir, and praying men call upon Deronda to experience history, but now it's named with feeling—"tragic and yet glorious." Whereas he looked at Mordecai and saw him as analogic artifacts—an old ivory carving, a forsaken temple—now Deronda "wondered at the strength of his own feeling; it seemed beyond the occasion—what one might imagine to be a divine influx in the darkness, before there was any vision to interpret." The sound carries him somewhere else to feel a place of deep passion, to imagine an experience of being beyond what is before him, to feel the presence of another realm. This is sound prior to sight, "before there was any vision to interpret," "a divine influx in the darkness." Deronda hears the sacred, divine presence.

What stands behind Eliot's very human acknowledgment of her "make-believe of a beginning"—that which she must do to begin her novel and that which is not "the true beginning"—is, I want to assert, a sacred account of "the true beginning." And that beginning is breath and sound. Genesis 3–4 states: "When God began to create heaven and earth—the earth being unformed and void, with darkness over the surface of the deep and *a wind from God* sweeping over the water—God said, 'Let there be light.' And there was light." And later: "The Lord God formed man from the dust of the earth. *He blew into his nostrils the breath of life,* and man became a living being" (emphasis mine, 13). According to the Torah, whatever the sacred is, it is before creation, already there because always, eternal. And whatever the sacred is, it is embodied as wind. From divine breath come sound and life. The sacred, the eternal, is "made flesh" as wind, breath, and sound.

David Abram, in his remarkable *The Spell of the Sensuous,* considers the holiness of wind for oral cultures: "The air for oral peoples is an archetype of all that is ineffable, unknowable, yet undeniably real and efficacious. Its obvious ties to speech—the sense that spoken words are structured breath (try speaking a word without exhaling at the same time), and indeed that spoken phrases take their communicative power from this invisible medium that moves between us—lends the air a deep association with linguistic meaning and thought" (226–27). Imagine the air as that which wanders outside and carries all that is most mysterious to and from us—know the presence of the Eternal moving outside us and within. Imagine the air as that which resides within and enables us to make sound—know speech and music as structured breath. Abram discusses the Hebrew *aleph-beth,* with its twenty-two consonants and absence of vowels, as the first alphabet and as still tied to its roots in orality with its emphasis on breath:

> Another, perhaps more significant, reason for the absence of written vowels in the traditional *aleph-beth* has to do with the nature of the vowels them- selves. While consonants are those shapes made by the lips, teeth, tongue, palate, or throat, that momentarily obstruct the flow of breath and so give form to our words and phrases, the vowels are those sounds that are made by the unimpeded breath itself. *The vowels, that is to say, are nothing other than sounded breath.* And the breath, for the ancient Semites, was the very mystery of life and awareness, a mystery inseparable from the invisible *ruach*—the holy wind or spirit. The breath, as we have noted, was the vital substance blown into Adam's nostrils by God himself, who thereby granted life and consciousness to humankind. It is possible, then, that the Hebrew scribes refrained from creating distinct letters for the vowel-sounds in order to avoid making a visible representation of the invisible. To fashion a visible representation of the vowels, of the sounded breath, would have been to concretize the ineffable, *to make a visible likeness of the divine.* It would have been to make a visible representation of a mystery whose very essence was to be invisible and hence unknowable—*the sacred breath, the holy wind.* And thus it was not done. (Emphasis mine, 241–42)

"The sacred breath, the holy wind" breathes life into being and manifests itself through sound sculpted by an alphabet that leaves room for the divine to be blown across its letters. Absent vowels let us hear the Eternal's pres- ence as we chant the vowels forward.

Maybe we can imagine the novel *Daniel Deronda* as a text with a space left open—vowelless—that is the space of sound that Deronda wanders into and that we must breathe into to try to hear. Eliot says it is a realm of voices. Here's Mirah: "Is it not wonderful how I remember the voices better than anything else? I think they must go deeper into us than other things. I have often fancied heaven must be made of voices" (371). And Mordecai's pouring of his words into Deronda's ears as the only possible transport for the transmigration of souls has everything to do with his belief that it is through voice that the soul travels through time:

> I know what I am outwardly—I am one among the crowd of poor—I am stricken, I am dying. But our souls know each other. They [our souls] gazed in silence as those who have long been parted and meet again, but when they found voice, they were assured, and all their speech is understanding. The life of Israel is in your veins . . . Is it not begun? Have I not breathed my soul into you? (572, 811)

For Mirah, heaven is made of voices remembered because still heard, the deepest things inside us; and for Mordecai, voice carries the soul and can be breathed into another when spoken. But Eliot claims that voice alone cannot hold the Eternal: it's what the voice voices, or chanting the sacred alphabet of sound, that creates a shared space between the human and the divine. Mirah's earliest recollections are of her mother's singing to her Hebrew hymns—this is her *aleph-beth* of being breathed into her—she repeats those hymns to remember her mother's presence and to feel her own life. Deronda understands the repetition of the chanted Hebrew liturgy to hold a tradition, over time, no matter where it is sung. When his mind wanders to imagine the synagogue in Genoa, he "saw faces there probably little different from those of his grandfather's time, and heard the Spanish-Hebrew liturgy which had lasted through the seasons of wandering generations like a plant with a wandering seed, that gives the far-off lands a kinship to the exile's home" (684). And Mordecai chants the prayers into Deronda again and again so that his body can carry the sounds of the Eternal forward. All of these instances are about making an aural spatialization of sacred time, sacred presence. Each instance holds the idea of how it is that through the rhythm of repetition the sounds of the past meet the present meet the future; how it is through the music of chanting the sounds of the Eternal that the divine presence is breathed, heard, passed on; how it is through the lyrics of Hebrew prayer—its *aleph-beth*—that we make contact with the Eternal.

I understand George Eliot's moments of profoundest exchange to happen through sound. In *Daniel Deronda,* the chanting of Jewish prayer creates an aural bridge between the human and the divine. Eliot does not call upon us to listen either to evolution or to the past—those, it seems, we can see. Instead, she calls us to hear what transcends human time, namely, the sounds of the Eternal. God embodied as Hebrew prayers chanted—the union of human and divine—happens in the space of the *Shema*. And this is what the *Shema*, the oldest and most holy of Jewish prayers, commands: *HEAR,* which means in Hebrew, *understand:*

"*Hear,* O Israel: The Eternal is our God, the Eternal One alone!"

Hear that God is eternal. Hear the Eternal is one. Hear the Eternal's sound. Hear to understand the something that is greatest and best on earth— beloved idea made flesh—

    Shema

PART III

Thomas Hardy and Nonintrospective
Consciousness

CHAPTER 5

"Now I Am Melancholy Mad"

Mood and *Jude the Obscure*

1. WINDOW-JUMPING

William James tells a story in *The Principles of Psychology* of two university students who feel tempted to jump out a window, an anecdote he uses to consider the power of "bad" or "unpleasant" temptation and more generally the "impulses of the will":

> In my university days a student threw himself from an upper entry window of one of the college buildings and was nearly killed. Another student, a friend of my own, had to pass the window daily in coming and going from his room, and experienced a dreadful temptation to imitate the deed. Being a Catholic, he told his director, who said, "All right! if you must, you must," and added, "Go ahead and do it," thereby instantly quelling his desire. This director knew how to minister to a mind diseased. But we need not go to minds diseased for examples of the occasional tempting-power of simple badness and unpleasantness as such . . . (II, 553–54)

Perhaps what is most memorable about Sue Bridehead is that she jumps out a window—twice.

Jude the Obscure, like all other Thomas Hardy novels, is remarkable for its insistence on impulse, for making impulse the primary mental state of its characters and its effects a primary motivating force of plot. On impulse, Michael Henchard sells his wife, Alec Stoke-D'Urbervilles rapes Tess, Sue Bridehead leaps out of windows, and Jude Fawley follows Arabella and her bantam egg upstairs to bed. None think of the consequences of their behavior; none when held by the force of impulse seem to think at all.[1] And Hardy offers no explanations and no analysis to help us make sense of their acts or decisions. Instead, Hardy narrates how impulse functions as a complex motivating force because of how it drives the minds and behavior of his characters—none more so than Sue Bridehead. James uses his example of the window-jumpers—one who acts, the other tempted and then quelled of the desire to act—to reveal what he calls our "vertiginous fascination" for the "badness" of an act, or how it is that we can fall prey to "diseased impulses and pathological fixed ideas" (II, 553). Resisting the temptation to analyze why at times we are fascinated by what is diseased or harmful, James allows it to be part beneficial. Like Gwendolen Harleth who, in the moment of crisis, lets Grandcourt drown, Sue leaps. However, whereas Gwendolen, almost catatonic from trauma, manages after to have a lengthy exchange with Deronda about the significance of what she did by not acting, Sue Bridehead feels the need for no such later working-through. Threatened with solitary confinement for a week in the Training School she attends at Melchester, Sue, Hardy writes, "had got out the back window of the room in which she had been confined, escaped in the dark across the lawn and disappeared" (142). Later, when in Jude's room, Sue reports what she did and what she felt prior to the leap, not what she thought or felt about making the leap itself: "'Walked through the largest river in the county—that's what I've done! They locked me up for being with you; and it seemed so unjust that I couldn't bear it, so I got out of the window and escaped across the stream!'" (144). What motivates the impulse—"'it seemed so unjust that I couldn't bear it'"—is a feeling. Hardy writes that it is because of strong feelings that *The Mayor of Casterbridge's*

---

1. Acting without thought, acting from some other energy, Hardy's characters seem to many readers less minded persons than "embodiments of sensation or force." Gilles Deleuze and Claire Parnet, for instance, write that Hardy's figures "are not people or subjects, they are collective sensations" (*Dialogue* 39–40). And William Cohen notes, "Hardy's character is less a person, or a picture of a person, than a dynamic force, at once human and not" ("Faciality and Sensation" 441). Attention to what constitutes the mindedness of Hardy's characters or to their absence of mind is what J. Hillis Miller first pays at the beginning of *Distance and Desire,* that critical work which for me marks the beginning of such attention: "'A naturalist's interest in the hatching of a queer egg or germ is the utmost introspective consideration you should allow yourself,' [Hardy] says in a private notebook entry of 1888" (1). In response to Hardy's words, Miller comments, "To be conscious is to be separated. The mind has a native clarity and distinctness which detaches it from everything it registers. Though Hardy finds that his consciousness separates him from the world, he does not turn away from what he sees to investigate the realm of interior space. He and his characters are distinguished by the *shallowness of their minds.* They have no profound inner depths leading down to the 'buried self' or to God" (emphasis mine, 3–4). However, this "shallowness of mind," when explored in terms of James's and Damasio's theories of consciousness, I want to suggest, reveals in ways easily missed or dismissed because of their nonintrospective nature a different understanding of what it means to be minded persons.

Michael Henchard lies to keep his Elizabeth-Jane near him, at whatever cost: "Henchard, scarcely believing the evidence of his senses, rose from his seat, amazed at what he had done. It had been the impulse of a moment . . . the sudden prospect of her loss had caused him to speak mad lies like a child, in pure mockery of consequences" (289). Like Henchard, Sue seems to know no fear of consequence and no willingness or capacity to try to bear the feeling of injustice. The second leap is from the bedroom window of the home Sue shares with her husband Phillotson. Unlike the first impulsive jump, reported after its occurrence, the second jump happens in real narrative time, reported through the third-person perspective of Phillotson's observing eyes:

> There was a cry from the bed, and quick movement. Before the school-master perceived where he was he perceived Sue starting up half-awake, staring wildly, and springing out upon the floor on the side away from him, which was towards the window. This was somewhat hidden by the canopy of the bedstead, and in a moment he heard her flinging up the sash. Before he had thought that she meant to do more than get air she had mounted upon the sill and leapt out. She disappeared in the darkness, and he heard her fall below. (226)

The narrative is a lengthy description of what Phillotson hears and sees of the moving image before him—a cry, a wild stare, a springing upon the floor, a momentary obstruction of view, a flinging up of the sash, a mounting on the sill, a leap out, a disappearance into the dark, a fall below. It is not Sue's mind that Phillotson describes, but traces of its direction in the moment, embodied in her wild starting, staring, springing, flinging, mounting, leaping, disappearing, and falling behavior. When he tries to imagine her mind, he reads Sue's thoughts incorrectly: "Before he had thought that she meant to do more than get air, she had mounted upon the sill and leapt out." While Phillotson perceives Sue, he does not accurately interpret her behavior and so does not recognize what her behavior reveals: her wild feelings of terror. Phillotson thinks as he thinks, as most would think when watching someone open a window—this is someone getting air. But the wild, starting, flinging, springing gestures before throwing up the sash would tell other observing minds that Sue is not acting like someone who just wants to take a deep breath. The trajectory of her movements is like that of a wild animal that feels trapped and must escape. William James writes, "[N]o actions but such are done for an end, and show a choice of means, can be called indubitable expressions of Mind" (I, 11). Aren't Sue's actions here—done for an end, through a choice of means—an "indubitable expression of Mind"? Whereas we count on the thought "I must not jump out the window" to be shared between minds, Sue's behavior negates that and makes imaginable that she thinks the unimaginable, "I must jump out the window." Why can't Phillotson read Sue's mind, in the sense of imagine in this moment and more generally that what Sue thinks may not be what others think, in the way that what Sue does is often not what others do? What does this failure of imagining mean about Phillotson and about the imaginability of Sue? Sue even says of herself, "So few could enter into my feeling" (215), an expression that reflects her ongoing experience as "unknowable." Sue's only thought, she later reveals, after he carries the strangely unscathed "white heap" lying on the gravel back into the house, is for her feelings about what she thought she saw: "'I was asleep, I think!' she began, her pale face still turned away from him. 'And something frightened me—a terrible dream—I thought I saw you—.' The actual circumstances seemed to come back to her and she was silent" (227). Sue in a dream state, somewhere between consciousness and sleep, awakens after the fall to conscious consideration of what happened. Was it "a terrible dream" that I saw you, or the awful truth? The thought of Phillotson standing there, in either her dream or real bedroom, is the only thought Sue has. There are no thoughts to follow the thought of Phillotson; only feelings follow, and then their embodiment in actions. From thought to feeling to enacted impulse, Sue jumps herself away from the thought of him, so powerful is "I thought I saw you"—as either a dream or in the flesh.

2. IMPULSES OF WILL

What alternative is there for Sue Bridehead but to jump, to be a Bertha Mason who leaps her way to freedom, but manages to live, at least for a little while? Sue describes her marriage to Phillotson, its basis in a contract that commands feeling, as a state of torture: "'What tortures me so much is the necessity of being responsive to this man whenever he wishes, god as he is morally!—the dreadful contract to feel in a particular way, in a matter whose essence is voluntariness!'" (212). *Jude the Obscure* is an anti-marriage novel—relentlessly so. Hardy is shrill in his attacks on marriage, repetitive in his returns to "the letter killeth," and predictable in ending everyone's life as one form or another of "death by marriage." Jude's parents (the Fawley cousins), Arabella and Jude, Sue and Phillotson—are all crushed from legal partnership, partnerships from which there are no escapes, only returns, until some final "death do you part." The exception, Arabella, knows "women must provide for a rainy day" (401), which means, Arabella knows how to survive—how to make use of whoever crosses her path or of whatever social system she finds herself a part of so as to claw her way to tomorrow. However the world of *Jude the Obscure* makes itself manifest to Arabella, she is its survivor; its practices are those to which she can adapt. Arabella the Ishmaelite alone lives to tell the tale. *Jude the Obscure* writes against the comic tradition of the English novel's promised end of happy marriage and in so doing breaks from and transforms its literary heritage and ends Hardy's novel-writing career.

What distinguishes Sue Bridehead is not that she is oppressed by her marriage to Phillotson—she is—or that she resists marrying Jude when she is free to do so—she does, again and again. Sue jumps not to be free, at least not to be free from the social forces that oppress her as a woman. Married or single, ecclesiastical lettering or teaching schoolgirls, confined in a room or walking along the road buying statues of Apollo and Venus, Sue is Sue, no matter the setting. No social force or convention or dogma defines or confines her, until the novel's horrific end traumatizes Sue into, as Jude calls her, the "'dear, sad, soft, most melancholy wreck of a promising human intellect that it has ever been my lot to behold!'" (389). But until she witnesses that closing scene of infanticide, Sue Bridehead is that most promising human intellect: she is the mouthpiece for Hardy as social critic and the mentor to Hardy as Jude on the hypocrisies of religious dogma, social law, and conventional wisdom. In Sue, Hardy has imagined a woman character unlike any other in the nineteenth-century English novel—a character who is more her "self" than she is representation of "woman." In a remarkable note in which Sue pleads with Phillotson to let her live separately from him, she writes, "'I know you mean my good. But I don't want to be respectable!'" (225). Sue questions the foundation of what Victorian culture takes to be what every woman wants because of its own defining and training of what every woman should want—to be respectable. If a woman does not want to be respectable, what can she want? And even more disturbing, who or what then is she? Unique, strange, mostly unknowable in the way that human beings are mostly mysteries, Sue cannot be read or understood through a social lens of expectation or prediction—she is not "like a woman"; she is not "one of us." Further, Sue does not evolve: she does not grow; she does not change; and she does not learn. In the way that *Jude the Obscure* is an anti-marriage novel, which makes it an anti-English novel, *Jude the Obscure* the Bildungsroman is, when focused on Sue, an anti-Bildungsroman. Sitting before Jude as his mirror, dressed in his clothes, in his bedroom—a room *into* which she leaps—Sue tells Jude who she is: "I am a negation of civilization"; "I have no fear of men and their books"; "I have remained as I began" (147–48).

Each is an expression of her self-understanding formed from before the novel: each holds something of how she imagines her identity. As a "negation of civilization," Sue tells Jude in the same scene, "'I have no respect for Christminster whatever, except, in a qualified degree, on its intellectual side . . . The medievalism of Christminster must go, be sloughed off, or Christminster itself will have to go" (150). That beacon of learning—the shining light that is for Jude Christminster—is for Sue in danger of becoming obsolete and must be revised if it is to be of any consequence or hold any purpose other than be an empty symbol. For Jude, such thinking is incomprehensible and provokes in him a sense of hurt outrage: how can she entertain such thoughts of his dream-vision? Sue describes how she made her own *new* New Testament and offers to make one for Jude by cutting up the Epistles and Gospels and arranging them into separate brochures by chronology. To Jude, this is sacrilege. Sue has "no fear of men, nor of their books" because, she says, "I have mixed with them . . . almost as one of their own sex" (147). Dressed as Jude, debating with him ideas about education and religion, Sue for Jude doesn't "talk quite like a girl" (147). She describes her days living with a young male student at Christminster as friendly intimates—"like two men almost"—not as lovers. What Sue reveals to Jude is a "curious unconsciousness of gender" (149). Even as she breaks the young man's heart by sharing close quarters but not her body with him, she does not break her own heart by acting as he expects or needs her to by being his lover. "I have remained as I began," Sue tells Jude. Called "cold-natured,—sexless—on account of it," Sue refutes how others read her choice to be intact with, "'Some of the most passionately erotic poets have been the most self-contained in their daily lives'" (149). Sue's resistance to physical lovemaking is not for her a sign of what she fails to feel. Rather, it reveals something of her need to *inhibit* impulse. "'I should shock you by letting you know how I give way to my impulses'" (204), Sue tells Jude, without telling him how she gives way. I take Sue's self-understanding of "I have remained as I began" to mean both that her "Bridehead" remains a maidenhead and that Sue remains Sue.

To remain as she began drives Sue, a drive that both pushes her out of windows and keeps her inside them. Admitting another inside her or allowing the ideas of the world to take up space inside her are what Sue refuses to do: Sue Bridehead refuses to accommodate in mind or body. She cannot bear to hold the thought inside her of unjust separation *from* Jude and jumps to him; she cannot bear to hold the thought inside her *of* Phillotson and jumps away from him. When Jude goes to visit Sue at Phillotson's schoolhouse and then again when the two return to Marygreen for their Aunt Drusilla's funeral, Sue positions herself *inside* a windowsill with Jude outside so that, as she says, "'I can talk to you better like this than when you were inside.'" Hardy writes, "Now that the window-sill was between them, so that he could not get at her, she seemed not to mind indulging in a frankness she feared at close quarters" (205). To be herself with Jude, Sue protects herself behind a casing—"so that he could not get at her." For Sue, to be gotten at means no longer to remain her self. The window for Sue is the necessary third when she is in the company of a man: it creates a semiporous boundary that both keeps him from getting in and allows her to go out—as herself. Called out by the cry of the rabbit caught in the gin, Sue again uses a window between them to keep herself from the rabbit's fate, caught and killed. Reaching out of the casement, Sue puts her hand on Jude's hand as they talk and "[i]n a moment of impulse," bends over the sill and lays her weeping face on his hair and kisses the top of his head. Before he can put his arms round her as, Hardy writes, "he unquestionably would have otherwise done" (215), Sue closes the casement. Sue refuses to be caught by Jude even as she reaches out to "catch" him, refuses, that is, until Arabella's animal presence and threat of renewed sexual relations with Jude leads Sue to acknowledge, "the little bird is caught at last" (268). Arabella, it seems, is stronger than a window. But until then, Sue inhibits her impulsion to touch, as her momentary touch incites his, and then explains to Jude why:

> "My liking for you is not as some women's perhaps. But it is a delight in being with you, of a supremely delicate kind, and I don't want to go further and risk it by—an attempt to intensify it! I quite realized that, as woman with man, it was a risk to come. But, as *me* with *you,* I resolved to trust you to set my wishes above your gratification." (240)

Our relationship, Sue tells Jude, is more than the generic "woman with man." Ours is particular to us, "*me* with *you.*" And what I feel for you is not like what other women might feel for you—it is what *I* feel for *you*—"a delight in being with you, of a supremely delicate kind." The complexity of Hardy's portrait of Sue and her feelings for Jude has everything to do with how he works to set Sue apart from the category "woman" in order to make her nature her own—unique, original, difficult to understand because she is like no one else and wants to remain so. The most extraordinary scene of symbolic boundary-making and -breaking in *Jude* happens in the clothes closet under the stairway of Phillotson's home, a little space in the dark where Sue builds a nest of her own. Having no actual lock, Sue fastens the door shut from the inside with a piece of string. Just a pull on the knob from the outside by Phillotson causes the string to break and the door to open, to the horror of each. "'You ought not to have pulled open the door! . . . It is not becoming in you! O, will you please go away; please will you!'" (221) she cries, upon his breaking the string that separates her from him. Sue's "eccentricity," her need for the presence of a physical third to mark off her separation from Phillotson, orders and regulates through inhibition impulse—hers and his. For someone whose fundamental drive is to remain as she began in a universe of minds where, as William James writes, "We do all these things because at the moment we cannot help it; our nervous systems are so shaped that they overflow in just that way; and for many of our idle or purely nervous and fidgety performances we can assign absolutely no reason at all" (II, 553), something more than our own bodies is needed to control our "nervous and fidgety performances" of impulse—a window, a piece of string.

Sue Bridehead finds windows to leap from or to stand behind as the means to enable or inhibit impulse. But always there is a prompt—"the impulse to window" does not just happen—it is a response. In his chapter simply entitled "Will," William James states that motives prompt us to act, "motives supplied by innumerable objects, which innervate our voluntary muscles by a process as automatic as that by which they light a fever in our breast" (II, 552). He continues:

> If one must have a single name for the condition upon which the impulsive and inhibitive quality of objects depends, one had better call it their *interest.* "The interesting" is a title which covers not only the pleasant and the painful, but also the morbidly fascinating, the tediously haunting, and even the simple habitual . . . It seems as if we ought to look for the secret of an idea's impulsiveness, not in any peculiar relations which it may have with paths of motor discharge,—for *all* ideas have relations with some paths,— but rather in a preliminary phenomenon, the *urgency, namely, with which it is able to compel attention and dominate in consciousness* . . . [T]he impelling idea is simply one which possesses the attention. (Emphasis mine, II, 558–59)

Objects motivate impulse. The more interesting the object, the more it compels attention, and the more power the object has to dominate consciousness, the more energy the mind focuses on the impelling feelings of physical-emotional urgency it motivates. The thought of Phillotson is so interesting to Sue, so compelling of her attention, so urgent in how it dominates her consciousness, that it motivates her to leap impulsively from a window. And the presence of Jude is so compelling that Sue impulsively kisses the top of his head in response, and then inhibits more. Hardy, a man haunted by objects, insists on their presence throughout his novels and poems, insists on their power to compel the attention and the response of his characters. J. Hillis Miller writes in *Distance and Desire,* "Almost every sentence Hardy ever wrote, whether in his fiction, in his poetry, or his more private writings, is objective" (1); and "The mind is held entranced by a vision of objects which seem themselves entranced, constrained" (4). A pig's pizzle, a bantam egg, Latin books, hairpiece, dimples, a photo of Jude are a few of the objects that focus the attention of Arabella and Jude on each other and that hold the course of their story—from their attraction to their dissolution. From the opening moment of *Jude the Obscure,* Hardy makes an object the source of motivation for the impulses that drive his characters' minds. The schoolmaster departing from the village is not the object of attention of the rector, the blacksmith, or the bailiff—but his piano is. Three sentences from the novel's beginning we read:

> [T]he only cumbersome article possessed by the master, in addition to the packing-case of books, was a cottage piano that he had bought at an auction during the year in which he thought of learning instrumental music. But the enthusiasm having waned he had never acquired any skill in playing, and the purchased article had been a perpetual trouble to him ever since in moving house. (9)

The unnamed schoolmaster is leaving, but the named "cottage piano" cannot leave: our attention is not, therefore, on the man, but on the trouble of his departure, this object that holds his waning enthusiasm, this source of "perpetual trouble." The object of interest shifts when we read of "a little boy of eleven" whose presence is described as "thoughtful" and who solves the problem of what to do with the piano—store it in Aunt Drusilla's great fuel-house. Now the object of the little boy's eyes and their tears—*his* departing teacher named Phillotson, which is to say, *their relationship*—become the text's object of attention. To make our way as readers toward the minds of Hardy's characters, we must do what Hardy writes his characters do—look at the objects of their attention as clues to the shape, tendencies, qualities of their minds. For James, what we notice is what brings order and character and particularity to each consciousness: "My experience is what I agree to attend to. Only those items which I notice shape my mind—without selective interest, experience is an utter chaos. Interest gives accent and emphasis, light and shade, background and foreground—intelligible perspective, in a word" (402). Hardy's attention to the objects of his characters' attention—to what they notice and how they act in relation to what they notice—defines not just a refutation to the authorial omnipotence of mind-reading but a vision of how consciousness works. Study the novel's representations of a character's object-attention and discern the "accent and emphasis, light and shade, background and foreground" of that character's mind.

For the little boy Jude, the troubling cottage piano is not a clue to any deficiency in his schoolmaster: rather, it is a means to stay connected to him, as is the parting gift Phillotson bestows of a book, as are the parting words of Phillotson to Jude:

> "My scheme, or dream, is to be a university graduate, and then to be ordained. By going to live at Christminster, or near it, I shall be at head-quarters, so to speak, and if my scheme is practicable at all, I consider that being on the spot will afford me a better chance of carrying it out than I should have elsewhere . . . I shan't forget you, Jude . . . Be a good boy, remember, and be kind to animals and birds, and read all you can. And if ever you come to Christminster remember you hunt me out for old acquaintance' sake." (10–11)

In this crushing moment of loss, Jude attaches himself to the words of his schoolmaster—words that define the dreams of the object of his attention. Jude makes another's dream his own: this act of object attention defines the accent, emphasis, lighted foreground of Jude's mind. Each of Phillotson's sentences about himself come to be the adopted "scheme or dream" of Jude—to be a university graduate and then to be ordained—to get there by living "on the spot"—at Christminster, or nearby. And each piece of advice Phillotson gives to Jude is adopted as his means to make Phillotson's dream his own—to be a good boy, to be kind to animals and birds, to read all he can, to hunt down Phillotson at Christminster, and most of all, to *remember*. Three times Phillotson tells Jude to remember his words and himself, and tells Jude he shall not forget him. On impulse, Jude stakes his life on Phillotson's words—by remembering and by acting to make the dream his own. In doing so, Jude the Patron Saint of Lost Causes comes to have a cause, and Jude the Orphan comes to have someone to remember and comes to imagine that he is held in mind by someone. Jude's narrative—his coming to consciousness—begins with the loss of the object and the adoption, in memory, of the lost object's hopes. What makes the lost object so interesting, so urgent, and so telling of the shape of Jude's mind is what makes its cause so motivating and defining for and of Jude. Attachment to the object—as desire to adopt the object and be adopted by the object—defines Jude's longing to have a self, to be Jude. Like Jude's attachment to Christminster, Jude's attachment to Sue first happens with the idea of her—"the photograph of a pretty girlish face, in a broad hat, with radiating folds under the brim like the rays of a halo" (78). Haunted by her angelic image, Jude quickens his course for Christminster, as much to find his ideal Sue, as to find his ideal father Phillotson—the fulfillment of his dreams. Jude will spend the course of his short, yet endlessly laborious twenty-nine years seeking what Hardy names these objects for Jude—"the spot"—

> It had been the yearning of his heart to find something to anchor on, to cling to—for some place which he could call admirable. Should he find that place in this city if he could get there? Would it be a *spot* in which, without fear of farmers, or hindrance, or ridicule, he could watch and wait, and set himself to some mighty undertaking like the men of old of whom he had heard? As the halo had been to his eyes when gazing at it a quarter of an hour earlier, so was the *spot* mentally to him as he pursued his dark way. (Emphasis mine, 25)

Phillotson, Christminster, Sue—are the places he holds in mind as ideals to which he can anchor his longings, objects to which he can attach "the embroidery of imagination upon the stuff of nature" (40), other presences with which he can merge, become one, and become someone—"'You [breezes] . . . were in Christminster . . . touching Mr. Phillotson's face, being breathed by him, and now you are here, breathed by me—you, the very same'" (23). Jude's consciousness comes into being as the dawning of feelings—tears of sorrow at Phillotson's departure, the awakening of wonder at the thought of Christminster the promised land, and "feeling more than ever his existence to be an undemanded one" (18). Objects create motivations—the impulse to act or to inhibit action—because they create feelings.

3. "AN EPICURE IN EMOTIONS"

Civilization—that collective of conventions, institutions, rules, and forms of social and mental training and regulation—is not for Sue an interesting object in the sense of "urgent" or "irresistible" and, therefore, not catalyzing of her impulses of will because it does not create in her feelings. Sue's attention to civilization as an object is questioning, analytic, critical. As a reflection of her thinking mind in the notice she pays it, civilization prompts from Sue a consistency of mind—the undominated social critic who remains in the presence of civilization as she began. But "Sue the consistent" is the wrong epithet, or at least is not how Jude and Philottson describe Sue

or how Hardy leads us to imagine her. However much civilization compels Sue to be its critic, its real inability to affect and influence her being
makes her attention to its codes and institutions background to her mind's
nature. But the urgency of her attention to Jude and Phillotson—to how
they affect her from one moment to the next—suggests a foreground as
alive and inconsistent and mysterious as any mind in fiction. In a moment
of shared exchange between the three, Sue's responses are immediate, passionate, and beyond even Sue's understanding:

> "Your cousin is so terribly clever that she criticizes it [Jude's model of
> Jerusalem] unmercifully," said Phillotson, with good-humoured satire. "She
> is quite skeptical as to its correctness."
>
> "No, Mr. Phillotson, I am not—altogether! I hate to be what is called a
> clever girl—there are too many of that sort now!" answered Sue sensitively.
> "I only meant—I don't know what I meant—except that it was what you
> don't understand!"
>
> "*I* know your meaning," said Jude ardently (although he did not). "And
> I think you are quite right."
>
> "That's a good Jude—I know *you* believe in me!" She impulsively
> seized his hand, and leaving a reproachful look on the schoolmaster turned
> away to Jude, her voice revealing a tremor which she herself felt to be
> absurdly uncalled for by sarcasm so gentle. She had not the least conception
> how the hearts of the twain went out to her at this momentary revelation
> of feeling, and what a complication she was building up thereby in the
> futures of both. (107)

Phillotson's gentle teasing, calling her "so terribly clever," creates feelings
in Sue she cannot tolerate. To be able to bear teasing requires a capacity
for irony—something Sue lacks, in particular about herself. And to be able
to bear another's skeptical response to her requires the capacity to tolerate doubt—something Sue cannot do when she is the one doubted. Not
having her words understood as she intends them, taken for being one of
a group (another one of those "clever girls"), thought insincere (being a
"clever girl" for the sake of being a clever girl, not because she believes
what she says) make Phillotson's words for Sue an object of attention of
such urgency that her own words, "there are too many of that sort now,"
cannot hold, let alone explain, that urgency. Such an outbreak of fragility
and sensitivity happens frequently when Sue hears herself described by
others, as in when Jude calls Sue a "flirt" and she declares herself to be
"the reverse of what you say so cruelly" (204). But she does not explain
her statements: they are her words of self-meaning, something close to a

private language, that only she understands and that sometimes even she does not understand. For William James, Sue's mental activity in the scene demonstrates the essential nature of consciousness: "[C]onsciousness is *in its very nature impulsive.* We do not have a sensation or a thought and then have to *add* something to it to get a movement. Every pulse of feeling which we have is the correlate of some neural activity that is already on its way to instigate a movement" (II, 526). And:

> The objects of our rage, love, or terror, the occasions of our tears and smiles, whether they be present to our senses, or whether they be merely represented in an idea, have this peculiar sort of impulsive power. The *impulsive quality* of mental states is an attribute behind which we cannot go . . . It is the essence of all consciousness (or of the neural process which underlies it) to instigate movement of some sort. (II, 550–51)

For James, consciousness is a physical process, a flow of neural activity that links the registering of object attention to emotional response to impulsive movement. His description of consciousness—in all its embodied reactivity—moves thought to the position of "current," or just one of the mental activities consciousness constructs in its motion between nerves. For Hardy's characters thought, if it happens at all, comes later in the current of impulsive movement that constitutes consciousness. "I am a feeler, not a reasoner" (232): these are Phillotson's words, Phillotson's self-conception, and could be that of any Hardy figure. I take the one great exception to this claim to be *The Mayor of Casterbridge*'s Elizabeth-Jane. Elizabeth-Jane is Hardy's embodiment of a mind that reasons. As large as Elizabeth-Jane's capacity is to feel acceptance and sympathy, feelings Hardy's characters do not for the most part have, Elizabeth-Jane's powers of reasoned deliberation help her to know patience and to know her own mind, qualities of existence Hardy's characters mostly live without. Elizabeth-Jane is Cordelia to Henchard's Lear. Mostly, a Hardy character exists in a mental landscape of "un-thinking consciousness" or "after-thought consciousness." "'I should never have thought it'" is Sue's refrain to Jude's inquiries into and expressions of reasons for doing things when they first meet, as if she does not have reasons and as if she never thinks. And so while Sue's mental flow makes her a model mind for James's claims about the nature of consciousness, in her inability to find her way to thought or to understanding what she means, Sue seems more unconscious than conscious—a product more of the automatic we associate with the unconscious than with the conscious mind. Antonio Damasio further refines William James's conception of consciousness by distinguishing between what he calls "core conscious-

ness" and "extended consciousness," a distinction that helps to reveal the
nature of Sue's mind:

> *Core consciousness* is generated in pulse like fashion, for each content of
> which we are to be conscious. It is the knowledge that materializes when
> you confront an object, construct a neural pattern for it, and discover
> automatically that the now-salient image of the object is formed in your
> perspective, belongs to you, and that you can even act on it. You come to
> this knowledge, this discovery as I prefer to call it, *instantly:* there is no
> noticeable process of inference, no out-in-the-daylight process that leads
> you there, no words at all—there is the image of the thing, and right next
> to it, is the sense of its possession by you. (Emphasis mine, *The Feeling* 126)

For the most part, Hardy's characters embody minds of core consciousness—in the pulselike "now" of feeling present to the object world and
feeling one's own presence now because of it. Core consciousness creates
the instant knowledge of being and being in the world in the moment,
without words, without introspection. Such a description of consciousness
suggests the mind of Sue—automatic, feeling, alive to and in the present
tense of experience. By contrast, "extended consciousness" in its extension
to minding the past and future of experience seems not to be Sue's:

> *Extended consciousness* is everything core consciousness is, only bigger and
> better, and it does nothing but grow across evolution and across a lifetime
> of experience in each individual. If core consciousness allows you to know
> for a transient moment that it is you seeing a bird in flight or that it is
> you having a sensation of pain, extended consciousness places these same
> experiences in a broader canvas and over a longer period of time. Extended
> consciousness still hinges on the same core "you," but that "you" is now
> connected to the lived past and anticipated future that are part of your
> autobiographical record. (Emphasis mine, *The Feeling* 196)

What is so striking about Sue is her absence of extended consciousness—of
autobiography. She tells the story of the other Christminster student, there
is that, but little else to mark that she had a lived, in the sense of remembered, life before Jude. Sue is there, fully formed because fully living in now,
without the shadow of a past and without a dream of the future. Marriage
threatens Sue in part because it defines and confines her to a future, that
which she cannot imagine because she cannot "mind." Sue cannot think
about tomorrow, much less, as she tells Jude, two years from now.

In response first to Phillotson and then Jude, Sue speaks, touches, and looks the inner workings from her mind out onto her body. The neural activity of every pulse of feeling creates the impulses of core consciousness that cause Sue to move her mouth, her hand, her eyes in their expression. Sue vibrates as a fidgety collection of nervous energy. The way the objects of her attention register inside Sue's mind-body as pulses of feeling that course through her till they find their way to expression as embodied action—impulse—make it so that Sue cannot do otherwise, be otherwise. They fill her and there is no room in her mind for an extension back to the past or ahead to the future. Sue's mental activity is peculiar to Sue, defining of Sue. Jude's surprised wonder at Sue's "impulsive quality of mental states"—that it is more than it is in others—leads him to recognition of its source:

> Jude was surprised to find what a revelation of woman his cousin was to
> him. She was so vibrant that everything she did seemed to have its source
> in feeling. An exciting thought would make her walk ahead so fast he could
> not keep up with her; and her sensitiveness on some points was such that
> it might have been misread as vanity. (102)

"Everything she did seemed to have its source in feeling." If in Hardy's universe Elizabeth-Jane is the embodiment of reason, and Tess is the embodiment of embodiment, Sue Bridehead is the embodiment of feeling. The feeling mind is the very core of core consciousness. Not governed by reason, logic, order, convention, or drives, Sue never knows the comforts that order, a ruling principle, history, or biology bring to existence. Instead, because Sue is ever alert to the objects that surround her, her natural state is excitation, untempered by judgment, patience, or another introspective state that would cause her to step back from feeling. Sue stays with a feeling until it changes to another feeling, which means she "lives" her core consciousness. This affects Phillotson as well, stirs him, exhausts him, drives him to despair: "'I hate such eccentricities, Sue. There's no order or regularity in your sentiments!'" (221). Sue has no means to self-soothe because the "ethereal, fine-nerved, sensitive girl" (218) of "nervous temperament" cannot. The "fibres of her nature" vibrate in passionate response to the world—not to its conventions, codes, rules, or other organizing principles that lend forms of order and the calm that order can bring—but to other people, and all the chaotic feelings that being in their company brings, without much analysis, reflection, memory, or imagination to temper her experience. Feelings of fright, flight, attack, attraction—the four fundamental feeling states we draw on for self-preservation and self-expansion—are the mind states that define Sue. But they define her experience without predictability and without the possibility of temperance, modification, or transformation. Phillotson comes to realize about Sue, "She was beginning to be so puzzling and unpredictable that he was ready to throw in with her other little peculiarities the extremest request which a wife could make" (224)—to live with another man. "The state of that mystery, her heart" (239), moves in inconsistent, changeable, incoherent, illogical, passionate response to the presence of others. Others make Sue feel. And Sue makes others feel. Being with Jude, touching Jude, kissing Jude causes him to want her, as sharing a schoolhouse and walking under an umbrella together prompts Phillotson's desires. No window casement can ensure the inhibition of feeling. Sue's emotional aliveness is contagious; her alertness to the presence of others and the feelings such moments create in her spread out and encourage even the forlorn or repressed to feel in relation to her, to give in to feeling states, to know their own aliveness. That she has an emotional life of such variety and power makes Sue anything but intact. By nature, Sue is relational because she is emotional and emotional because she is relational. Moody because others affect her, Sue is inconstant, inconsistent, and not intact.

Feelings are not consistent, logical, or long-lasting. Hardy in *The Mayor of Casterbridge* describes the movement of time in terms of the course of a character's emotions, as if time and emotion are made from the same stuff— embodiments of *movement* and *change*—"Her emotions rose, fell, undulated, filled her with wild surmise at their suddenness; and so passed Lucetta's experience, of that day" (162). And William James writes, "*Bodily changes follow directly the perception of the exciting fact, and . . . our feeling of the same changes as they occur is the emotion*" (II, 449). Learning for the first time that Jude is married to Arabella, a woman still alive, Sue moves through a wild zigzag of emotions in response. In two pages, Sue expresses or just feels *anger:* "'Why didn't you tell me before!'"; *jealousy:* "'I suppose she—your wife—is—a very pretty woman, even if she's wicked?'"; *the desire to hurt:* "'I at least don't regard marriage as a Sacrament. Your theories are not so advanced as your practice!'"; *pity:* "When she saw how wretched he was she softened"; *sadness:* "For once Sue was as miserable as he, in her attempts to keep herself free from emotion, and her less than half-success"; and *recovered:* "They moved on a dozen paces and she showed herself recovered" (166–67). In response to the news of Jude's former attachment, Sue moves through six feeling states. No single state is more true or real or representative of Sue; rather, each emotion is a different response, a different cast of mind. For James,

> Objects do excite bodily changes by a preorganized mechanism . . . [and]
> the changes are so indefinitely numerous and subtle that the entire organ-
> ism may be called a sounding-board, which every change of consciousness,
> however slight, may make reverberate. The various permutations and com-
> binations of which these organic activities are susceptible make it abstractly
> possible that no shade of emotion, however slight, should be without a
> bodily reverberation as unique, when taken in its totality, as is the mental
> mood itself. (II, 450)

Angry, jealous, attacking, pitying, sad, recovered, Sue is a sounding board of
indefinitely numerous changes in consciousness, changes in feeling states.
Embodying what Hardy once calls in *The Mayor of Casterbridge* Lucetta's
"Protean variety in her phrases, moods, opinions, and also principles" (174),
Sue as a "totality" holds the changes of consciousness that come with
changes of feeling, from one to the next, making the permanence or
consistency of "the mental mood" a fantasy. In Sue Bridehead, mood gives
way to protean variety of undulating emotions.

"A state of mind in which an emotion or set of emotions gains ascen-
dancy"—*mood*—denotes one feeling mind state that comes to be predominant, as in a prevailing "attitude" or "disposition," "humor," "temper," or
"vein."[2] The mood of verbs acknowledges that verbs "act" with forms of
intention, or feeling states—indicative, subjunctive, imperative, interroga-
tive. It is a remarkable quality of language that it acknowledges that verbs
have feelings, feelings that reflect those who use them to communicate.
But the moods are constant, in that mood "is" indicative or "wishes" to
be subjunctive or "must" be imperative, steady feeling states, until another
verb arrives and acts in a different feeling way. We imagine moods not just
as states of mind or of verbs, but as textual and contextual atmospheres,
atmospheres that are possible to create in the minds of their witnesses
because of the arrangement of the elements that form their composition,
perhaps through their elements of sound most of all. About literary mood,
Gabriele Schwab writes, "Since moods are formed and operate unconsciously, their transference in the reading process tends to rely on subtle,
mostly unconscious, perception of formal qualities. This is why the sound
qualities and musical elements (*melos*) that endow poetic language with a
'voice-feeling' play the most fundamental role in the transference of literary

---

2. My definitions of "mood" come from Webster's Dictionary.

moods."[3] The atmosphere of the literary text must be made in its words: how it "voices" its mood states creates the feeling of "the weather indoors," as Fred Vincy calls it. Works of art, like the weather outdoors of a dark and stormy night, tend to remain bound to a predominant voice-feeling or mood.[4] And like the night and storm that end to usher in the dawn light and the change in mood that change of state engenders, the temporal works of art (dance, music, literature) can over the course of their movement through time shift energies and qualities of expression. In each, the mood that predominates or the mood into which things emerge to mark progressive or regressive change depends on a logic or order in the design of its steady state or in the design of its change—an ordering consistency. Mood helps us to make sense of or to discern the meaning of how we are to interpret text and context. We often associate sudden mood shifts with a sense of uncertainty or doubt as to their reality, as in: if mood is about shifts of thoughts and feelings, and because a mood can come on quickly, can any particular mood really ever capture or fully hold what I think and feel about "x"? We imagine or hope that over time, the "true" response will emerge that represents the "true self," precisely because the labile quality of mood will have worn itself out and in its stead will remain the steady state, the one steady mood of self, what Christopher Bollas calls those moods that are "characterological—those that are repeated forms of being states."[5]

But for Jude to understand mood as a state of ascendant emotion or as characterological is not possible when he considers Sue. At the wedding scene of Sue and Phillotson in which Jude "gives Sue away," according to her wishes after she has just rehearsed the wedding vows with Jude himself, he despairs about Sue's nature, "[P]ossibly she would go on inflicting such pains again and again, and grieving for the sufferer again and again, in all her colossal inconsistency" (175). Fluctuating between inflicting pain and grieving for the sufferer is what Sue's mind does—again and again. There

3. "Words and Moods: The Transference of Literary Knowledge," 115. Schwab's fine essay draws on the work of the psychoanalyst Christopher Bollas to explore the nature of literary mood and how it can create states of uncanny dawning—urgent feelings of the "unthought known."

4. Francesco Marroni writes of how Hardy's landscapes have moods, moods that at times become inseparable from those who dwell there. Focusing on *The Return of the Native*, Marroni names "melancholy" the predominant mood of Hardy's Wessex, where the "torments of a trapped soul long for escape" (84–85), and claims "the narrator reveals to the reader that, essentially, his heroine is conceived and imagined as a landscape of melancholy" (86). Eustacia Vye and Egdon Heath are themselves and in relation to each other, for Marroni, landscapes of melancholy.

5. *The Shadow of the Object* 99. Bollas continues, "Musing on the often-heard comment 'I am not myself today' Ralph Greenson in his, 'On Moods and Introjects' in *Explorations in Psychoanalysis*, explores how such a comment points out the close connection between the questions 'How are you?' and 'Who are you?'" (101).

is no one ascendant mental mood of Sue, just the "colossal inconsistency" of her mercurial emotional states. For the psychoanalyst Philip Bromberg, the idea of "getting into a mood" reveals that the mind may be by nature discontinuous and decentered, that each mood rather than representing a negation of the "real" self holds "its own reality, and sometimes its own 'truth'":

> We speak of a person as being in different "moods," or as being emotionally "labile," or as not being "himself." These metaphors are useful, particularly with patients at specific moments. But because they are based on affective shifts as emanating from a unitary, centered self that is temporarily decentered, an analyst's traditional posture and listening stance has tended to focus on the *content* of mental states without much particular regard for the basic discontinuity in structural *context*—the states themselves . . . *I am offering the view that for any human being, feeling differently at different moments about the same thing, or "getting into a mood," represents a shift to a state of consciousness with its own internal integrity, its own reality, and sometimes its own "truth."* (Emphasis mine, "'Speak!'" 533)

For Bromberg, feeling differently at different moments, "getting into a mood," reveals consciousness to be by nature not a solitary or centered state of being, but rather a collection of discontinuous multiple self-states that lacks a central mental mood or primary state of consciousness. Bromberg grants the possibility that each mood has its own integrity as a self state, and so represents how a consciousness in that moment is feeling. We may read Sue Bridehead as an extreme embodiment of Bromberg's view of any human being who feels differently at different moments about the same thing, whose multiple states of consciousness each reveal their own integrity and truth. But we may also read Sue Bridehead's nervous flights of emotion as representative not just of the human mind's tendency toward a discontinuity of feeling states, but as suggestive of a mood disorder—a hypomanic tendency of mind.

One of the leading figures in the field, Kay Redfield Jamison, charts what is known of the nature, manifestation, experience, and meanings of mood disorders in a remarkable collection of essays, *Night Falls Fast: Understanding Suicide; An Unquiet Mind: A Memoir of Moods and Madness; Touched with Fire: Manic-Depressive Illness and the Artistic Temperament;* and *Exuberance: The Passion for Life.* As both physician and patient of manic-depressive illness, Jamison offers profound knowledge of its experience, its mystery, and its importance in our attempts to understand the human mind and the nature of human experience. Her own experiences of manic flight seem to resemble Sue's impassioned movements from start to end of *Jude the Obscure*. Here's Jamison: "Even now, I can see in my mind's rather peculiar eye an extraordinary shattering and shifting of light; inconstant but ravishing colors laid out across miles of circling rings; and the almost imperceptible, somehow surprisingly pallid, moons of this Catherine wheel of a planet . . . I saw and experienced that which had been only dreams, or fitful fragments of aspiration" (*An Unquiet Mind* 90). What does Sue see in her mind's eye? Why does she buy her statues of Venus and Apollo? We do not see the colors in her mind and we do not know why she wants these pagan sculptures near. Hardy remains in relation to Sue only through Jude's eyes—and Hardy occupies Jude's eyes from the position of third-person narrator. From the moment of Jude's first real meeting eye-to-eye with Sue, we stay inside Jude's mind as he looks at Sue's "untranslatable eyes" and then tries to translate them and Sue's nature: "She looked right into his face with liquid, untranslatable eyes, to combine, or seemed to combine, keenness with tenderness, and mystery with both" (90). Our source to Sue's mind, therefore, acknowledges that his reading of her is at best one that reveals a seeming truth, a truth dominated by mystery. Because we do not read from inside Sue's mind, we do not know how she experiences the world or how it feels for her to move rapidly from one feeling state to the next—and yet we are a witness to them. We observe and listen with Jude to how her body and language and more often than not voice reveal the quality of her mood states—"The voice, though positive and silvery, had been tremulous" (100); "The emotional throat-note had come back, and she turned her face away" (150); "Jude knew the quality of every vibration of Sue's voice, could read every symptom of her mental condition; and he was convinced that she was unhappy" (189); "The *tremolo* in her voice caused her to break off" (204); "He knew her mood; the look of her face, when she subscribed herself at length thus. But whatever her mood, he could not say she was wrong in her view" (207); "[T]aking up in her voice the emotion that had begun in his" (237)—these are some of the physical traces that Jude experiences as Sue in "a" mood, however brief, likely to change, or untranslatable.[6] That Sue is a "creature of moods," that

---

6. Hardy's descriptions of Sue's voice as the means through which Jude and we are to experience her feeling states demonstrate Gabriele Schwab and Geoffrey Hartman's idea that voice most of all creates mood. Schwab writes in "Words and Moods": "When Hartman describes literary transference as an 'exchange of feelings' enabled by the power of poetic language to conduct a 'voice-feeling,' he points to the most subliminal aspect of this emotional involvement, namely the formation of literary moods . . . Voice leaves its traces in written language in the form of sounds, rhythms, tonality, pitch, and intonation . . . Since these are the qualities of voice that we experience before the acquisition of a symbolic system of meaning and codes, they are particularly prone to carrying mnemonic resonances with the wordless worlds that carry our earliest 'grammar of being'" (111).

her heart is a "mystery," that as Jude says, she has been "fearless, both as thinker and a feeler" (345), that she is for Jude "a woman-poet, a woman-seer, a woman whose soul shone like a diamond" (350), that her sensitivity makes criticism unbearable, that her "tight-strained nerves" push her out windows and move her through the world with sometimes irritable, sometimes radiant energy combine to create the portrait of a maniclike mood disorder.

Exploring the relation of the artistic temperament to hypomania with regard to mood, thinking, and behavior, Jamison writes in *Touched with Fire:*

> *Mood* in hypomania is usually ebullient, self-confident, and often transcendent, but it almost always exists with an irritable underpinning. Hypomanic mood, although elevated, is generally both fluctuating and volatile. Manic mood, frequently characterized as elated and grandiose, is often as not riddled with depression, panic, and extreme irritability. The perceptual and physical changes that almost always accompany hypomania and mania generally reflect the close and subtle links that exist between elevated mood, a sense of well-being, expansive and grandiose thought, and intensified perceptual awareness . . .
>
> Manic and hypomanic *thought* are flighty and leap from topic to topic; in milder manic states the pattern of association between ideas is usually clear, but, as the mania increases in severity, thinking becomes fragmented and often psychotic. Paranoid, religious, and grandiose delusions are common, as are illusions and hallucinations . . .
>
> Among the particularly dramatic and extreme clinical features of acute mania are its associated frenetic, seemingly aimless, and violent actions. *Bizarre, driven, paranoid, and impulsive patterns of behavior* are common. (Emphasis mine, 28–31)

Sue's maniclike mood states, thoughts, and behaviors recall those Jamison describes, in particular, when Sue loses her mind to the trauma of the infanticide and when she jumps out of windows. But as well the energy of her "mania" pushes her to want more, to feel more, to experience more. Hardy demonstrates her mental attitude by how she responds to Jude's suggestion that they press on in the enjoyment of the day together rather than be safe and sure: "Sue, who was inclined for any adventure that would intensify her sense of the day's freedom, readily agreed" (137). Sue describes something of her emotional needs when she says later to Jude in the company of shepherds, no less: "'Outside all laws except gravitation and germination . . . I crave to get back to the life of my infancy and its freedom . . . You don't know what's inside me . . . 'The Ishmaelite'" (139). Sue the Ishmaelite, unlike Arabella the Ishmaelite, is less a figure of survival than a figure of the wild and uncivilized who wants to follow only natural law and experience the freedom of the infant before social law shapes her being. But the fantasy of returning to infancy is not enough for Sue. She wants to experience the new, to feel what she has not yet felt, to know a limitless or boundless emotional life, to be an "epicure in emotions"—"'I like to do things like this . . . They are interesting, because they have probably never been done before . . . My curiosity to hunt up a new sensation always leads me into scrapes'" (173). Sue is an original. This is how she knows herself. This is how she is herself. Thinking of, doing, and feeling what others have not, Sue has a capacity for invention and discovery and experience that knows few bounds because her emotions press her to "move out" in her feeling exploration of them. Sue's aliveness is the aliveness of her maniclike mood states and all the change they cause her to know.

4. "THE TONE OF HIS MIND"

But what of Jude? As alive and full of promise as Jude is, his story is that he is "obscure": his dreams are borrowed and he is forgotten, again and again:

> Somebody might have come along that way who would have asked him his trouble, and might have cheered him by saying that his notions were further advanced than those of his grammarian. But nobody did come becomes nobody does; and under the crushing recognition of his gigantic error Jude continued to wish himself out of the world. (31)

The felt-quality of being crushed—the rooks trying to feed, the earthworms under foot, the rabbit's leg in the trap—Jude knows this feeling because it is the feeling that gave birth to his mind. "'I don't remember you in the least'" (101). Phillotson's first words to Jude after their long separation and Jude's long journey of yearned-for reunion with his ideal ends with a slap. Jude has remembered, but Phillotson has not. Jude's mind has been shaped by holding Phillotson and his dream in mind, as Jude's own, but Phillotson never shared in that fantasy of father–son bond and dropped Jude completely from his mind: "'I don't remember you in the least'" can offer Jude no hope of having held any "spot" in Phillotson. The loss of his attachment to Phillotson, the recognition of his existence as "undemanded," the absence of anyone present to recognize him and the more global absence of anyone at all crush Jude. For Jude it is the loss of the known object—or the ongoing absence of the unknown longed-for object—that creates the shape of his mind, a mind motivated to find a way out of the feelings of obscurity that crush him.

Jude the Obscure is an empty book, or rather empties out, as Jude finds himself time and again reactive to and unadopted by what or whom he seeks. What Jude has, like Sue, is a great power to feel—idealizing, sympathetic, erotic, romantic—and to study. Like the self-taught Hardy, Jude knows more Latin and Greek than the Christminster students who have gained admission into the world he so badly seeks, as he scrawls Job's words on the gates of that world, "'I have understanding as well as you; I am not inferior to you: yea, who knowth not such things as these?'" (118). But without Christminster, Jude cannot sustain what he knows, cannot support his sense of self. Always seeking a new attachment to enable him to come into being and always rejected or forgotten or just not noticed by the object world, Jude never fixes his mind on a way of being all his own—apart from the object world and its power to approve, accept, or dismiss and reject:

> Deprived of *the objects of both intellect and emotion,* he could not proceed to his work. Whenever he felt reconciled to his fate as a student, there came to disturb his calm his hopeless relation with Sue . . . he sat more or less all the day, convinced that he was at bottom a vicious character, of whom it was hopeless to expect anything. (Emphasis mine, 119)

Without his ideal objects of intellectual and emotional attachment—Christminster and Sue—Jude falls to the opposite pole of idealization, that is, imagines himself a "vicious character, of whom it was hopeless to expect anything." What can the Bildungsroman named *Jude the Obscure* be but a novel of un-building, un-forming, un-becoming? If Jude begins his story with heroic thoughts and dreams, he ends his days an antihero, dead not from a worthy opponent, but from the rain. Slapped across the face by a pig's pizzle, by the angry farmer from whose crops he let the rooks feed, by Phillotson's forgetting him, by seeing Sue and Phillotson together with his arm around her waist under an umbrella, by reading the letter of rejection from the Head of a Christminster College—Jude recurrently experiences being struck. Not only can he form no dream of his own, he is punished for his borrowed dreams, a punishment he carries inside as a state of being unminded, unmoored—obscure—the very quality of being an "absence," "nonpresence," "difficult to discern," "an unstressed vowel." "His fixed idea was to get away to some obscure spot and hide, and perhaps pray" (123).

The ideal spot becomes the obscure spot and the adopted dream becomes his fixed idea to hide. Jude's schizoid pattern of attaching himself to an ideal vision—"It had been his standing desire to become a prophet," experiencing the deflation of that vision—"He always remembered the appearance of the afternoon on which he awoke from his dream," and falling into a despair from which he cannot recover—"'And it is too late, too late for me!'" (399), defines how Jude returns to the melancholy mood as his mental refrain. If Sue's mind tends toward the manic pole of mood disorder, Jude's mind tends toward the depressive pole. Manic depression, a disease of polar mood states, when fluctuating toward the manic pole ignites brain chemistry to create high feelings of euphoria, grandiosity, flightiness, and volatility, and when fluctuating toward the depressive pole slows brain chemistry to create flat feelings of lifelessness, meaninglessness, and despair. Jamison writes: "Manic depression distorts moods and thoughts, incites dreadful behaviors, destroys the basis of rational thought, and too often erodes the desire to live. It is an illness that is biological in its origins, yet that feels psychological in the experience of it; an illness that is unique in conferring advantage and pleasure, yet one that brings in its wake almost unendurable suffering and, not infrequently, suicide" (*An Unquiet Mind* 6). Sue and Jude hold between them the extreme poles of human mood and create between them the manic-depressive energy of *Jude the Obscure,* the bipolar moodiness of its narrative universe "that brings in its wake almost unendurable suffering and [. . .] suicide."

As she does with mania, Jamison describes the mood, thinking, and behavior of melancholia:

> The depressive, or melancholic states are characterized by a *morbidity and flatness of mood along with a slowing down of virtually all aspects of human thought, feeling, and behavior that are most personally meaningful.* Occasionally these changes reflect only a transient shift in mood or a recognizable and limited reaction to a life situation. When energy is profoundly dissipated, the ability to think is clearly eroded, and the capacity to actively engage in the efforts and pleasures of life is fundamentally altered, then depression becomes an illness rather than a temporary or existential state . . . Mood, in the more serious depressive states, is usually bleak, pessimistic, and despairing. A deep sense of futility is frequently accompanied, if not preceded, by the belief that the ability to experience pleasure is permanently gone. The physical and psychological worlds are experienced as shades of grays and blacks, as having lost their color and vibrancy. Irritability, quick anger, suspiciousness, and emotional turbulence are frequent correlates of depressed mood; morbid and suicidal thinking are common . . . (Emphasis mine,

Touched with Fire 18, 21, 23)

If Jude's movements are motivated by a great desire for expansion, the world's refusal to accommodate his wishes incite in him an existential despair that accompanies each adventure and each stop shy of the gate. At the end of the second part of the novel, with a full four parts still to come, Jude awakens to the melancholy madness of being dream-broken because hope-broken, a mood that never fully leaves him:

> [W]hen he awoke it was as if he had awakened in hell. It *was* hell—"the hell of conscious failure," both in ambition and in love. He thought of that previous abyss into which he had fallen before leaving this part of the country; the deepest deep he had supposed it then; but it was not so deep as this. That had been the breaking in of the outer bulwarks of his hope: this was of his second line. (124)

Hell is not failing in ambition and love. Hell is knowing failure, feeling hope break and dreams end, consciously living without meaning, purpose, and possibility—being The Obscure. "'Well, here I am, just come home; a fellow gone to the bad; though I had the best intentions in the world at one time. Now I am melancholy mad'" (125). The mood of melancholy madness sounds the tone of Jude's mind and masters him. Julia Kristeva writes in *Black Sun,* "For if it is true that those who are slaves to their moods, beings drowned in their sorrows, reveal a number of psychic or cognitive frailties, it is equally true that a diversification of moods, variety in sadness, refinement in sorrow or mourning are the imprint of a humankind that is surely not triumphant but subtle, ready to fight, and creative . . ." (22). Jude is without this "diversification of moods." With the "breaking in of the outer bulwarks of his hope" followed by the fall of what he calls "his second line," Jude is out of fight and has nothing within from which to create.

Jude's melancholy mood defines the nature of his character, and for Hardy, is Jude's "fate"—an idea Hardy attributes to Novalis in *The Mayor of Casterbridge:*

> Character is Fate, said Novalis, and Farfrae's character was just the reverse of Henchard's, who might not inaptly be described as Faust has been described—as a vehement, gloomy being, who had quitted the ways of men without light to guide him on a better way. (112)

Can the novel be a tragic art form? Hardy's greatest response to that question, *The Mayor of Casterbridge: The Life and Death of a Man of Character,* is a tragedy not because of Fate, but because of how Hardy writes "Character is Fate": the life and death of a man bound to his "vehement and gloomy," impulsive, contrary, grandiose, passionate character. It is Michael Henchard's character that fates him to "quit the ways of men without light to guide him on a better way"—character—that makes possible *The Mayor of Casterbridge*'s tragic representation of life and death. Much of what Hardy makes possible for the novel as an aesthetic form hinges on how he writes and conceives of "character"—not just in his reimagining of the novel as tragic but in his reimagining of the idea of character itself.[7] Hardy writes character as mood. The mysteries of identity—what it is to be unknowable to another and to oneself—is what Hardy gives full attention to in his narrative worlds. Hardy resists explaining his characters because much of their beings and actions can't be explained—they "just act," by impulse. However much context, conscience, and consciousness affect his characters' lives, for Hardy what fundamentally constitutes character is *temperament,* a distinctly modern understanding of character as the emotional tendencies of mind. While Hardy's understanding of temperament looks back to the ancient theory of the humours, in defining the existence and importance of character temperament and in claiming its embodiment, the complexity of Hardy's modern understanding of emotion and how we experience emotion fundamentally recasts and opens out that ancient model. A singer of his temperament, one whose voice prompts others to know their emotions, Donald Farfrae turns his temperament out into the world and creates a spatial sound for others to meet him there:

Young Farfrae repeated the last verse. It was plain that nothing so pathetic

7. James Wood writes about the origins of novelistic characterization: "The novel begins in the theater, and novelistic characterization begins when the soliloquy goes inward. The soliloquy, in turn had its origin in prayer" (*How Fiction Works* 139). If John Bunyan's 1679 *Pilgrim's Progress* narrates prayer as soliloquy and defines novelistic characterization to be moral emblem, my sense is the characters of the English eighteenth- and nineteenth-century novel follow Bunyan's pattern-setting. Theirs are in essence moral identities, which, while tested and tried by experience, inevitably and reliably surface in response to what befalls them. And yet, however fixed a character's "goodness" or "badness"—through prayer, the soliloquy turned inward, the hard spiritual work of the development of conscience—character as moral identity can change for the better, even be saved. But English theater presented the novel with two fundamental forms for imagining the nature of character: as moral embodiment and as the embodiment of humours—sanguine, choleric, melancholic, phlegmatic. No such path of character change through spiritual labor is possible when character is understood through the theory of the humours. Only through physical treatment—a change in diet, a physical expunging of fluids (blood, bile, and phlegm)—will the humours change and change how they define character. The Puritan beginnings of the English novel let go of the idea of character as temperament in favor of moral identity, I would assert, because of the path toward change it holds open, through the difficult mental labor of spiritual awakening—an awakening based in acceptance of God's truth as opposed to a nonmeditative, physical letting-go.

had been heard at the King of Prussia for a considerable time. The difference of accent, the excitability of the singer, the intense local feeling, and
the seriousness with which he worked himself up to a climax, surprised
this set of worthies, who were only too prone to shut up their emotions
with caustic words . . . They began to view him through a golden haze
which *the tone of his mind* seemed to raise around him . . . He seemed to
feel exactly as [Elizabeth-Jane] felt about life and its surroundings—that
they were a tragical, rather than a comical thing; that though one could
be gay on occasion, moments of gaiety were interludes, and no part of the
actual drama. It was extraordinary how similar their views were. (Emphasis
mine, *The Mayor of Casterbridge* 51, 53, 55)

"The tone of his mind" raises a golden haze around Donald Farfrae, a tone
made visible through the audibility of his singing. The particular temperament of Farfrae—how his mind feels—must act, must make music. And his
voice prompts those who hear to feel him feeling, to join him feeling, to
discover what it means to feel again: Farfrae's singing enters his listeners
like an emotional contagion. The tone of mind—temperament—affects
not just how one mind experiences life, but how a community of minds
experiences life, as separate or as shared, as comical or as tragical.

How emotions are experienced, what moods emerge, what patterns of
behavior result are for Hardy what constitutes character and are for the
psychiatrist Kay Jamison what constitutes personality. For both, temperament distinguishes the nature of one mind from another. Jamison writes
in *Exuberance: The Passion for Life:* "Psychology has always, if insufficiently,
concerned itself with individual differences in personality and temperament.
Basic emotions such as joy, anger, and fear are universal, but individuals vary
enormously in the *nature, quickness, and intensity of their emotional responses*"
(emphasis mine, 97). She continues:

Temperament, which can be broadly defined as the relatively stable pattern
of moods and behaviors first manifest early in life, has been more fully
described by psychologist Gordon Allport as the "class of raw material
from which personality is fashioned." Personality generally denotes the
unique or most distinctive aspects of an individual, characteristics shaped
by innate forces operating under the influence and constraints of upbringing and environment. "Temperament," according to Allport, is the "internal
weather" in which personality evolves. "The more anchored a disposition
is in native constitutional soil the more likely it is to be spoken of as a
temperament. . . . [*It comprises*] *the characteristic phenomena of an individual's
emotional nature, including his susceptibility to emotional stimulation, his customary*

strength and speed of response, the quality of his prevailing mood, and all peculiarities of fluctuation and intensity of mood." These phenomena, Allport assumed, were largely inherited. In practice the terms "temperament" and "personality" are often used interchangeably, although temperament is assumed to be more genetically determined. (Emphasis mine, 100–101)

"Nature, quickness, intensity" of emotional response, the qualities of how emotions are experienced, along with their range, what patterns of moods and response emerge and take hold as dispositions and behaviors defines temperament—or how the mind experiences being alive. Psychology takes temperament to be genetically determined, as does Hardy, but to which he adds "views of life" to make character "fate." Little Father Time is Hardy's walking embodiment of how temperament acts as fate:

> [H]is morbid temperament . . . "It was his nature to do it. The doctor says there are such boys springing up among us—boys of a sort unknown in the last generation—the outcome of new views of life. They seem to see all its terrors before they are old enough to have staying power to resist them. He says it is the beginning of the coming universal wish not to live." (336–37)

Named for a category—those boys who seek the end of life because they cannot bear to live with the temperament to which they are born—Little Father Time is temperament as allegory, temperament as tragic fate—the Child who Fathers the end of Time. Hardy sets the morbid temperament of Little Father Time, the genetic offspring of Jude's partnering with Arabella, in relation to two other offspring of partnering: the loosening into the world of the temperament "Greek Joyousness" (297) created between Sue and Jude, and "the antipathetic, recriminatory mood of the average husband and wife of Christendom" (296) created between Arabella and Cartlet. "Horribly sensitive," Sue and Jude are figures "unsuited to marriage" by temperament, Hardy writes, unsuited because they feel: "'[T]heir supreme desire is to be together—to share each other's emotions, and fancies, and dreams'" (231). Arabella and Cartlet are suited to marriage because of their absence of feeling, or because of their shared mood of recrimination. Morbidity, Joy, Antipathy—the desire to die, the desire to live, the absence of desire—these are the temperaments that characterize the moods of *Jude the Obscure,* textual moods born into Hardy's narrative world by the general temperaments that characterize shareable states or natures of being: the Little Father Times, the Married, the Lovers.

However particular Jude is, particular enough to be the eponymous subject of a novel, his descent into obscurity negates that particularity because his is a story about not becoming, but being The Obscure. His is a story that can be told about him and from his viewpoint because it is shared—it is "our" story—the hell of conscious failure. Writing about the winter lyric, "The Fallow Deer at the Lonely House," Susan M. Miller describes not just how but why Hardy brings us inside the viewpoint of one to prompt our recognition of the other who "escapes our notice": "Hardy asks us to identify with a point of view that could not have told the whole story as it is told, and with this defiance of narrative logic he calls our attention to the astonishingly vivid presence of the world that is always escaping our notice" (103). One character of *Jude the Obscure,* one temperament, is not shareable or generalizable, is not, Hardy asserts, to be found anywhere else. Mad, bright, nervous, always in motion, always changing, scintillating as a star, Sue Bridehead "could not have told the whole story as it is told," but her "astonishingly vivid presence walks the world with the fibres of her nature [. . .] strained like harp-strings" (225). Perhaps Hardy's most poetic and difficult account of Sue's nature comes after the scene of infanticide, in a moment of Sue's convalescence. It is the closest Hardy comes to entering Sue's mind, to imagining her internal metamorphosis from feeling a charmed haunting by life to feeling life a paranoid haunting:

> Vague and quaint imaginings had haunted Sue, in the days when her intellect scintillated like a star, that the world resembled a stanza or melody composed in a dream; it was wonderfully excellent to the half-aroused intelligence, but hopelessly absurd at the full waking; that the First Cause worked automatically like a somnambulist, and not reflectively like a sage; that at the framing of the terrestrial conditions there seemed never to have been contemplated such a *development of emotional perceptiveness* among the creatures subject to those conditions as that reached by thinking and educated humanity. But affliction makes opposing forces loom anthropomorphous; and those ideas were now exchanged for a sense of Jude and herself fleeing from a persecutor. (Emphasis mine, 342)

What distinguishes Sue from others, what gives her character, is her "development of emotional perceptiveness," a temperament that enables her to experience the world as a "stanza or melody composed in a dream." But the "First Cause," that Force or Will that brought forth the world, did not bring forth Sue, nor did thinking and educated humanity. She is made of some other material, from some other sphere—the fibers of harp strings, the realm of emotion. Unprotected, that very emotional perceptiveness that enables Sue to hear the world as a song strikes her down when confronted by the murder of her young, causes her to transform the music of being alive into a shaming, relentless persecutor. To be alive, Hardy writes, is to feel crushed—to hear the mad melancholy mood that is the tone of Jude's mind. Yet, for Hardy, temperament determines *how* that melancholy madness *lives* in the mind—whether it beats down or is beaten down, whether one experiences life as Michael Henchard or Donald Farfrae, Jude Fawley or Sue Bridehead. "'I am beaten, beaten!'" Sue comes to declare finally, but not till the bitter end, after all her children are dead.

"The emotions have no place in a world of defect, and it is a cruel injustice that they should have developed in it" (458), despairs Hardy. If for Hardy what is most beautiful about being human is our emotions, what Hardy writes as a "chronicler of mood and deeds" (288) in all his novels is the tragedy of feeling in a flawed world.

CHAPTER 6

"That Blue Narcotic Haze"

Dreams, Dissociation, and *Tess of the D'Urbervilles*

"I don't know about ghosts," she was saying; "but I do know that our souls
can be made to go outside our bodies when we are alive . . . A very easy
way to feel 'em go," continued Tess, "is to lie on the grass at night and look
straight up at some big bright star; and, by fixing your mind upon it, you
will soon find that you are hundreds and hundreds o' miles away from your
body, which you don't seem to want at all."
—Thomas Hardy, *Tess of the D'Urbervilles*

All major turns of plot in Thomas Hardy's *Tess of the D'Urbervilles* occur in
some relation to sleep—the death of Prince, Tess's rape, Angel's burying of
Tess, Tess's capture at Stonehenge. Sleep rehearses loss before the event, as
the loss of conscious awareness. And sleep prepares for loss—of virginity, of
love, of life—upon awakening to its real experience. A different movement
of consciousness happens in moments of daydreaming in the novel. Tess
transfixed wearing flowers; Tess mesmerized as if in another world while
working on the threshing machine; Tess dreaming out of a window. These
waking dreams set her consciousness in another place that make a space for
her to occupy, alone, apart from the world before her, before Alec forces
her attention in each instance back on him, her consciousness forced to be
defined in relation to him. Significantly, when Tess moves into these states
of liminal consciousness, or waking dreams, she goes, as she says "outside
her body," a state she claims she can will. Lying down on the grass as if
asleep or even dead and fixing her mind on a big, bright star, Tess says
that her mind travels far from her body, that which "you don't seem to
want at all." Why does Tess not seem to want her body at all, her beautiful
body, which everyone else seems to want most of all?

1. A STORY OF "O"

Tess of the D'Urbervilles is a novel of evolutionary metamorphosis—meta-morphosis that emerges from the ebb and flow, forward and back, forward and back—circles and circles that plot not just repetition, but evolution. "O" is the fundamental geometry of the novel, perhaps of all Hardy's novels. The "O-O-O" sound the landlady overhears leaking out from inside the shared apartment of Tess and Alec in Sandborne we see, drawn on the page before our eyes, and etched as the plot's course over and over again. The "O" holds motion, a circling motion that retraces itself as it widens over increasing space and time. Tess walks or rides from her home in Marlott to the Chase, returns to Marlott and goes to River Var, returns to Marlott and then moves to Flintcomb-Ash, makes her final return home to Marlott to finish drawing the widening circle's arc with four new places linked together by her movement from one to the next.

Kingsbere/Sandborne/Stonehenge/Wintoncester—these are Tess's tem-porary destinations until she is no more and Liza Lu stands there in her stead, hand in hand with Angel. Tess, caught and executed, metamorphoses into Liza Lu, who, with Angel, continues to trace the human march first begun by Eve, caught and punished, who, with Adam, is sent out of Eden. The motion of the "O" is one of return and extension. Taken as a whole, Hardy's narrative defines a physical universe of "O": time is a mix of the past that repeats in the present as it changes into the future; space con-tracts and expands; motion extends and returns. And it is an experiential universe of the "O": the inescapability of the "no way out" of a limited set of possibilities finds its way out by chance to new possibilities through substitution, replacement, and reconstitution. Like the phases of the moon that trace physical change in relation to what came before, the novel plots experiential change over time, holding onto the same presence as it trans-forms into difference with chance encounters. The novel evolves from Phase One to Phase Seven, from "The Maiden" to "Fulfilment," from the stabbing death of Prince to the stabbing rape of Tess to the stabbing murder of Alec, from passion-hearted to hardhearted to tender-hearted Angel, from seducer to preacher to jailer Alec, from Joan Durbeyfield to Tess to Liza Lu—each new position a repeated replacement that marks the same but different.[1]

---

1. J. Hillis Miller opened the way to seeing Hardy's structuring formal repetition, a repetition that for Miller creates "immanent design": "Taken together, the elements form a system of mutually defining motifs, each of which exists as its relation to the others. The reader must execute a lateral dance of interpretation to explicate any given passage, without ever reaching, in this sideways movement, a passage which is chief, original, or originating, a sovereign principle of explanation. The meaning, rather, is suspended within the interaction among the elements. It is immanent rather than transcendent" (*Fiction and Repetition* 127). For Miller what is made by the repetitions back and forth

Adaptation, Darwin's understanding of how life seeks to ensure its survival through successful combinations of repetition, chance, and change, I
understand in Hardy's narrative universe as metamorphosis with a purpose.
Both are visions of evolution. The evolution that stands above all others in
Tess, ineluctable as time, is not social history. What is man-made, that story
of named lineal descent, can be passed on in words, distorted, manipulated,
bought and sold, and so made possible in Hardy's narrative universe to
come to nothing—to devolve. The novel teases us to imagine at its opening
that this will be a story of historical evolution: "'Don't you really know,
Durbeyfield, that you are the direct lineal representative of the ancient and
knightly family of the D'Urbervilles, who derive their descent from Sir
Pagan D'Urberville, that renowned knight who came from Normandy with
William the Conqueror, as appears by Battle Abbey roll?'" (7–8). Hardy
makes knowing the relation between "Durbeyfield" and "D'Urberville" and
"Stoke-D'Urbervilles" the social story of evolution that names the book,
Tess of the D'Urbervilles, or words its meaning. But the process of naming
is false or at least weak because man-made, as Hardy most coarsely defines
the process in the regrafting of the "extinct" family name "D'Urberville"
by Mr. Simon Stoke.[2] Deeper, far deeper than the social male narrative of
patrilineal descent lies THE story of evolutionary metamorphosis of this
Bildungsroman that encloses and enfolds them all—the natural female narrative of girl to woman. If "D'Urbervilles" is the name annexed or regrafted,
"Tess" is the name that emerges, grows, and holds meaning. Hardy tells this
evolutionary metamorphosis as Tess's story, a metamorphosis that is both
natural to her like the phases of the moon and socially "grafted" upon her.

Attributing from where or how Tess emerges, grows, and holds meaning,
Hardy determines three core evolutionary paths. There is that of Tess born
from her mother's body and nature, not from her father's lineage: "There

is a meaningfulness that comes from within, the interaction itself of the patterns, traces, designs that
reflect one another, and, when held together, reveal sameness and difference, together. Miller's work,
bound to a poststructuralist seeing of "either/or/and," resists naming any structures of meaning that
would seem to account for the relationship between sameness and difference and that might define to
what end they are bound. By contrast, Gillian Beer brings to Miller's formal account of how Hardy
writes a name for how Hardy plots—"Darwin's plots." In intellectual echo, Hardy's novels intertwine
repetition, chance, and change to plot their stories, as Darwin weaves them together to account for
the nature of experience. Here's Beer: "Hardy and Darwin concur in that chance and change are not
intermitting conditions in their work. Rather they are the permanent medium of experience and
thus of language. But both of them also insist on repetition as a basic organization for all experience
within the natural order" (229). For Beer, Darwin's natural order is Hardy's narrative order.

2. Hardy writes: "Conning for an hour in the British Museum the pages of works devoted to
extinct, half-extinct, obscured, and ruined families appertaining to the quarter of England in which
[Mr. Simon Stoke] proposed to settle, he considered that *D'Urberville* looked and sounded as well as
any of them: and D'Urberville accordingly was annexed to his own name for himself and his heirs
eternally" (39). I read "conning" both as studying and as "swindling." Given that this is a passage
about dead-names and the possibility of their annexation, I read "eternally" as the italicized "*eternally.*"

still beamed from [Joan Durbeyfield's] features something of the freshness, and even the prettiness of her youth; rendering it evident that the personal charms which Tess could boast of were in main part her mother's gift, and therefore unknightley, unhistorical" (20). Not just Tess's physical nature, but her tendencies to dream find their way from Joan to Tess: "There was a dreaminess, a preoccupation, an exaltation, in the maternal look which the girl could not understand" (21). Tess holds in her physical and mental forms evolutionary states of times past with the time present that is, like memory, a composite of shifting-sameness, wholly composed of now, and wholly composed of before. But as well there are Tess's features now at sixteen that Hardy describes in relation to their earlier look, flashes of which come forward in her now: "Phases of her childhood lurked in her aspect still. As she walked along to-day, for all her bouncing womanliness, you could sometimes see her twelfth year in her cheeks, or her ninth sparkling from her eyes; and even her fifth would flit over the curves of her mouth now and then" (15–16). Like the architectural remains that are strewn throughout Hardy's novels, buried and uncovered, waiting to be restored, or just standing there like harbingers of the past in the present, Tess embodies time in the phases of evolution traced on her being, an evolution that holds who her mother once was, the girl she still is, and the woman she is becoming.[3] But before this dyad of evolutionary paths that trace the emergence and growth of Tess, Hardy writes this sentence: "Tess Durbeyfield at this time of her life was a mere vessel of emotion untinctured by experience" (15). These are new words, prior words Hardy writes to constitute what "Tess Durbeyfield" holds. The metaphor "vessel of emotion" makes Tess a container of fluid emotion, or a ship floating on or traveling through emotion. "Untinctured by experience" makes the vessel of emotion at once "pure" in that it is not "tinted" or "stained" or "impregnated" with experience—and vulnerable. Between "Tess Durbey-field" and "vessel of emotion" lies the phrase "at this time of her life," and its shadowy suggestion that Tess is not *yet* tinctured by experience. Experience is what happens to Tess because she is alive, embodied in the world and in time. It is this third evolutionary path that carries to Tess chance and so, too, variety, difference, and the possibility of adaptation—or its failure. Chance, therefore, brings to the Hardy narrative universe the co-present possibilities of adaptation and of tragedy.

3. Jules Law writes about how history is embodied as the "aestheticized historicization" of Tess's body in "Sleeping Figures: Hardy, History, and the Gendered Body."

2. TINCTURE

For Tess to experience, to be vulnerable to time and all that passes with it, there must exist a real outside her mind, a real she must engage in order to be in the world and in time. But what is the real outside her mind? Why engage what "tints" or "stains"? An emerging understanding of the real involves, according to the psychoanalyst Philip Bromberg, "the way in which one's capacity to see things as others see them develops, stabilizes, and coexists with one's values, wishes, fantasy life, impulses, and spontaneity; in other words, these assumptions concern the conditions through which subjective experience of reality (including reality about one's self) is freed to move beyond the limits of egocentrically conceived personal truth" (*Standing* 4). Bromberg makes experience—the movement from and between one's personal truth to know and be in the world—not necessarily staining but a fundamental part of what makes possible mental development from child to adult. What is at stake in being beautiful? In being the world's embodied beautiful of emerging female sexuality? And how is Tess to bring her "vessel of emotion," her "values, wishes, fantasy life, impulses, and spontaneity" to the world and the world's reality to her personal truth to trace that path of mental development in relation to her physical development? Hardy's descriptions of Tess demand not just recognition of her sexual presence as Female, but Male response to them: the "luxuriance of aspect, a fullness of growth, [. . .] made her appear more of a woman than she really was" (42), *even* to a man "with the least fire in him" (151). The embodied effect of Tess on that man with the least fire in him, the angel-man Angel, Hardy writes, is that of the *real*—"real vitality, real warmth, real incarnation" (150). All this aliveness presses on him to experience the real embodiment of Woman through how her presence makes him feel his own real embodiment as Man—"distracted, infatuated, maddened" (151), not as the angel Angel, but as the man Angel.

I read Tess as Hardy's embodiment of the life force that is Female, as wet and green and milky as the fecund world of the Talbothay Dairy, her real home, that space where her being and her being in the world know contiguity and congruence. Entering the Var Vale, "beautiful Tess" is met by cries east and west, not because the Valley is conscious of her arrival, but to announce milking time (105). Tess's entrance to the Var Vale is not marked as separate from the scene of milking; rather, Tess enters and begins immediately to get her hand and mouth in, by milking and drinking in the milk. Her hand helps make the milk flow while her mouth opens to the milk's flow into her—she makes milk and is made of milk—she milks the landscape and is made of the landscape's milk, this land of milk and honey. Embodied in space and time, Tess is aware of neither. She is present; she is now—the figure in relation to whom all space exists and through whom all time passes—complete. Listening to the notes of Angel's harp in the garden, Tess feels the sounds made visible, as she breathes them in—the garden and Tess harmonize to Angel's music:

> Tess was conscious of neither time nor space. The exultation which she had described as being producible at will by gazing at a star, came now without any determination of hers; she undulated upon the thin notes as upon billows, and their harmonies passed like breezes through her, bringing tears into her eyes. The floating pollen seemed to be his notes made visible, and the dampness of the garden the weeping of the garden's sensibility. (123)

Here in this garden filled with the harp notes of Angel, Tess's wishes, fantasy life, impulses, and spontaneity coexist with and in the way the world is now. Angel, the outsider, who has come to Talbothay not as a farmer but as a gentleman who seeks to learn farming, sounds in his harp the notes that bring Tess and the garden they share to him. He plays and she and the billows undulate in response. The harmonies as breezes surround and fill Tess, surround and fill the garden's air with floating pollen—his notes made visible. She weeps and the garden weeps in postorgiastic response. For the Var Vale in heat, Angel, this David with his harp, is the longed-for outsider in response to whom the maddening state of desire emerges and grows. If Angel seeds the garden with his notes, so too do his notes seed Tess. Tess knows in Var Vale what it means to be Var Vale—a galaxy of big bright stars—the Milky Way.

Milking creates a potion all its own—the smell, the touch, the taste of the cradle of life—the sensuous atmosphere of fertility release embodied calls for the touching nearness of union and creation. Eight chapters later of almost continuous milking, Hardy writes of the spell cast by the cows on their milkers in the Var Vale:

> Amid the oozing fatness and warm ferments of the Var Vale, at a season when the rush of juices could almost be heard below the hiss of fertilization, it was impossible that the most fanciful love should not grow passionate. The ready bosoms existing there were impregnated by their surroundings . . . The air of the place, so fresh in the spring and early summer, was stagnant and enervating now. Its heavy scents weighed upon them, and at mid-day the landscape seemed lying in a swoon . . . And as Clare was oppressed by the outward heats, so he was burdened inwardly by a waxing fervour of passion for the soft and silent Tess. (149)

Hardy's prose pants with desire and the oppressive near-but-not-here relief of orgasm. The steady state of milking has drawn, not just from the milkers but from the whole Var Vale—passion—"the hiss of fertilization." The milkers are impregnated by their surroundings; the landscape lies down in a swoon; Angel waxes with a fervor of passion for the "soft and silent Tess." Milking its way to a state of continuous sexual longing, the Var Vale is in heat—"Ethiopic scorchings browned the upper slopes of the pastures" (149)—without relief—"The rains having passed the uplands were dry" (149). Hardy's achingly alive prose never veers from its sensuous vivacity. Whether in heat, in fecundity, or in barrenness, *Tess of the D'Urbervilles* insists on embodied life bearing down in all its presence and power. Hardy never lets life as a force go away. His imagination cannot let it—his mind feels the pulsations of life happening and his language finds its way to images that pulse life back.

But the aliveness of Tess, her remarkable embodiment, her oneness with space and time and being, cannot hold in Hardy's universe. The fundamental principle of Darwin's account of the natural order understands natural selection as the best adaptive strategy to ensure that life lives. Natural selection "uses" Tess, incorporates from her what is most highly adaptive, and discards what remains. Played out as narrative, Tess finds herself time and again chosen for the very aliveness that mirrors Hardy's writing and depiction of life—both at their most generative—and then punished. How Tess is both the embodiment and victim of the very aliveness that most defines Hardy's creative force and life's creative energy stages itself in metonym, as the drama of Tess's mouth.

3. KISSING

We cannot kiss our own lips. Our mouths can't know the pleasures of kissing without having other mouths to kiss. In "Plotting for Kisses," the psychoanalyst Adam Phillips writes about this, "Because the mouth, unlike the body parts it sucks, is acutely alive to its own pleasure, it therefore seeks . . . by that same narcissistic logic its curious reunion through another's lips" (99). The mouth must seek other mouths—touch them and feel touched by them—to know its own pleasure. And it is acutely alive to its own pleasure because of the amount of the brain's cerebral cortex devoted to it.[4] Figure

4. The cerebral cortex is home to all the brain's "higher functions," which include the generation of movement, the processing of sensation and vision, the construction of the world, thinking, planning, language, spatial relations, attention, decision-making, memory. "Lower functions" happen in the brain stem, which include breathing, eye movement, reflexes, postural adjustments,

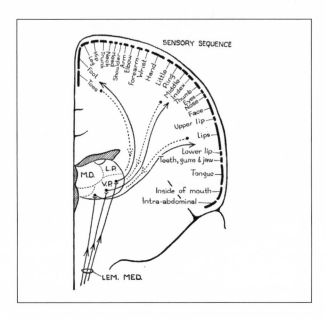

FIGURE 3 *Original description of figure:* Sensory sequence in the Rolandic cortex shown on a cross section of the cerebral hemisphere. Lengths of the black lines in the cortex indicate the approximate extent of the representation of sensation for each part. Afferent impulses pass upward from the periphery through the thalamus to the postcentral gyrus. From there, the impulses are returned by a hypothetical tract, indicated by the broken lines, to the centrencephalic system. This would provide for integration with the other sensory streams of impulses derived from both hemispheres. SOURCE: *Epilepsy and the Functional Anatomy of the Human Brain,* Wilder Penfield and Herbert Jasper (Boston: Little, Brown and Company 1954), 71.

3, from the study *Epilepsy and the Functional Anatomy of the Human Brain* by neurologists Wilder Penfield and Herbert Jasper, is a representation in cross-section of the cerebral cortex's sensory strip and reveals through the length of the dark black line attached to body part the amount of sensation the brain devotes to each part. The upper lip, lower lip, teeth, gums, jaw, tongue, and inside of the mouth compose at least a third of the chart—the lips and tongue have the longest black lines attached to them.

Conceived somewhat differently, Penfield's "homunculus," shown in figure 4, represents by size the extent of the cortex's motor strip occupied by

blood pressure, heart regulation, neural-hormonal aspects of being. The thalamus serves intermediate functions between the cerebral cortex and brain stem. The cerebellum acts as a "motor computer" to regulate the accuracy and coordination of motion, and the basal ganglia regulate the smoothness and speed of motion.

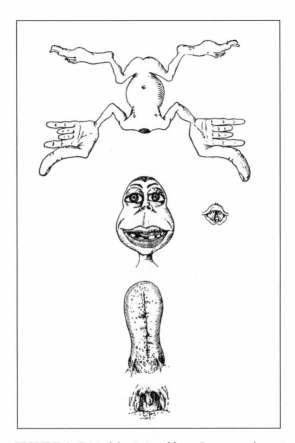

FIGURE 4 *Original description of figure:* Sensory and motor homunculus. This was prepared as a visualization of the order and comparative size of the parts of the body as they appear from above down upon the Rolandic cortex. There are certain unavoidable inaccuracies in the drawing. It does not show the differences between sensory and motor representation. . . . SOURCE: *Epilepsy and the Functional Anatomy of the Human Brain,* Wilder Penfield and Herbert Jasper (Boston: Little, Brown and Company 1954), 70.

each body part and by arrangement the order of the parts of the body as found in the cortical sequence. The massive lips of the homunculus and the large erect tongue underneath represent the large amount of brain devoted to the mouth's movements, and make even more vivid how important a role the mouth plays in how we experience. To survive and flourish we must want to suck at the breast and put food in our mouths: the human brain has evolved to make the oral experiences of sucking and eating some of our greatest sensory pleasures.

For Adam Phillips:

> Kissing is integral to the individual's ongoing project of working out what mouths are for. In that craving for other mouths that is central to the experience of adolescence and seems to begin then, the individual resumes with new found appetite and inhibition his oral education, connected now with an emerging capacity for genital sexuality. There is the return of the primary sensuous experience of tasting another person . . . [T]he kiss is the image of reciprocity, not domination—but one that is also unprecedented, since it includes tasting someone else's mouth . . . When we kiss we devour the object by caressing it; we eat it, in a sense, but sustain its presence. Kissing on the mouth can have a mutuality that blurs the distinction between giving and receiving. (96–97)

In *Tess,* the plotting figure Alec desires to devour Tess's mouth, a desire he first suggests in his forced strawberry-feeding of Tess and then makes literal in his relentless forced feedings on Tess. Alec's "plotting for kisses" is about wanting to eat her alive so as to rid himself of the need to kiss her peony mouth with its "little upward lift in the middle of her red top lip"—her mouth shaped as an embodied kiss moving through space. But not wanting him to touch her with his mouth, Tess cries she wants nobody to kiss her. Here is the drama of their mouths:

> "Let me put one little kiss on those holmberry lips, Tess; or even on that warmed cheek, and I'll stop—on my honour, I will!" . . . "But I don't want anybody to kiss me, sir!" she implored, a big tear beginning to roll down her face, and the corners of her mouth trembling in her attempts not to cry . . . He was inexorable, and she sat still, and D'Urberville gave her the kiss of mastery. No sooner had he done so than she flushed with shame, took out her handkerchief, and wiped the spot on her cheek that had been touched by his lips . . . She had, in fact, undone the kiss as far as such a thing was physically possible. (55–56)

This is not about seeking the kiss of reciprocity but of domination, even annihilation. Tess keeps his mouth from entering hers: Alec kisses her cheek, a kiss she erases with a wipe of the hand. Alec's desire to annihilate through the kiss of mastery is met by Tess's annihilating touch of the erasing hand in return. Theirs is a power struggle about self-defense. For Alec to penetrate Tess by force, by crossing the boundary of her mouth and gaining entrance inside her, means for Tess to experience a loss of self. For Tess to be alive in the world, forcing Alec to feel by her sheer presence a hunger for her, means for Alec to experience lack. The kiss of mastery, to master the other through the mouth, is the kiss that seeks to make the other "mine." Possession is not about wanting the other; rather, it is about *not* wanting the other. If he could just kiss himself, Alec might again know his feeling of self-mastery before he laid eyes on Tess, and again know no lack, no deficiency, no vulnerability.

Stealing kisses happens for Hardy in spring-carts and spring-wagons. Something about their movement up and down and forward, something about the proximity of its passengers, something about the word "spring" itself conveys and is a conveyance of kissing, makes the spring-ride a met-onym for Hardy of the kiss.[5] From first sitting alone with Alec atop the horse-driven spring-cart to then finding herself in the same scene but beside Angel, Tess succumbs freely to Angel's kiss on her cheek. Hardy writes:

> Clare resolved never to kiss her until he had obtained her promise; but somehow, as Tess stood there in her prettily tucked-up milking-gown, her hair carelessly heaped upon her head till there should be leisure to arrange it when skimming and milking were done, he broke his resolve, and brought his lips to her cheek for one moment. She passed downstairs very quickly, never looking back at him, or saying another word. (182–83)

Hardy writes nothing of how either experienced the kiss. Instead, he juxta-poses the careless heap of hair and the leisurely look of Tess to the bring-ing of Angel's lips to Tess's cheek. It is his resolve that is broken, not her resistance. Later, on yet another spring-wagon ride and incited by Angel's words "'Do you care for me? I wish you would prove it some way,'" Tess kisses Angel. "She clasped his neck, and for the first time Clare learnt what an impassioned woman's kisses were like upon the lips of one whom she loved with all her heart and soul, as Tess loved him" (190). Angel's child-like momentary touch of his lips on her cheek becomes Tess's passionate kisses on his lips. Tess brings her mouth to his and in the passionate touch of her kisses makes them lovers. Hardy writes Angel as the maiden and Tess as the "maiden-no-more": the most Angel can manage is brushing his lips onto her cheek; he cannot enter Tess's mouth. In response to Angel's "show me" words of temptation, she must do it for him.[6] The consequence

5. Riding a horse together leads to and acts as the metonym for sex in the novel. However silent the moment of penetration, the prior horse ride of Alec and Tess is Hardy's articulation of Alec's elided "ride" of the sleeping Tess.

6. Alan Lerner and Frederick Loewe make musical in reverse the woman's need to invoke the man's sexual energies when Eliza Doolittle sings to Freddy Ainsford Hill, "Haven't your lips longed for my touch? Don't say how much—show me!" in *My Fair Lady*. As surprising as it is to witness this scene of passionate temptation between Eliza and Freddy on the streets of London is it surprising to

of this has everything to do with how Angel imagines Tess's mouth, an imagining that keeps him apart from her, still inside himself. I return to Hardy's words about how Angel experiences the embodied Tess in greater detail—as what "her face was to him":

> How very lovable her face was to him. Yet there was nothing ethereal about it; all was real vitality, real warmth, real incarnation. And it was in her mouth that this culminated. Eyes almost as deep and speaking he had seen before, and cheeks perhaps as fair; brows as arched, a chin and throat almost as shapely; *her mouth he had seen nothing to equal on the face of the earth.* To a young man with the least fire in him that little upward lift in the middle of her red top lip was distracting, infatuating, maddening. He had never before seen a woman's lips and teeth which forced upon his mind with such persistent iteration the old Elizabethan simile of roses filled with snow. (Emphasis mine, 150–51)

The realness of Tess's face in all its aliveness culminates in her mouth. "Her mouth he had seen nothing to equal on the face of the earth": Tess's mouth is what makes her face Tess and nowhere else on the *face of the earth,* for Angel, is there such a mouth. Strangely, it is the very distinctiveness of Tess's lips that prompts his mind to erase her distinction, her separation from him. Angel does this by making Tess's mouth an analog of his learning—"the old Elizabethan simile of roses filled with snow." What sets Tess apart as "other" in the eyes of Angel leads him to experience her as what he already knew in his mind, leads him back to words he had read and memorized before, which now, in the presence of her mouth, are "forced upon his mind with such persistent iteration." Tess is for Angel an embodiment of his mind's eye.

For Alec and for Angel, all of Tess, and most of all her mouth, call not just their bodies into being or into knowing their maleness, but call their minds into being as well, meaning how each experiences himself. Tess's mouth, therefore, acts for Alec and for Angel as the mirror that casts back a reflection of each man's self—not of her. "Because the mouth, unlike the body parts it sucks, is acutely alive to its own pleasure, it therefore seeks . . . by that same narcissistic logic its curious reunion through another's lips" (Phillips 99). The words of Adam Phillips define the narcissistic logic of Alec and Angel—Tess's mouth is the locus for where each man can achieve reunion with himself—kissing her lips, each man can know his

---

read Angel's role of passive temptation, and Tess's role of aggressive passion because of their exchange of accepted-acceptable maiden-man positions in each.

own mouth, from the inside. Alec's object hunger drives him, obsesses him to the point where he loses all self-mastery. It is a plague that pushes him to possess Tess at all cost, as if his life depends on it. Alec experiences Tess as the reflected embodiment of his own lack—an object in the world that mirrors what he is missing, forces him to experience himself as not whole. His narcissistic grandiosity and rage are the very behaviors that enable him to defend against the haunting feeling of lack they conceal. Angel experiences Tess as the reflected embodiment of his own perfection—an object in the world that mirrors forward his desire for perfectibility, enables him to experience himself as ideal. Heinz Kohut, whose theories on narcissism and "selfobject" transference transformed psychoanalytic thinking and practice post-Freud, writes in "The Psychoanalytic Treatment of Narcissistic Personality Disorders—Outline of a Systematic Approach":

> The *idealizing transference* is the therapeutic revival of the early state in which the psyche saves a part of the lost experience of global narcissistic perfection by assigning it to an archaic (transitional object), the idealized parent imago. Since now all bliss and power reside in the idealized object, the child feels empty and powerless when he is separate from it and attempts, therefore, to maintain a continuous union with it. (88)

While Kohut writes about idealizing transference, or the need for an ideal object, as what gets called up in the therapeutic treatment of narcissistic personality disorder, it is Kohut's more global recognition of the human need for mirroring—the self's need for mirroring objects—that helps make sense of Alec's and Angel's relation to Tess. Kohut goes on to describe a narcissistic transference particularly suggestive of Alec's relation to and treatment of Tess:

> If the child's relationship to the idealized object is, however, severely disturbed, e.g., if he suffers a traumatic (intense and sudden, or not phase-appropriate) disappointment in it, the child does not acquire the needed internal structure, but his psyche remains fixated on an archaic object imago, and the personality will later, and throughout life, be dependent on certain objects in what seems to be an intense form of *object hunger*. The intensity of the search for and of the dependency on these objects is due to the fact they are striven for as a substitute for missing segments of the psychic structure. These objects are not loved for their attributes, and their actions are only dimly recognized; they are needed in order to replace the functions of a segment of the mental apparatus which has not been established in childhood. (Emphasis mine, 89)

It is not the etiology of Alec's narcissism that concerns Hardy; it is its manifestation: Alec's "intense form of object hunger" and the mad striving he feels to consume Tess to satiate that hunger and regain his self-mastery. What is that moment of satiation for Alec? Lying before him, wrapped in the thick darkness of fog that holds "the moonlight in suspension," Tess is for Alec a "pale nebulousness at his feet, which represented the white muslin figure he had left upon the dead leaves. Everything else was blackness alike. D'Urberville stooped and heard a gentle regular breathing. She was sleeping soundly" (73). We understand the satiation to be sexual penetration—the baby Sorrow is its objective reification. But we don't read the moment. What we read is oral penetration: before her sliding down off the horse, "he had stolen a hearty kiss" (71); and before her lying down in the grass, Alec holds the bottle of alcohol to her mouth "unawares." "Tess sputtered and coughed, and gasping 'It will go on my pretty frock!' swallowed as he poured, to prevent the catastrophe she feared" (72). Hardy leads us to trace a line in our minds from one moment of visualized forced entry to the next—until its invisible end is visible to our imaginations—the rape of Tess. But the pattern Hardy traces is thick with suggestion. The stolen kiss and the bottle poured down her mouth rehearse another satiation Alec will take from the pale nebulousness of Tess—the infant sucking at the breast. As rape turns the creation of life into annihilation, so this scene of sucking turns the sustaining of life into destruction. First reported by the psychoanalyst Isakower in 1938, "Isakower's phenomenon" refers to a patient's repeated pre-sleep visionary state in which "the visual sensation of a large, doughy, shadowy mass, usually round" appears. Isakower understood the sensation to be the memory of a crushing breast that "obscures the boundary between self and outside world . . . Often there are feelings [in those who report such a recollection] of floating or loss of equilibrium."[7] What I'm suggesting is that the pale nebulous "breast" Tess to the hungry Alec is not nourishing but crushing, not defining of himself but obscuring, not helping him to regain his balance, but causing him to lose it. Alec's intense object hunger for Tess may be about his longing to feel complete, but his experience of Tess is one of insatiability, or of being crushed by the hunger that feels no end.

I take Alec's unrelenting need to possess the object as the futile drive toward self-mastery to be a near-relation to Angel's need to know the object is "pure"—a pure reflection of his own perfection. How else can we make sense of Angel's abandonment of Tess, when they share confessions of their pasts, when they tell parallel stories of their experience, when "he seemed

7. See Philip Bromberg's *Standing in the Spaces,* 98.

to be her double" (224)? The shock of the moment, when Angel says, "You were one person and now you are another" (228), is deeper than cultural expectation, deeper than the annihilation of a social ideal. For Angel, "The essence of things had changed" (228): the crisis is *ontological*. Tess separates her self, her experience, from his, and cries out, "'What have I done—what *have* I done? I have not told of anything that interferes with or belies my love for you. You don't think I planned it, do you? It is in *your own mind* what you are angry at, Angel, it is not in me. O, it is not in me'" (emphasis mine, 231). Tess has not failed him—she loves him—she has not changed. But Tess as an idealizing selfobject has failed him. And so Angel has changed. The perfection he saw reflected back of his own mind—his perfect mind—has vanished. Here Kohut describes what happens when there is a breach in the idealizing narcissistic transference from patient to analyst, a breach suggestive of that between Angel and Tess:

> In the undisturbed transference the patient feels powerful, good, and capable. Anything that deprives him of the idealized analyst creates a disturbance of his self-esteem; he feels powerless and worthless, and if his ego is not assisted by interpretations concerning the loss of the idealized parent imago, the patient may turn to archaic precursors of the idealized parent imago or may abandon it altogether and regress further to reactively mobilized archaic stages of the grandiose self. The retreat to archaic idealizations may manifest itself in the form of vague, impersonal, trancelike religious feelings; the hypercathexis of archaic forms of the grandiose self and the (autoerotic body) self will produce the syndrome of emotional coldness tendency toward affectation in speech and behavior, shame propensity, and hypochondria. (94)

When in the presence of the ideal selfobject Tess, Angel feels strong, powerful, good. But when ideal Tess becomes real Tess, her own separate self, Angel collapses. All he exhibits to Tess by day is emotional coldness and by night is a trancelike sleepwalking burial of his ideal selfobject in the grave, "'Dead! dead! dead!'" (246). With the death of his own mirrored perfection, Angel abandons the mirror. Why stay to have to look upon "the shade of his own limitations" (265)?

Adam Phillips's account of the mouth's desire to seek reunion with itself—through a mouth not its own but made its own through extension—outgrows Kohut's understanding of narcissistic disorder in the very woman onto whom the men kiss their self-projections. This strange fact—to experience oneself requires that one experience others as other to oneself, not as extensions of oneself—is missed by everyone except Tess. For the philosopher Edmund Husserl, we live in states of "reciprocal co-existence," in which our self-apprehensions are mediated all the time by how we perceive and experience the presence of others and by how others perceive and experience us.[8] About this, Dan Zahavi writes in his essay "Beyond Empathy":

> [S]ubjectivity is not a "motionless identity with itself"; rather, it is essential to subjectivity to open itself to an other and to "go forth from itself." It is precisely my own experience as such that makes me open for what I am not. Subjectivity is not hermetically sealed up within itself, remote from the world and inaccessible to the other. Rather, it is above all a relation to the world, an openness toward others is secured the moment I define myself and the other as co-existing relations to the world. (Zahavi 163)

According to phenomenology, without knowing in the sense of feeling the incarnate presences "other" and "world" as separate from the self, and as informing, affecting, and co-making of the self, we would have no conscious experience of subjectivity. Descartes' *cogito* becomes—in phenomenology's retelling of the nature of experience—"I am, I exist because I feel my presence in the world as I feel the presence of others in the world as other to me."

Tess knows this as what it means to love. Perhaps the most poignant moment of the novel happens as the result of Angel's failure to hear Tess's imperative: "Love myself as I love yourself in all changes and disgraces" (228). Tess knows what it means to love Angel—for himself, not as her idea of an angel, but as Angel, himself, over time, in the world, through all that will happen without and within him—in all changes and disgraces. But Angel cannot yet imagine this because he has no intersubjective understanding of Tess, as Tess. To love Tess as herself would require that Angel accept that she is not himself, accept that she is not the holder of his perfectibility, and imagine a love beyond narcissism.

Angel's failure, like Alec's failure to hear Tess or to honor the meaning of Tess's words as expressive of the claims of her own subjectivity apart from his, is nothing new. That mouth makes words, tells herself, makes available her subjectivity as more than lips making a kiss in the air. Here's Tess to Alec: "'I don't want anybody to kiss me, sir!' she implored" (55–56). Or here's Angel and Tess: "She was no longer the milkmaid, but a visionary essence of woman—a whole sex condensed into one typical form. He called her Artemis, Demeter, and other fanciful names half teasingly, which she did

---

8. See Zahavi's discussion of Husserl, 160.

not like because she did not understand them. '*Call me Tess,*' she would say askance" (emphasis mine, 130). Tess's words are not heard by Alec in that they seem not to inform him of a feeling subjectivity apart from his own, or at least they do nothing to alter the course of his subjectivity—"he was inexorable"—he takes her kiss away. And Angel may come to say the name "Tess," but means by it his "visionary essence of woman." He cannot hear Tess call herself "Tess" or hear how she means herself because he is not yet present to Tess as "Tess"—a being apart from himself who names and means her own self. Angel does not yet understand the reciprocal coexistence of subjectivity. From imagining her lips as "roses filled with snow" to naming her "Artemis" or "Demeter," to defining her as "virtuous as a vestal," Angel transforms Tess's lips, name, and being to be his names, his ideas, his vision. Alec fills Tess's lips with his body and Angel fills Tess's lips with words: both men respond to Tess's mouth as a space that demands filling. The "O-O-O" shape of her mouth is too dangerous left open or too inviting to resist projection because its very presence and all that its presence urges questions the very nature of subjectivity as intact or as world-making.

What would it mean to kiss the lips that held such a sound?[9] This question is not possible to ask in the world of *Tess of the D'Urbervilles*. While Angel may not be able to hear Tess's words, we cannot imagine her voice—Hardy does not write it. In part, this is because of the insistence of Hardy's visual imagination: Hardy does not make present the quality of voices in *Tess of the D'Urbervilles*.[10] Tess's words fall on deaf ears. If George Eliot predicates the possibility of intersubjective understanding on one's capacity to hear voice and from it experience a commingling of minds within one's mind, the failure of Hardy's men to hear Tess precludes their recognition of her mind, separate from their own. The presence in the world of Tess's mouth—those distracting, infatuating, maddening lips—is seen but not heard by Alec and Angel. Overwhelmed by the sight of her maddening lips and all that her mouth stirs, neither can hear the voice that her mouth emits and what it holds. Their failure to hear Tess say "Call me Tess," and to understand whose being she voices, is one not just of intersubjectivity, but of subjectivity.

Tess incites Alec and Angel to feel their sexual power and urgency. Her

9. Ann Patchett's lyrical novel *Bel Canto* makes the mouth of a great lyric opera singer the site of intersubjective fantasy when it asks on its opening page in the voice of all the listening present, "What would it mean to kiss the lips that held such a sound?" This is *the* question of Patchett's novel. By contrast it is not a question in *Tess of the D'Urbervilles*.

10. By contrast, *The Mayor of Casterbridge* does make voice present and a means through which character demonstrates itself and makes itself able to be experienced, for Donald Farfrae most of all.

embodied presence sounds nature's call in their bodies to procreate—*that call* they can hear and, in knowing response, vibrate back. This is the highly adaptive "use" of Tess: it is what her aliveness creates in the world; it is how her aliveness is world-creating. But her very aliveness—that which gives the man his feeling of aliveness—simultaneously takes it away. Tess's presence functions as the narcissistic wound that causes each man to become conscious of his failure to be whole or to be perfect without her—a consciousness that demands the sacrifice of her aliveness by annihilation, abandonment, or replacement.

4. "AN ESCAPE WHEN THERE IS NO ESCAPE"

Before Tess's "Rally," before the moment in the Talbothay garden when she and the world are impregnated with the notes of Angel's harp, have come earlier scenes outdoors, in other gardens and woods, experiences that come to trace not a natural but a "coarse" pattern onto "the beautiful feminine tissue, sensitive as gossamer, and practically blank as snow" that defines Tess. Although Tess is renamed from "Maiden" to "Maiden No More," Hardy does not define the change in her as a metamorphosis of development from "maiden to woman." She is no more who she was. Without a new noun to replace "maiden," we must wonder not just "*who* is she?" or "*what* is she?" but "*is* she?" What comes before the evolutionary metamorphosis of Phase Three is the wounding and tincturing of Phases One and Two, not the change from "a" to "a + b," but the change from "a" to "~a" = "wounded or not a." The shock of "a precipitous disruption to self-continuity" (S. A. Pizer) or "an overwhelming threat to the integrity of the self that is accompanied by annihilation anxiety" (Bromberg) are states that define trauma.[11] I understand Tess's transformation from "Maiden" to "Maiden No More" to trace not just a coarse pattern but a course that undoes pattern, or threatens with its annihilation the intact pattern that defines self-continuity. And yet, later, Tess rallies. We know that she will come to walk away from the forced, traumatic loss of her maidenhood and of her child Sorrow. After the rape, after the death of Sorrow, following "two silent reconstructive years," still young and alive, Tess recognizes the possibility of a second chance, that there is an escape from being not-Tess:

> Yet even now Tess felt the pulse of hopeful life still warm within her; she might be happy in some nook which had no memories. *To escape the past*

11. For a fuller account of trauma, see Bromberg's *Standing in the Spaces,* page 11.

and all that appertained thereto was to annihilate it, and to do that she would have to get away . . . [A]nd some spirit within her rose automatically as the sap in the twigs. It was unexpended youth, surging up anew after its temporary check, and bringing with it hope, and the invincible instinct towards self-delight. (Emphasis mine, 99–100)

To move her body away from what came before is for Tess to "escape the past"—to annihilate it rather than to be annihilated by it. To leave the past is to walk into the future, to have a future. While Tess's mind leads her to this recognition of how to leave the past—to make it "not"—it is her body, her youth, with its "invincible instinct towards self-delight," that surges up and carries her forward to live "the pulse of hopeful life still warm within her."

But what if the past cannot be escaped? What if "life" holds the present captive and annihilates the future? What if there is no walking away? Like Angel who sleepwalks his way from what he knew to what he now knows, when conscious life leaves her no out, Tess sleeps her way to, if not through, her rape and commits murder in a hypnoid trance—finds an escape when there is no escape. In *The Dreaming Brain*, the dream researcher and neuropsychiatrist J. Allan Hobson writes of the brain activity that makes possible the temporary existences that constitute our fluid, changing states of mind:

Imagine that all twenty billion [brain] cells, each communicating with at least ten thousand others, is also sending messages at that same rate of speed within the system itself. The noise, if possible to describe, [. . .] would be a deafening roar, more like the "buzzing confusion" of William James's metaphor for consciousness. But this incessant activity all proceeds silently, with only our relatively peaceful consciousness as its product. The music of these spheres within our head is consciousness. Consciousness is the continuous subjective awareness of the activity of billions of cells firing at many times a second, communicating instantaneously with tens of thousands of their neighbors. And the organization of this symphony of activity is such that it is *sometimes externally oriented (during waking), sometimes oblivious to the world (during sleep), and sometimes so remarkably aware of itself (during dreams) that it recreates the world in its own image.* (Emphasis mine, 132–33)

What is remarkable is that any discernible, unified mental state ever comes into being—be it oriented to the world during waking, oblivious to the world during sleeping, or recreating the world in its own self-image during dreaming. The death of Prince, Tess's rape, Angel's burying of Tess while sleepwalking, Tess's capture at Stonehenge—the memorable events of plot represent change, not the slow evolutionary change of continuity, but the abrupt, sudden change of discontinuity. If the living plot of *Tess of the D'Urbervilles* is the story of Tess's evolutionary metamorphosis from girl to woman, the "unliving" showstopping plot that accompanies that evolutionary metamorphosis is *loss*. Sleep marks the loss of conscious awareness. And, in the world of *Tess,* sleep marks the losses that will follow awakening. But sleep strangely, remarkably, brings to life not just the nightly presence of death in the loss of consciousness, but the reanimation of life in dreams. Hobson's dreaming-brain research has led him to a psychophysiological theory of how dreams are formed, the "activation–synthesis hypothesis":

[S]pecifically, that the form of dreams is related to the form of brain activity in sleep; and that the brain is first turned on (activated) during sleep and then generates and integrates (synthesizes) its own sensory and motor information. The sensory and motor signals that the brain automatically generates are both the driving force and the directional vector of the dream plot, which is synthesized in light of the individual's past experiences, attitudes, and expectations.

The activation-synthesis hypothesis thus proposes a specific brain mechanism that is both necessary and sufficient for dreaming to occur. This mechanism is both more and less deterministic than previous theories of dreaming have been.

More deterministic because the automaticity and the fixed quality and quantity of dreaming that it produces make dreaming an integral part of vegetative life rather than a mere reaction to life's vicissitudes. Dreaming is seen, by activation synthesis, as an endogenous process with its own genetically determined dynamics. There may be no covert informational meaning to the process; on the contrary, information processing may be just one of the many functions served by dreaming.

Less deterministic because the activation-synthesis theory supposes an open system of information processing, which is capable not only of reproduction and distortion of stored information but of the elaboration of novel information. Activation synthesis thus includes creativity among its assumptions. This theory sees the brain as so inexorably bent upon the *quest for meaning* that it attributes and even creates meaning when there is little or none to be found in the data it is asked to process. In this sense, the study of dreaming is the study of the brain-mind as an autocreative mechanism.

In using physiology to understand dreaming, I aim to show that the most remarkable property of mind—an aspect that is most essentially human, *the capacity to imagine, to hope, to create—is physically given and physically based*. The brain is neither a closed system with its own set of fixed determinacies nor slave to information received from the outside world. It is a dynamic and self-sustaining organ capable of generating its own information. *It is designed to deal with the external world by having ideas about the external world. The brain therefore constantly imposes its own truth upon the external world*. (Emphasis mine, 15)

Hobson's theory defines brain physiology as designed to dream, as an "integral part of vegetative life," rather than as just a response to that which we cannot tolerate in daily consciousness. Turned on when we sleep and ignited by the generation and integration of sensory and motor information, the dreaming brain continues the experience of physically processing life experiences, even when we are not having them. It's as if the brain cannot shut down its integration of information collection. Sleep gives the brain a chance to continue the integration and synthesis of material that occurred during the wakeful hours of the day. However, it does more than just process or store like a computer—the dreaming brain *generates ideas* about its ongoing collection of sensory and motor information in relation to "past experiences, attitudes, and expectations." For Hobson, this makes dreams a manifestation of our experience as brain-minded beings: dreams synthesize material living with the generation of ideas we have about that living. Hobson concludes that what most distinguishes the human and differentiates one human being from another—"the capacity to imagine, hope, and create—is physically given and physically based." For Hobson, our abilities to imagine, hope, and create are a part of how the human brain works, not just a response to environmental factors or states that are only reflective of experience.

Tess does not have sleeping dreams; at least she never recalls her dreams or reports them. However, Tess engages in *waking forms of creation of the dreaming brain*. As much as Tess sleeps, she falls into states undefined by Hobson, hypnoid states oblivious to the world, between being awake and asleep. Often Hardy describes them as half-states: "half-paralysis"; "half-forgotten"; "half-dream"; "half-consciously"; "half-hypnotized." For Tess, these half-states of dreaming wakefulness define a half-world to which her mind goes, a somewhere between fantasy and labor, the concrete and the abstract, wakefulness and sleep, life and death. Tess falls away from the world by looking down, looking away, turning her attention from what is before her. Such moments create chances for her mind's departure. Elaine Scarry writes in *Dreaming by the Book* of the relation of falling to skating to imagining in a moment of analysis of Seamus Heaney's "Crossings xxviii" poem: "[F]or skating is like falling through the world . . . As stumbling is the motion of all skating, so skating is the motion of all imagining: 'A farewell to surefootedness, a pitch / Beyond our usual hold on ourselves'" (212). Tess's "farewell to surefootedness" is her departure from where she is. But as well, her falls away hint at the deeper falls Tess so often falls prey to—falling down or falling asleep or falling in love or falling from grace or falling from the gallows. Briefly, inadvertently, Tess loses hold of the vigilance of care, lets go of the ongoing effort the world requires of her attention. When Tess allows herself to drift something always happens because the condition of aliveness in Hardy's narrative universe is change. For the most part, Hardy does not disturb Tess when she goes to her half-world. He marks it by naming it "half-x," but does not describe her experience there. We gaze upon her when she's there, tranquil, away from and yet still a part of "the" world, lost in "pondering silence" or "abstraction" or "reverie." Hardy may move in as close as to observe, "she rode along with an inward and not an outward eye" (44), or he may note, "[s]he thought, without exactly wording the thought" (84)—views that mark Tess's presence in this half-world but not descriptions of how she lives there. Tess does not word her presence there—and neither does Hardy. Instead, Hardy makes Tess simultaneously present to and observable as a presence in the world and in her half-world, but remains outside Tess's experience of the between. Therefore, so do we. Tess is somewhere between the boundaries of being.

The closest Hardy comes to naming Tess's half-world is what he calls the predawn moment of "the marginal minute of the dark" (49). And some time after Tess returns from being "maiden" to being "maiden no more," Hardy describes a moment when Tess seeks out the evening half-world of *twi-light*:

> She knew how to hit to a hair's-breadth that moment of evening when the light and the darkness are so evenly balanced that the constraint of day and the suspense of night neutralize each other, leaving absolute mental liberty. It is then that the plight of being alive becomes attenuated to its least possible dimensions. She had no fear of the shadows; her sole idea seemed to be to shun mankind—or rather that cold accretion called the world, which so terrible in the mass, is so unformidable, even pitiable in its units. (85)

Between light and dark, at the halfway marker of a hair's breadth, Tess finds an opening and walks through it into the half-world. That evening door opening into the woods makes possible what Tess seeks—"absolute mental liberty"—free of mankind, free of the "cold accretion called the world," free of "the plight of being alive"—freedom from embodiment. For Tess, the half-world is some other world of mind freed of body—the *absolute mental liberty* of being disembodied.

Tess "words the thought" of her half-world, knows how to go there and knows why—once. I return to those words from the chapter's opening frame:

> "I don't know about ghosts," she was saying; "but I do know that our souls can be made to go outside our bodies when we are alive . . . A very easy way to feel 'em go," continued Tess, "is to lie on the grass at night and look straight up at some big bright star; and, by fixing your mind upon it, you will soon find that you are hundreds and hundreds o' miles away from your body, which you don't seem to want at all." (120)

What Tess describes—this state of splitting mind from body in order to take her mind away from her body to a desired place—is *dissociation*. Philip Bromberg writes, "[D]issociation is basic to human mental functioning and is central to the stability and growth of personality. It is intrinsically an adaptational talent that represents what we call 'consciousness' . . . [T]he psyche does not start as an integrated whole, but is nonunitary in origin—a mental structure that begins and continues as a multiplicity of self-states" ("'Speak!'" 520–21). Whereas psychoanalysis has understood dissociation to be a normal defense that marks how an intact observing ego chooses to limit its capacity for self-reflection as a form of adaptation to the moment, Bromberg begins with a different understanding of the human mind as not intact, but decentered, shifting, and nonlinear (*Standing* 7). Tess's daydreaming states of mind—transfixed wearing flowers, mesmerized while working on the threshing machine, dreaming out a window—are states that at once mark her as nonunitary and as separate from the minds around her, but as distinctive, too. Dissociation limits self-reflection, prevents the mind from forming symbols to represent its current, "live" experience, takes the mind to some other state that is somewhere else than in conscious self-reflection. Bromberg writes:

> [D]issociation as a defense, even in a relatively normal personality structure, limits self-reflection to what is secure or needed for survival of selfhood, while in individuals for whom trauma has been severe, self-reflection is extremely curtailed in order that the capacity to reflect back does not break down completely and result in a collapse of selfhood. What we call

annihilation anxiety represents the latter possibility. Thus, paradoxically, the defensive division of the self into unlinked parts preserves identity by establishing more secure boundaries between self and "not-self" through dissociative unlinking of self-states, each with its own boundaries and its own firm experience of not-self. Consequently, dissociative patterns of relating come to define personal boundaries of selfhood in a very powerful way. (*Standing* 12)

When the boundaries of Tess's being—that which defines her to have a state of self-continuity—come under attack so that in order to continue to have her self she must split into selves, Tess sleeps, daydreams, and dissociates. Her body does one thing while her mind goes somewhere else. Whereas Austen's Emma retires from the social world so as to imagine her self-conscious presence into that social world—through *association*—Hardy's Tess while present in the world uses her imagination to escape from it—through *dissociation*. Commanded to be fed strawberries by Alec, after first refusing, Tess parts her lips, takes in the strawberries, and "eats in an abstracted half-hypnotized state whatever D'Urberville offered her." Gathering rose blossoms, Alec gives them to Tess to put into her bosom. "She obeyed like one in a dream." He moves back from her and watches her "pretty and unconscious munching through the skeins of smoke that pervaded the tent . . . that blue narcotic haze" that stands between her and "the 'tragic mischief' of her drama" (42). Seemingly still inside that blue narcotic haze, Tess boards the van for home and "did not know what the other occupants said to her as she entered, though she answered them; and when they started anew she rode along with an inward and not an outward eye" (44). Called "quite a posy" by one of the passengers, Tess focuses her attention back out and blushes from the recognition of herself as a "spectacle," marked as in bloom, and then "she fell to reflecting again." That "fall into reflection" causes Tess to look down and a rose to prick her chin. William James distinguishes between three theories of the hypnotic state: 1) of Animal Magnetism, where direct passage of force from operator to subject causes the subject to become a controlled puppet; 2) of Neurosis, where predisposed patients fall into a peculiar pathological state caused by special physical agents; and 3) of Suggestion, to which we all fall prey of yielding to outward suggestion, affirming what we conceive, and acting in accordance with what we expect.[12] Tess enacts the hypnotic state of animal magnetism, ceding control of her will to the force of Alec and

12. See James's chapter 27, "Hypnotism," in *The Principles of Psychology*, Volume II, especially pages 596–601.

the forces of nature. Obeying like one in a dream or a trance, Tess allows Alec to enter the boundary of her mouth, as falling into reflection causes the rose to prick her chin, as falling asleep makes it possible for Prince to be stabbed and Tess to be raped. All of these moments of falling away from conscious attention may be read as the openings that make possible the trauma that pursues Tess so relentlessly. Her abandonment of conscious attention makes the boundary between herself and the world porous and undefended. And the world in *Tess* seeks to penetrate boundaries—most of all through sex, birth, and death—life's great "breakthrough" moments.

To escape when there is no escape—Tess shifts her attention away from what or who is before her toward her inward self. She forfeits conscious attention to her body—"'that which you don't seem to want at all'"—to continue to have her mind, to travel away from the scene of wounding and loss so that even when her body is trapped, like a caged bird, Tess can still call herself "Tess." Losing Angel a second time, after each has suffered so much, the retraumatization of her greatest loss, switches Tess not to the "off" position of sleep, but to the "on" position of Lady Macbeth. Her "unspeakable despair" finds its way to speech, as a soliloquy, as a dirge: "'O you have torn my life all to pieces . . . made me a victim, a caged bird . . . My own true husband will never, never—O God—I can't bear this!—I cannot!'"(381). What she cannot bear to behold or contain—Hardy's great tragic idiom of the "too late"[13]—demands enactment, demands that her body act. In a hypnoid reversal trance of animal magnetism, Tess turns on her "master": Tess must annihilate or be annihilated.

5. "A SPLENDID STAR"

As natural and ineluctable as it is for Hardy to write and his characters to experience being embodied in the world, Hardy's characters also long to travel from embodiment to the immaterial, to a place of disembodied or inner-embodied experience—what Hardy calls "the power of viewing life here from its inner side" (168). For a moment, Hardy makes possible Angel's view of life from the inner side when he sees inside Tess's mouth:

> She was yawning, and he saw the red interior of her mouth as if it had been a snake's . . . her face was flushed with sleep, and her eyelids hung heavy over their pupils. The brimfulness of her nature breathed from her.

13. On the idea of "the tragedy of the too late," see Franco Moretti's essay "Kindergarten," in *Signs Taken for Wonder.*

> It was a moment when a woman's soul is more incarnate than at any other
> time; when the most spiritual beauty bespeaks itself flesh; and sex takes the
> outside place in the presentation. (169)

Tess's yawn opens the way to viewing her from the inside out, the cavity of the mouth and the tongue. But more than that, her very nature is
breathed out into the world. Tess's "spiritual beauty bespeaks itself flesh"
and "sex takes the outside place." What are hidden—Tess's nature, spirit,
sexuality—reveal themselves for a moment through the opening of her
mouth. Tess breathes her immaterial self out through a yawn, and Angel
views Tess from her inner side.

Hardy presents Tess's mouth as a *portal* through which one can view
"a woman's soul" AND as a *presence* of "nothing ethereal," the culmination
of the real, through which one can see in reflection the embodiment of
one's own self. For Alec, Hardy writes no moment of viewing Tess from
the inner side, her soul breathed out before him. For Angel there are both
views. What Angel must continue to work through if he and Tess are to
have any chance of having each other is what both views mean. About
Tess, Hardy writes, "Beauty to her, as to all who have felt, lay not in the
thing, but in what the thing symbolized" (297). If Angel is one who feels,
he must go deeper than the view of Tess as a thing of beauty: he must
move from her beauty to its inner side to view what her beauty "symbolized." What Angel must attempt, therefore, is an escape from the "shade
of his own limitations": an escape that requires he be in the company of
one with a more expansive, forward-viewing mind, a "cosmopolitan mind"
(341). The cosmopolitan mind "*viewed* the matter [of Tess, her past, and
Angel] in quite a different light from Angel; that what Tess had been was
of no importance beside what she would be" (emphasis mine, 341). "Beauty
or ugliness of character," Angel comes to see, is not just determined by
past "achievements," but also by "aims," "impulses," and "things willed"
(340)—by the nature of *future-directed feelings.* Angel's heart, a prisoner of
history, metamorphoses from harshness to tenderness when he views Tess
from the inner side of "what she would be." He can now call her by the
right name: "'I did not think rightly of you—I did not see you as you
were! . . . I do now, dearest Tessy, mine'" (378). "Tenderness was absolutely
dominant in Clare at last" (385). Angel has made his own escape from the
inescapable "what was" to the freedom of "what will be" by viewing Tess
forward from the inner side of tenderness.

Why does Beauty sleep? Tess sleeps and daydreams her way to and some-times through the most oppressive moments of her life—as if she can stop or at least forestall their occurrence through her mind's escape. "'All is trouble outside there; inside here content,'" Tess tells Angel (390). Now Angel, too, can lie down "inside here" with Beauty. The "O" of Tess's open lips—the portal of her sleeping mouth "like a half-opened flower"—parts toward Angel's tender sleeping cheek. Now they can fall into a shared sleep together of five days and nights "wrapped in profound slumber" under "stars in serene dissociation from the two wisps of life."

   "'Which do we live on—a splendid one or a blighted one?'" Abraham asks his sister Tess to judge the universe they inhabit. "'A blighted one,'" Tess responds. If in the book of *Genesis,* Abraham's son Isaac is not sacri-ficed by the hand of his father, in the book of *Tess*—a narrative universe of the blighted star—Prince is sacrificed by Tess's sleeping body and Tess is sacrificed when her body sleeps. But for a little while, when wrapped in profound slumber with her Angel, or traveling to her half-world of dreams away from the beautiful body which she does not seem to want at all, Tess finds her way to a splendid star.

CODA

The Neurology of Narrative

Kay Young, Ph.D.
Jeffrey L. Saver, M.D.

The oral storytelling tradition of philosophy made evident by the dialogues of Socrates and parables of Plato goes underground with the writings of Aristotle. Our sense of what it means to do philosophy comes from Aristotle and his legacy, where the structure of storytelling is replaced by the construction of logical propositions, descriptions of abstractions, and assertions of general "truths." And so what are we to make of the following?: "The more isolated I become, the more I come to like stories" (Aristotle, fragment 688). These are Aristotle's words, Aristotle's desire for stories. They prompt us to think of Aristotle's story—that he has a story, that he has an autobiographical "I" that has narrated his desire for narrative as a means of lifting him out of the loneliness of what it means to be the solitary thinker who contemplates himself into the philosophical mood. Stories, it would seem, offer Aristotle comfort, call it company, or the sense that others somehow are present by virtue of what it is stories tell, or by how they tell. They as well prompt in him the reference to an "I," an "I" who does not rise to the textual surface of his strictly philosophical writings, as in the *Ethics* or *Poetics*. What's of particular interest to us about this fragment of Aristotle's is the intertwining of the "I" and the stories, that they are in relation to one another, that one offers the other the chance at individual presence and mutual recognition. And we have come together in our own intertwining to begin to work through what that relation is about, or perhaps more accurately, *why* that relation is.

The parameters that define what it is narratives accomplish are too vast to disclose, though we can allude to their variety—medical histories, legal testimonies, psychological portraits, texts of pure fiction, news stories, autobiographies, conversations. The structure of the story surfaces in positions where it both announces and is silent about its presence. When we choose to be in the company of a story by reading a novel or seeing a film, the narrative sets itself off as a narrative, not as a part of our lives; we stand in relation to it as audience to its "performance" as an aesthetic work. However, the storytelling we experience as an event in life can lose its appearance as narrative by virtue of its integration in life. So used to having conversations that function as stories are we that we lose an attention to their nature. So inescapably bound are we to consciousness that we lose sight of how consciousness most often leads us to think. While we can be trained to think in geometrical shapes, patterns of sounds, poetry, movement, syllogisms, what predominates or fundamentally constitutes our consciousness is the understanding of self and world in story. Roland Barthes in his "Introduction to the Structural Analysis of Narratives" comments first about the place of narrative within culture and then about its primacy within the self:

> [N]arrative is present in every age, in every place, in every society; it begins with the very history of mankind and there nowhere is nor has been a people without narrative. All classes, all human groups, have their narratives, enjoyment of which is very often shared by men with different, even opposing, cultural backgrounds. [Barthes in footnote 1 notes that "this is not the case with either poetry or the essay, both of which are dependent on the cultural level of their consumer."] Caring nothing for the division between good and bad literature, narrative is international, transhistorical, transcultural: *it is simply there, like life itself.* (Emphasis ours, 79)

> Although we scarcely know more about the origins of narrative than we do about the origins of language . . . it may be significant that it is at the same moment (around the age of three) that the little human "invents" at once sentence, narrative, and the Oedipus. (124)

This movement in Barthes from his consideration of the presence of narrative within culture to his musings about the origins of narrative in the "little human" arriving simultaneously with the sentence and sexuality—or, from life as narrative to one's life as narrative—suggests the coming to narrative is a necessary feature of human development. And to the extent that culture is human development writ large, narrative becomes an inescapable constituent of culture. Most narrative theory works to define the nature of the story—the problematics of the interactions of teller, tale, and audience, the epistemological ambiguities of the relations of the text to the "reality" to which it refers or seeks to re-present. Barthes's nod toward the question of what the relation is between the structuring of consciousness in story to the productions of those stories as representations of self and culture takes up momentarily what is for the most part not considered. For us the question to which he alludes sounds like a series of questions: Why does the "I" tell his or her self as a story? Why does the "I" have a story to tell at all? How does the drive to narrate enable the production of autobiography, and as well dictate its form—as stories?

In his work on artificial intelligence, Roger Schank seeks to define intelligence in order to then recreate it. He asserts in *Tell Me a Story* that "storytelling and understanding are functionally the same thing" (24), that "intelligence is bound up with our ability to tell the right story at the right time" (21). Schank proposes the binding together of abilities to tell, hear, and retrieve stories appropriately, usefully, or innovatively with levels of intelligence. What enables the making of memories is, he claims, the telling of stories: "We need to tell someone else a story that describes our experience because the process of creating the story also creates the memory structure that will contain the gist of the story for the rest of our lives" (115). While we will not hold on to the words of the telling, our retention of the story's core will make a cognitive space or an environment for thought that can be drawn upon when the gist of the story serves a new purpose. To be without stories means in Schank's telling to be without memories; this means something like to be without a self.

Such a condition describes children before the age of three or four, who cannot remember their autobiographic experience. However, with emerging access to language that enables children to have conversations with adults about the past (and with anatomic maturation of mnestic networks) comes the ability to form and register memories. What's at issue then is how the bringing of narrative to experience enables a sense of self founded on a series of recollections—to be without one's stories is to be without knowledge of one's life. While we have each experienced infancy, without our stories of it we have no access to it, no memories of it, and so on some level have had no infancy. Not all memory works toward the production of life stories: "*generic memory,*" or what creates the familiar through its repeated appearance, works as the background or setting for the norm against which the unfamiliar can be distinguished; "*episodic memory,*" that which occurs as a specific event tied to its own time and place, may be remembered if it is significant; "*autobiographical memory*" comes into being from out of the episodic and generic—selected incidents from the episodic become woven together to form a kind of plot set in the time and place of the generic (Squire, Knowlton, and Musen 1993, Markowitsch 2000). It is these autobiographical memories that construct the "story of one's life." Episodic and generic memories are alone recalled in early childhood, on their own, but not as elements of composed stories. Words come in time to replace just the recollection of images or sound. And narrative-motivated words—meaning, on the most primitive level, words that come together to act as a story with a coherent sense of wholeness bound to a beginning, middle, and end, as a series of events situated diachronically and with referential particularity, wrapped together by a governing sense of consequence or logic, enacted by agents (the self as the primary agent or recipient of others' agency), and structured by a discourse that defines point of view or the "how" of the telling—replace "unstoried" words.

Yet, the question still remains, why in order to have life stories must we rely on the production of narratively framed autobiographical memories? What is it about the nature of the human brain that necessitates that the memories we draw on as evidence for who we are work as narratives? For, as the psychologist Jerome Bruner in "The Narrative Construction of Reality" and the cognitive literary theorist Mark Turner in *The Literary Mind* assert, narrative organizes not just memory, but the whole of human experience—not just the life stories of the past, but all of one's life as it unfolds. Bruner describes narrative as an instrument of mind that constructs our notion of reality, and asserts that the experience of life takes on meaning when we interact with it as an ongoing story, as our story.[1] But Bruner fails to address the neurobiological underpinning of the centrality of narrative in human cognition: the questions still remain, how and why does the brain cause us to experience life and our individual lives as narratives at all?

Recent advances in cognitive neuroscience suggest that the creation of narrative in the human central nervous system is mediated by a regionally distributed neural network. Fundamental components of this network include 1) the amygdala-hippocampal system, where episodic and autobiographic memories are initially arranged; 2) the left peri-Sylvian region, where language is formulated; and 3) the frontal cortices and their subcortical connections, where individual entities and events are organized into real and fictional (imagined) temporal narrative frames.

Studies employing functional imaging in normal volunteers and clinical reports assessing alterations in cognition in individuals who have suffered

---

1. See Jerome Bruner's "The Narrative Construction of Reality" in *Critical Inquiry*, 18.1 (Autumn 1991): 1–22, and his *Actual Minds, Possible Worlds,* and *Acts of Meaning* for a full treatment of his theory of the narrative construction of reality.

TABLE 1. FORMS OF DYSNARRATIVIA

Clinical Manifestation	Neuroanatomic Substrate
Arrested narration	Amygdala–hippocampal system
Unbounded narration	Amygdala–hippocampal system plus frontal systems
Undernarration	Orbitofrontal cortices
Denarration	Dorsolateral/mesial frontal cortices

focal brain injuries provide a convergent view of how the brain narratively organizes experience. To illustrate this emerging schema, we will describe and discuss four types of *"dysnarrativia,"* states of narrative impairment experienced by individuals with discrete focal damage in different regions of the neural network subserving human self-narrative (see table 1).

The first two types appear in individuals with global amnesia—loss of the ability to form new memories. Individuals with bilateral brain damage restricted to the amygdala–hippocampal system develop an isolated memory disturbance. Such injuries most commonly result from stroke, viral infection, or alcoholic vitamin deficiency. Amnestic patients have intact language, visuospatial, and executive function, and an intact immediate attention span. They can register and hold new ideas for 30 to 90 seconds, but no longer. Their accessible corpus of autobiographic experience is restricted to that acquired up until, or a few years before, their injury.

In recounting their autobiographic experience, most amnestic individuals provide *"arrested narratives"*: they are able to frame coherently their life from before their injury and not beyond, though this narrative may be 30 years out of date. Formal scientific reports, evocative "romantic science" portraits, and personal encounters with individuals with this condition unite in depicting individuals largely frozen in time, aging somatically but not psychologically (Milner, Corkin, and Teuber 1968, Ott and Saver 1993, Luria 1987, Sacks 1985). Their interests, obsessions, narrative self-interpretations, and dispositions are stable over decades.

A smaller group of amnestic individuals develop confabulation, restlessly fabricating narratives that purport to describe recent events in their lives but actually have little or no relationship to genuine occurrences. Usually these individuals have suffered, in addition to amygdala–hippocampal system damage producing amnesia, additional injury to frontal-lobe structures that are responsible for monitoring the veracity of responses and inhibiting inaccurate replies (Shapiro et al. 1981, Schnider and Ptak 1999). These individuals exhibit *"unbounded narrative,"* generating self-stories unconstrained (or barely constrained) by memories of actual events. Unaware of their memory disorder, they also generally appear unaware that they are creating factitious responses to fill in memory gaps. Often within the space of a few minutes they will provide several mutually contradictory narratives in response to the same question. Confabulating amnestic individuals offer an unrivaled glimpse at the power of the human impulse to narrative. The astonishing variety of plots they create arises not from a desire to impress, entertain, instruct, or deceive, but simply from a desire to respond to another human being's query with a story, albeit in unusual circumstances. These unique storytelling circumstances are a complete freedom to draw upon all materials for narrative content (free of limiting memories) and a willingness to accept all self-generated narratives as veridical.

A third type of dysnarrativia appears in individuals with bilateral damage to the ventromedial frontal lobe. These individuals have intact access to autobiographic memories, but are impaired at inhibiting immediate, impulsive responses. Classic case descriptions and neuropsychologic studies of these individuals suggest that they fail to construct and explore internal "as-if" narrative scenarios (Stuss and Benson 1986). They do not consider the multitude of potential outcomes of conjectured response options. They make "*under-narrated*" choices, often resulting in disastrous financial and social consequences. The paradigmatic patient with this disorder, Phineas Gage, was a railroad worker who survived an explosion that drove a tamping bar through his skull and brain. Following the accident, however, his personality was completely transformed, from temperate, dedicated, and religious to impulsive, vacillating, and irreverent. In his physician's haunting phrase, "He was no longer Gage" (Harlow 1868). Defects in fictive self-narrative construction destabilize and distort the human personality.

Recent studies suggest that at least some individuals with ventromedial frontal damage suffer a different, more subtle, yet equally disabling and revealing form of undernarration. One function of the ventromedial frontal brain region is to interweave emotional limbic centers with highly abstracted and integrated information in the dorsolateral frontal area. Damage may disconnect emotional and reasoning systems. Affected individuals are able to construct abundant internal narratives regarding response options, but fail to invest the resulting scenarios with affective tone (Saver and Damasio 1991, Bechara, Damasio, and Damasio 2000). Their decision making is not guided by automatic, bodily generated, emotional markers valorizing one result over another. Their overreasoned but emotionally undernarrated choices are frequently self-deleterious.

The last form of dysnarrativia we will examine appears in moderate form in individuals who have injury to the dorsolateral frontal cortices, and in extreme form in individuals with injury to the mesial sectors of the frontal lobe. The dorsolateral frontal cortices receive input from all higher order sensory association areas in the human cortex, and are critical for the planning and temporal organization of conduct and for guiding behavior by internal representations. Individuals with bilateral injury to this region are impaired in high-level cognitive programs that extract meaning from ongoing experience, organize the mind's mental contents coherently, and elaborate plans for sequenced action. Their behavioral repertoire is reduced and they become apathetic, with an apparent empty indifference to events in the surround (Blumer and Benson, 1975). The mesial frontal cortices and their pallidal and other connections are crucial for generating the drive toward motion and action. Individuals with bilateral injury to this region often develop an apathetic, abulic state, a listless loss of spontaneous activity (Mega and Cohenour 1997). They are unable to provide (and likely fail to generate internally) a narrative account of their experiences, wishes, and actions, although they are fully cognizant of their visual, auditory, and tactile surround. These individuals lead "*denarrated*" lives, aware but failing to organize experience in an action-generating temporal frame. In the extreme, they do not speak unless spoken to and do not move unless very hungry. These patients illustrate the inseparable connection between narrativity and personhood. Brain-injured individuals may lose their linguistic, mathematic, syllogistic, visuospatial, mnestic, or kinesthetic competencies and still be recognizably the same persons. Individuals who have lost the ability to construct narrative, however, have lost their selves.

Thus, the differing ways in which the multiregional neural system subserving narrative can break down—the dysnarrativias—highlight why narrative is the fundamental mode of organizing human experience.[2] Narrative

2. Determining the component operations of cognitive processes by analyzing the distinctive ways in which mental operations decompose after brain injury to discrete neural systems—the "lesion method"—is a time-honored and highly productive investigative strategy in neurology and neuropsychology. In addition to affording understanding of the neural substrates of narrative, this approach provides unique insights into the brain basis of "decoupling." Decoupling emerged as a central theme of the "Imagination and the Adapted Mind Conference," organized by Leda Cosmides, Paul Hernadi, and John Tooby, held at the University of California, Santa Barbara, August 26–29, 1999. Decoupling may be defined as the separation of mental action from physical action. Decoupling allows an individual to explore different response options in imagined mental scenarios without engaging the motor apparatus and actually enacting each envisioned behavior. Decoupling is clearly an evolutionarily advantageous process. Many conference participants suggested that the evolutionary origin of the human abilities to imagine and create literature and the arts may be traced to this functionally advantageous capacity.

Several neurologic illnesses produce breakdowns in the decoupling process, and help to illuminate the cognitive subcomponents of decoupling and their neural bases. We will outline a preliminary taxonomy of disorders in the regulation of decoupling (see table 2). These disruptions may be separated into two broad classes: disruption of elements of the decoupling apparatus itself, and disorders of the frequency of activation of an intact decoupling apparatus.

TABLE 2. DYSREGULATION OF DECOUPLING—A PRELIMINARY TAXONOMY

Disorders Impairing Decoupling

	Motor Output Inhibition	Judgement of Veridicality	Correct Activation of Semantic Stores
Normal imagination	+	+	+
Dreaming	+	—	—
REM behavior disorder	—	—	+
Delusions	—	—	—

Disorders of Frequency of Activation of Decoupling

Ventromedial frontal syndromes	Underutilization
Obsessive-complusive disorder/depression	Overutilization

     Critical cognitive components of the decoupling apparatus include 1) inhibition of motor output in imagined scenarios, 2) judgment of veridicality (assessing whether the scenario is actually currently taking place in real life, or is an imagined past, current, or future possibility), and 3) correct activation of semantic stores and/or perception of incoming stimuli to formulate an accurate perception of real or imagined events. In normal, waking mental enactments of imagined scenarios, all three of these elements are intact. While imagining different response options to particular environmental challenges (e.g., how to escape a bear, where to go for dinner, what to say to a stranger), individuals inhibit a motor response, correctly judge that their imagined scenarios are fictive, not real, and construct scenarios that are relatively true to key features of the real-world challenge being considered.

     The disorders of the decoupling apparatus include normal dreaming, the REM sleep behavior disorder, and delusional states. During REM dreaming, judgment of veridicality is often impaired and dreamers believe the dream world is a genuine reality. In normal dreaming, fortunately, the brain prevents motor enactment of actions appropriate in the dream reality but inappropriate in genuine reality through active pontine inhibition of spinal cord motor neurons, precluding motor output. In the REM sleep behavior disorder, lesions of the pons disrupt this motor inhibition, and dreamers physically enact their dreamed movements, often causing physical harm to themselves or their bed partners. In psychotic-delusional states, waking individuals form incorrect beliefs and perceptions regarding genuine reality, judge them as veridical, and act on them motorically and dysfunctionally.

     Exemplars of disorders of the frequency of activation of an intact decoupling apparatus include patients with ventromedial frontal syndromes, obsessive-compulsive disorder, and depression. Some individuals with bilateral ventromedial frontal injuries become stimulus bound, reacting immediately and impulsively to environmental cues without first mentally rehearsing varying possible scenarios of response and consequence. They demonstrate *underutilization* of the decoupling apparatus. Conversely, individuals with obsessive-compulsive disorder and ruminative depression may repeatedly replay certain scenes in their mind, unable to detach themselves from a limited set of preoccupying scenarios of action and response. These individuals demonstrate a form of *overutilization* of the decoupling apparatus. Many individuals with obsessive-compulsive disorder appear on functional imaging to have overactivity of ventromedial frontal circuits, further suggesting that the ventromedial frontal region is critical for activation of decoupling.

framing of the past allows predictions of the future; generating imaginary narratives allows the individual to safely (through internal fictions) explore the varied consequences of multitudinous response options. The potent adaptive value of narrative accounts for its primacy in organizing human understanding (as opposed to pictorial, musical, kinesthetic, syllogistic, or multiple other forms). Consciousness needs a narrative structure to create a sense of self based on the features of storytelling, such as coherence, consequence, and consecution.

Studies of the forms of neurologic disintegration of human narrative capacity carry an additional important implication for interpreting autobiographic literature. These conditions reveal that narrative framing and recall of experience is a dynamic, variable, and vulnerable process. Even single individual memories are resynthesized from widely distributed components. Picturing one's first encounter with a cat, for example, requires activating visual fragments of a feline form stored in the occipital cortex, tactile representations residing in the somatosensory cortices, audible contours of cat sounds in the auditory cortex, motoric programs for petting and carrying in the motor cortex, and often also retrieving emotional associations, metaphoric connections, and literary representations (Damasio 1989). Each of the stored components is vulnerable to change over intervening years, colored by new experience. Each act of resynthesis emphasizes different features depending on the individual's emotional, cognitive, and social frame at the time of recall (Zola). Modern neuroscience has demonstrated that retrieving memories is not the simple act of accessing a storehouse of ready-made photos in a stable neural album, preserved with complete fidelity to the moment of their formation. Rather, each act of recall is a re-creation, drawing upon multiple, dynamically changing modular fragments to shape a new mosaic. Numerous consequences follow for literary interpretation, of which we will mention just one. All memories are suspect, at the neural level. Fidelity-stable recall and self-interpretation of the past is not a property of the human brain and mind. The varied subjectivity of literary autobiographic productions has its root in the inescapable subjectivity of the brain's narrative and memory system. This variability of memory, however, does not detract from the primacy of narrative recall in organizing human experience. Texts that tell our "life stories," such as autobiographies, function as the written versions of what we first did when we brought narrative language to experience orally in order to approach a coherent identity called "the self." Not only does the activity of story production prompt, then, the production of memories, but it as well encourages an arranging of events into a state of coherence, consecution, and consequence—features of what constitute a narrative. We come to see our lives as understandable because of their apparent integration, logic, even order: our narratives and their consequent memories tell us that our lives were so. Autobiography and its related forms exemplify the phenomenon Jerome Bruner seeks to be defined. He writes: "My objective has been merely to lay out the ground plan of narrative relations. The daunting task that remains now is to show in detail how, in particular instances, narrative organizes the structure of human experience—how, in a word, 'life' comes to imitate 'art' and vice versa" (21). The narrative art form "autobiography" instructs us in our identities by virtue of its narrative form, which it imposes as a structure and vision on our lives, and exists in the form that it does as a consequence of how our brains function. Hence, autobiography stands as an embodiment of how art imitates life and life imitates art.

The comfort Aristotle takes in stories when he feels alone finds its power perhaps in his rediscovery of a connection to himself not prompted by how he philosophizes. To desire narrative reflects a kind of fundamental desire for life and self that finds its source in our neurologic makeup. The particular drive to narrate one's life story in the aesthetic form of autobi-ography reflects not only the need to create memories and so house within a notion of self formed from this collection of experiences told and in the telling remembered, but as well the need to create a notion of self that is understandable in the ways in which the narrative structure itself designs coherence. Autobiography imposes narrative's form on the consciousness of an "I's" experience, and exists as a consequence of how the "I's" brain organizes experience. What then an autobiography is, how it is told, and the drive we feel toward its narration we conclude to be brain-based and deeply human.

⚜

ACKNOWLEDGMENTS

Parts of this book have appeared elsewhere.

A portion of chapter 1 was published as "*Imaginado la Coscienza di Emma*" in a special issue of *il cannochiale: IL VALORE COGNITIVO DELL'ARTE,* edited and translated by Brunella Antomarini, 2 (2000): 157–66.

Chapter 2 was published in an earlier form as "Feeling Embodied: Consciousness, *Persuasion,* and Jane Austen" in *Narrative* (January 2003): 78–92.

A shorter version of chapter 3 was published as "*Middlemarch* and the Problem of Other Minds Heard" in a special issue of *LIT: Literature Interpretation Theory: Victorian Realism,* guest edited by Margaret E. Mitchell, 14 (2003): 223–42.

The coda, "The Neurology of Narrative," was first published in a special issue of *SubStance: On the Origin of Fictions,* guest edited by H. Porter Abbott, 94/95 (2001): 72–84.

Figures 1 and 2 are reproduced here from Herman Helmholtz's *On the Sensations of Tone as a Physiological Basis of Music,* translated by Alexander J. Ellis (New York: Dover Press [1954]): 136, 140.

Figures 3 and 4 are reproduced here from Wilder Penfield and Herbert Jasper's *Epilepsy and the Functional Anatomy of the Brain* (Boston: Little, Brown and Co. [1954]): 70, 71.

I owe profound and ongoing thanks to my teachers—to Philip Fisher, a remarkable teacher and scholar, who taught me how to read Austen, Eliot, and Hardy and how to think about the novel; to Stanley Cavell whose voice as philosopher continues to sound within me the call to search for meaning and to give it my voice; to Martha Nussbaum who first made the relation between the novel and philosophy a necessary part of my life; to Elaine

Scarry whose recognition of and moving attention to the representation of that which we imagine cannot be represented models for me the best of what scholarship in the humanities should seek to do; and to Jim Phelan and Peter Rabinowitz for their sustained interest in and engaged reading of my work and for bringing it to the attention of others. The Mellon Fellowship in the Humanities, what is now the Woodrow Wilson Fellowship, supported me throughout my graduate studies at Harvard—I owe my graduate education and career to their generosity and commitment to me and to the humanities. Over the course of the many years of writing this book, two intellectual homes emerged for me—the Institute of Contemporary Psychoanalysis, Los Angeles, and the Literature and Mind Initiative at the University of California, Santa Barbara. I am deeply grateful to my colleagues and friends from both worlds for sustaining me intellectually with the company of their far-reaching, generative minds and for their unfailing support. My thanks to the photographer Arash Afshari for his fine work and desire to make every image just right. Sandy Crooms, the wonderful Acquisitions Editor at The Ohio State University Press, has made every step of this book's production easier to move through and more enjoyable than I ever could have imagined. I am grateful for her committed, positive editorial support through all stages of this book's birth. Maggie Diehl's and Kristen Ebert-Wagner's skillful, gracious editorial attention has made this a better book—I am indebted to them for their knowledge of language and suggestions for how to better mine. My deep gratitude to Janna Thomspon-Chordas for the beautiful cover design and her responsive attention to my color palate and to Jennifer Shoffey Forsythe for the striking textual design. Together, they have made my book a work of art. Many thanks are due my students Erica Firman, Geoff McNeil, and Summer Star for their patient, thoughtful, careful research assistance. To Dashiell Fellini, who reminds me daily of what matters and asks like a refrain, "When will you get to work writing that bestseller?" At last I can answer, "Today." To Nelly, thank you for your sweet face and the quiet of your company through every writing moment. I owe the greatest thanks to the brilliant neurologist-philosopher Jeffrey Saver for knowing everything and for sharing your knowledge with such profoundly moving generosity. To my mother, the artist Eleanor Young, a lifetime of thanks for showing me what it means to imagine. My first words of dedication are my last—for my father—who taught me the power and wonder of an idea.

BIBLIOGRAPHY

Abbott, H. Porter, guest ed. "The Neurology of Narrative." *SubStance: On the Origins of Fictions* 94/95 (2001): 72–84.

Abram, David. *The Spell of the Sensuous.* New York: Vintage/Random House, 1996.

Aristotle. *Fragmenta.* Edited by V. Rose. Stuttgart, Germany: Teubner, 1967.

Armstrong, Nancy. *How Novels Think: The Limits of Individualism from 1719–1900.* New York: Columbia University Press, 2005.

Austen, Jane. *Emma.* Harmondsworth, Middlesex, UK: Penguin, 1985.

———. *Mansfield Park.* Harmondsworth, Middlesex, UK: Penguin, 1985.

———. *Northanger Abbey.* Harmondsworth, Middlesex, UK: Penguin, 1995.

———. *Persuasion.* Harmondsworth, Middlesex, UK: Penguin, 1985.

———. *Pride and Prejudice.* Harmondsworth, Middlesex, UK: Penguin, 1972.

———. *Sense and Sensibility.* Harmondsworth, Middlesex, UK: Penguin, 1995.

Bain, Alexander. *The Senses and the Intellect.* London: Longman, Green, and Co., 1894.

Baker, William. *George Eliot and Judaism.* Salzburg, Austria: Edwin Mellen, 1975.

Barthes, Roland. "Introduction to the Structural Analysis of Narratives." *Image-Music-Text.* Translated by Stephen Heath. New York: Hill and Wang, 1977.

Bechara A., Damasio H., Damasio A. R. "Emotion, Decision Making and the Orbitofrontal Cortex." *Cerebral Cortex* 10 (2000): 295–307.

Beer, Gillian. *Darwin's Plots.* Cambridge: Cambridge University Press, 2000.

Bennett, Alan. *The History Boys.* London: Faber and Faber, 2006.

Bluestone, George. "Limits of the Novel and Film." In *Film Theory and Criticism,* edited by Gerald Mast and Marshall Cohen. New York: Oxford University Press, 1985. 384–89.

———. *Novels into Film.* Berkeley and Los Angeles: University of California Press, 1966.

Blumer, D. and D. F. Benson. "Personality Changes with Frontal and Temporal Lesions." In *Psychiatric Aspects of Neurologic Disease.* New York: Grune & Stratton, 1975. 151–70.

Bollas, Christopher. "The Aesthetic Moment and the Search for Transformation." In *Transitional Objects and Potential Spaces,* edited by Peter L. Rydnytsky. New York: Columbia University Press, 1993. 40–50.

———. *The Shadow of the Object: Psychoanalysis of the Unthought Known.* New York:

Columbia University Press, 1987.

Booth, Wayne C. *The Rhetoric of Fiction*. Chicago: University of Chicago Press, 1983.

Bray, Joseph. "The Source of 'Dramatized Consciousness': Richardson, Austen, and Stylistic Influence." *Style* 35, no. 1 (Spring 2001): 18–33.

Bromberg, Philip M. "'Speak! That I May See You': Some Reflections on Dissociation, Reality, and Psychoanalytic Listening," *Psychoanalytic Dialogues* 4, no. 4 (1994): 517–47.

———. *Standing in the Spaces: Essays in Clinical Process Trauma and Dissociation*. London: Analytic, 2001.

Bruner, Jerome. *Acts of Meaning*. Cambridge, MA: Harvard University Press, 1992.

———. *Actual Minds, Possible Worlds*. Cambridge, MA: Harvard University Press, 1987.

———. "The Narrative Construction of Reality." *Critical Inquiry* 18, no. 1 (1991): 1–22.

Butte, George. *I Know That You Know That I Know: Narrating Subjects from* Moll Flanders *to* Marnie. Columbus: The Ohio State University Press, 2004.

———. "Shame or Espousal? *Emma* and the New Intersubjectivity of Anxiety in Austen." In *Jane Austen's Business: Her World and Her Profession,* edited by Juliet McMaster and Bruce Stovel. New York: St. Martin's, 1996. 54–65.

Campbell, Sue. *Interpreting the Personal: Expression and the Formation of Feelings*. Ithaca, NY: Cornell University Press, 1997.

Capuano, Peter. "An Objective Aural-Relative in *Middlemarch*." *SEL* 47, no. 4 (Autumn 2007): 921–41.

Carey, Benedict. "Amnesiacs May Be Cut Off From Past and Future Alike." *The New York Times,* January 23, 2007, health and fitness section.

———. "You're Checked Out, But Your Brain Is Tuned In." *The New York Times,* Tuesday, August 5, 2008, health section, D5.

Carey, Benedict and Natalie Angier. "Sleep." *The New York Times,* Tuesday, October 23, 2007, Science Times, D1–D8.

Cavell, Stanley. "Knowing and Acknowledging." *Must We Mean What We Say?* Cambridge: Cambridge University Press, 1976. 238–66.

Chalmers, David. *The Conscious Mind: In Search of a Fundamental Theory*. New York: Oxford University Press, 1997.

———. "Facing Up to the Problem of Consciousness." *Journal of Consciousness Studies* 2, no. 3 (1995): 200–219.

———. "The Puzzle of Conscious Experience." *Scientific American* 273, no. 6 (December 1995): 80–86.

Churchland, Patricia and Paul Churchland. *On the Contrary: Critical Essays, 1987–1997*. Cambridge, MA: MIT Press, 1998.

Churchland, Paul. *Matter and Consciousness*. Cambridge, MA: MIT Press, 1984.

Clark, Edwin and L. S. Jacyna. *Nineteenth-Century Origins of Neuroscientific Concepts*. Berkeley: University of California Press, 1987.

Clueless. Dir. and Screenplay Amy Heckerling. Perf. Alicia Silverstone. Paramount Pictures, 1995.

Cohen, William A. *Embodied: Victorian Literature and the Senses*. Minneapolis/St. Paul: University of Minnesota Press, 2008.

———. "Faciality and Sensation in Hardy's *The Return of the Native,*" *PMLA* 121, no. 2 (2006): 437–52.

Cohn, Dorrit. *Transparent Minds: Narrative Modes for Presenting Consciousness*. Princeton, NJ: Princeton University Press, 1978.

Crick, Francis. *The Astonishing Hypothesis: The Scientific Search for the Soul.* New York: Charles Scribner's Sons, 1994.

Da Sousa Correa, Delia. *George Eliot, Music and Victorian Culture.* New York: Palgrave Macmillan, 2003.

Damasio, Antonio. *Descartes' Error.* New York: G. P. Putnam's Sons, 1994.

———. *Looking for Spinoza: Joy, Sorrow, and the Feeling Brain.* New York: Harcourt, 2003.

———. *The Feeling of What Happens: Body and Emotion in the Making of Consciousness.* New York: Harcourt Brace, 1999.

———. "Time-Locked Multiregional Retroactivation: A Systems Level Proposal for the Neural Substrates of Recall and Recognition." *Cognition* 33 (1989): 25–62.

Dames, Nicholas. *Amnesiac Selves: Nostalgia, Forgetting, and British Fiction, 1810–1870.* Oxford: Oxford University Press, 2001.

———. *The Physiology of the Novel: Reading, Neural Science, and the Form of Victorian Fiction.* Oxford: Oxford University Press, 2007.

Darwin, Charles. *The Expression of the Emotions in Man and Animal.* New York: Greenwood, 1955.

Deleuze, Gilles and Claire Parnet. *Dialogues.* Translated by Hugh Tomlinson and Barbara Habberjam. London: Athlone, 1987.

Descartes, René. *Meditations on First Philosophy.* Translated by Donald A. Cress. Indianapolis, IN: Hackett, 1993.

Dennett, Daniel. *Brainstorms: Philosophical Essays on Mind and Psychology.* Montgomery, VT: Bradford, 1978.

———. *Consciousness Explained.* Boston: Back Bay, 1992.

Didion, Joan. *The Year of Magical Thinking.* New York: Alfred A. Knopf, 2005.

Duchenne de Boulogne, G. B. *The Mechanism of Human Facial Expression.* Translated by R. Andrew Cuthbertson. Cambridge: Cambridge University Press, 1990.

Eakin, Emily. "I Feel Therefore I Am." *The New York Times,* Saturday, April 19, 2003, A19.

Edelman, Gerald and Giulio Tononi. *A Universe of Consciousness.* New York: Basic Books, 2000.

Elfenbein, Andrew. "Cognitive Science and the History of Reading." *PMLA* 121 (2006): 484–502.

Eliot, George. *Adam Bede.* Harmondsworth, Middlesex, UK: Penguin, 1985.

———. *Daniel Deronda.* Harmondsworth, Middlesex, UK: Penguin, 1995.

———. "Liszt, Wagner, and Weimar." *George Eliot: Selected Critical Writings.* Edited and with an Introduction by Rosemary Ashton. Oxford: Oxford University Press, 1992.

———. *Middlemarch.* Harmondsworth, Middlesex, UK: Penguin, 1994.

———. *The Mill on the Floss.* Harmondsworth, Middlesex, UK: Penguin, 1985.

Etz Hayim: Torah and Commentary. Edited by David L. Lieber and Jules Harlow. New York: The Rabbinical Assembly, 2001.

Feagin, Susan L. *Reading with Feeling: The Aesthetics of Appreciation.* Ithaca, NY: Cornell University Press, 1996.

Fireman, Gary D., Ted E. McVay, Jr., and Owen J. Flanagan, eds. *Narrative and Consciousness: Literature, Psychology, and the Brain.* Oxford: Oxford University Press, 2003.

Fisher, Philip. *The Vehement Passions.* Princeton, NJ: Princeton University Press, 2002.

Fletcher, Loraine. "Emma: The Shadow Novelist." *Critical Survey* 4, no. 1 (1992): 36–44.

Fry, Carroll. "'The Hunger of the Imagination': *Discordia Concors* in *Emma*. *Persuasions* 29 (2007): 209–15.

Gallagher, Catherine. "George Eliot: Immanent Victorian." *Representations* 90 (Spring 2005): 61–74.

Genette, Gérard. *Narrative Discourse*. Translated by Jane E. Lewin. Ithaca, NY: Cornell University Press, 1985.

Gorman, Anita G. "The Body as Index of Emotion." *The Body in Illness and Health: Themes and Images in Jane Austen*. New York: Peter Lang, 1993. 127–62.

Gray, Patricia M., Bernie Krause, Jelle Atema, Roger Payne, Carol Krumhansl, and Luis Baptista. "The Music of Nature and the Nature of Music." *Science Magazine* 291, no. 5501 (January 5, 2001): 52–54.

Gregory, Richard L., ed. *The Oxford Companion to Mind*. Oxford: Oxford University Press, 1987.

Grey, Beryl. *George Eliot and Music*. New York: St. Martin's Press, 1989.

Hall, G. Stanley. *Founders of Modern Psychology*. New York: D. Appleton and Co., 1912.

Hardy, Barbara. *Particularities: Readings in George Eliot*. Athens: Ohio University Press, 1983.

Hardy, Thomas. *Jude the Obscure*. London: Penguin, 1998.

———. *The Mayor of Casterbridge: The Life and Death of a Man of Character*. London: Penguin, 1997.

———. *Tess of the D'Urbervilles: A Pure Woman*. Harmondsworth, Middlesex, UK: Penguin, 1998.

Harlow, J. M. "Recovery from Passage of an Iron Bar through the Head." *Publications of the Massachusetts Medical Society* 2 (1868): 327–47.

Hearne, Vicki. *Animal Happiness*. New York: HarperCollins, 1994.

Helmholtz, Hermann L. F. "On the Physiological Causes of Harmony in Music." Translated by A. J. Ellis. In *Helmholtz on Perception: Its Physiology and Development*, edited by Richard M. Warren and Roslyn P. Warren. New York: John Wiley & Sons, 1968. 42–44.

———. *On the Sensations of Tone as a Physiological Basis for the Theory of Music*. Translated by Alexander J. Ellis. New York: Dover, 1954.

Hobson, J. Allan. *The Dreaming Brain*. New York: Basic Books, 1988.

———. "Sleep and Dream Suppression Following a Lateral Medullary Infarct: A First-Person Account." *Consciousness and Cognition* 11 (2002): 377–90.

Hogan, Patrick Colm. *Cognitive Science, Literature, and the Arts*. New York: Routledge, 2003.

James, William. *The Principles of Psychology*. Vols. I and II. New York: Dover, 1890.

Jamison, Kay Redfield. *Exuberance: The Passion for Life*. New York: Vintage/Random House, 2004.

———. *Night Falls Fast: Understanding Suicide*. New York: Vintage/Random House, 2000.

———. *Touched with Fire: Manic Depressive Illness and the Artistic Temperament*. New York: Free Press Paperback, 1994.

———. *An Unquiet Mind: A Memoir of Moods and Madness*. New York: Vintage/Random House, 1995.

Jones, Wendy. S. "*Emma*, Gender, and the Mind-Brain." *ELH* 75 (2008): 315–43.

Keen, Suzanne. *Empathy and the Novel*. Oxford: Oxford University Press, 2007.

Keysers, Christian and Valeria Gazzola. "Social Neuroscience: Mirror Neurons

Recorded in Humans." *Current Biology* 20 (2010): 353–54.

Kohut, Heinz. "The Psychoanalytic Treatment of Narcissistic Personality Disorders—Outline of a Systematic Approach." *Psychoanalytic Study of the Child* 23 (1968): 86–113.

Kristeva, Julia. *Black Sun: Depression and Melancholia.* Translated by Leon S. Roudiez. New York: Columbia University Press, 1989.

Kosslyn, Stephen, William L. Thompson, and Giorgio Ganis. *The Case for Mental Imagery.* Oxford: Oxford University Press, 2006.

Lakoff, George and Mark Johnson. *Metaphors We Live By.* Chicago: University of Chicago Press, 2003.

———. *Philosophy in the Flesh.* New York: Basic Books, 1999.

Langer, Susanne. *Feeling and Form.* New York: Charles Scribner's Sons, 1953.

———. *Philosophy in a New Key.* 3rd ed. Cambridge, MA: Harvard University Press, 1956.

Law, Jules. "Sleeping Figures: Hardy, History, and the Gendered Body." *ELH* 65, no. 1 (1998): 223–57.

LeDoux, Joseph. *The Emotional Brain.* New York: Touchstone, 1996.

Lehrer, Jonah. *Proust Was a Neuroscientist.* New York: Mariner, 2008.

Levine, George. *The Realistic Imagination.* Chicago: University of Chicago Press, 1981.

Lodge, David. *Consciousness and the Novel.* Cambridge, MA: Harvard University Press, 2001.

Luria, A. R. *The Man with a Shattered World.* Cambridge, MA: Harvard University Press, 1987.

Mandel, Miriam B. "Fiction and Fiction-Making: *Emma.*" *Persuasions* 13 (December 16, 1991): 100–103.

Marshall, David. "True Acting and the Language of Real Feeling: *Mansfield Park.*" *Yale Journal of Criticism* 3 (1989): 87–106.

Markowitsch, Hans. "Memory and Amnesia." In *Principles of Behavioral and Cognitive Neurology,* 2nd ed., edited by M. Mesulam. New York: Oxford University Press, 2000. 257–93.

Marroni, Francesco. "Thomas Hardy and the Landscapes of Melancholy." In *Literary Landscapes, the Landscape in Literature,* edited by Michele Bottalico, Maria Teresa Chialant, and Eleonara Rao. Rome: Carrocci, 2007. 80–87.

Mast, Gerald and Marshall Cohen. *Film Theory and Criticism.* New York: Oxford University Press, 1985.

McGinn, Colin. *The Mysterious Flame: Conscious Minds in a Material World.* New York: Basic Books, 1999.

McKeon, Michael. *The Origins of the English Novel, 1600–1740.* Baltimore: The Johns Hopkins University Press, 2002.

McMaster, Juliet. "*Emma:* The Geography of a Mind." *Persuasions* 29 (2007): 26–38.

Mega, M. S. and R. C. Cohenour. "Akinetic Mutism: Disconnection of Frontal-Subcortical Circuits." *Neuropsychiatry, Neuropsychology, and Behavioral Neurology* 10 (1997): 254–59.

Merleau-Ponty, M. *Phenomenology of Perception.* Translated by Colin Smith. New York: Humanities Press, 1962.

Miller, Andrew H. "Reading Thoughts: Victorian Perfectionism and the Display of Thinking." *Studies in the Literary Imagination* 35, no. 2 (Fall 2002): 79–89.

Miller, J. Hillis. *Fiction and Repetition: Seven Novels.* Cambridge, MA: Harvard University Press, 1985.

———. *Others.* Princeton, NJ: Princeton University Press, 2001.

———. "The Roar on the Other Side of Silence: Otherness in *Middlemarch.*" *EDDA* 3 (1995): 236–45.

———. *Thomas Hardy: Distance and Desire.* Cambridge, MA: Harvard University Press, 1970.

Miller, Susan M. "Thomas Hardy and the Impersonal Lyric." *Journal of Modern Literature* 30, no. 3 (Spring 2007): 95–107.

Milner B., S. Corkin, and H. L. Teuber. "Further Analysis of the Hippocampal Amnesic Syndrome: 14 Year Follow-Up Study of H.M." *Neuropsychologia* 6 (1968): 215–34.

Minter, David Lee. "Aesthetic Vision and the World of *Emma.*" *Nineteenth-Century Fiction* 21(1966): 49–59.

Modell, Arnold H. *Imagination and the Meaningful Brain.* Cambridge, MA: MIT Press, 2003.

Moore, Barbara. "Imagining the Real: The Development of Moral Imagination in *Emma.*" *Persuasions* 25 (2003): 233–38.

Moretti, Franco. "Kindergarten." *Signs Taken for Wonder.* New York: Verso, 2006. 157–81.

Nagel, Thomas. *The View from Nowhere.* Oxford: Oxford University Press, 1986.

———. "What is it like to be a Bat?" *The Philosophical Review* 83 (1974): 435–50.

Nurbhai, Saleel and K. M. Newton. *George Eliot, Judaism and the Novels: Jewish Myth and Mysticism.* Houndmills, Basingstoke, Hampshire, UK: Palgrave, 2002.

Nussbaum, Martha. *Upheavals of Thought: The Intelligence of Emotions.* Cambridge: Cambridge University Press, 2001.

O'Farrell, Mary Ann. *Telling Complexions: The Nineteenth-Century English Novel and the Blush.* Durham, NC: Duke University Press, 1997.

Orange, Donna. *Emotional Understanding: Studies in Psychoanalytic Epistemology.* New York: Guilford, 1995.

Ott, B. and J. L. Saver. "Unilateral Amnesic Stroke: Six New Cases and a Review of the Literature." *Stroke* 24 (1993): 1033–42.

Palmer, Alan. *Fictional Minds.* Lincoln: University of Nebraska Press, 2004.

———. "Intermental Thought in the Novel: The *Middlemarch* Mind." *Style* 39, no. 4 (Winter 2005): 427–39.

Patchett, Ann. *Bel Canto.* New York: Perennial/HarperCollins, 2001.

Penfield, Wilder and Herbert Jasper. *Epilepsy and the Functional Anatomy of the Human Brain.* Boston: Little, Brown, 1954.

Phillips, Adam. *On Kissing, Tickling, and Being Bored: Psychoanalytic Essays on the Unexamined Life.* Cambridge, MA: Harvard University Press, 1993.

Piaget, Jean. *The Principles of Genetic Epistemology.* Translated by Wolfe Mays. New York: Basic Books, 1972.

Picker, John M. *Victorian Soundscapes.* Oxford: Oxford University Press, 2003.

Pinch, Adela. *Strange Fits of Passion: Epistemologies of Emotion, Hume to Austen.* Stanford, CA: Stanford University Press, 1996.

Pinker, Steven. *How the Mind Works.* Harmondsworth, UK: Penguin, 1997.

Polanyi, Michael. *Personal Knowledge: Towards a Post-Critical Philosophy.* Chicago: University of Chicago Press, 1962.

Prewitt, Julia Brown. "Jane Austen: In Search of Time Present." *Persuasions* 22 (Annual 2000): 136–56.

Rabbi Yitzchak Ginsburgh, assisted by Rabbis Avraham Arieh Trugman and Moshe Yaakov Wisnefsky. *The Alef-Beit: Jewish Thought Revealed Through the Hebrew Letters.* Lanham, MD: Jason Aronson, 1995.

Ramachandran, V. S. and William Hirstein. "The Science of Art: A neurological Theory of Aesthetic Experience." *Journal of Consciousness Studies* 6 (1999): 15–51.

Raphael, Linda S. *Narrative Skepticism: Moral Agency and Representations of Consciousness in Fiction.* Cranbury, NJ: Associated University Press, 2001.

Richardson, Alan. *British Romanticism and the Science of Mind.* Cambridge: Cambridge University Press, 2001.

———. "Of Heartache and Head Injury: Reading Minds in *Persuasion*." *Poetics Today* 23, no. 1 (2002): 141–60.

———. *The Neural Sublime: Cognitive Theories and Romantic Texts.* Baltimore: The Johns Hopkins University Press, 2010.

Rose, David. *Consciousness: Philosophical, Psychological and Neural Theories.* Oxford: Oxford University Press, 2006.

Sacks, Oliver. "The Lost Mariner." In *The Man Who Mistook His Wife for a Hat.* New York: Summit Books, 1985. 22–41.

Sartre, Jean Paul. *The Imaginary: A Phenomenological Psychology of the Imagination.* Translated by Jonathan Webber. London: Routledge, 2004.

———. *Imagination.* Translated by Forrest Williams. Ann Arbor: University of Michigan Press, 1962.

———. *The Psychology of Imagination.* New York: Citadel, 1961.

Saver J. L. and A. R. Damasio. "Preserved Access and Processing of Social Knowledge in a Patient with Acquired Sociopathy due to Ventromedial Frontal Damage." *Neuropsychologia* 29 (1991): 1241–49.

Scarry, Elaine. *Dreaming by the Book.* Princeton, NJ: Princeton University Press, 2001.

Schank, Roger. *Tell Me a Story.* New York: Charles Scribner's Sons, 1990.

Schnider, A. and R. Ptak. "Spontaneous Confabulators Fail to Suppress Currently Irrelevant Memory Traces." *Nature Neuroscience* 2 (1999): 677–81.

Schwab, Gabriele. *Subjects Without Selves: Transitional Texts in Modern Fiction.* Cambridge, MA: Harvard University Press, 1994.

———. "Words and Moods: The Transference of Literary Knowledge." *SubStance* 84 (1997): 107–27.

Shapiro, B. E., M. P. Alexander, H. Gardner, and B. Mercer. "Mechanisms of Confabulation." *Neurology* 31 (1981): 1070–76.

Siegel, Jerome M. "Why We Sleep." *Scientific American* 289, no. 5: 92–97.

Smiley, Jane. *13 Ways of Looking at the Novel.* New York: Alfred A. Knopf, 2005.

Spencer, Herbert. *The Principles of Psychology.* New York: D. Appleton and Co., 1872.

Sperlinger, Tom. "'The Sensitive Author': George Eliot." *The Cambridge Quarterly* 36, no. 3 (2007): 250–72.

Spinoza, Benedict de. *On the Improvement of the Understanding; the Ethics; Correspondence.* Translated by R. H. M. Elwes. New York: Dover, 1955.

Squire, L. R., B. Knowlton, and G. Musen. "The Structure and Organization of Memory." *Annual Review of Psychology* 44 (1993): 453–95.

Stern, Daniel. *Diary of a Baby.* New York: Basic Books/HarperCollins, 1992.

———. "The Sense of a Subjective Self: II. Affect Attunement." *The Interpersonal World of the Infant: A View from Psychoanalysis and Developmental Psychology.* New York: Basic Books, 1985. 138–61.

Stern, Donnel B. "The Eye Sees Itself: Dissociation, Enactment, and the Achieve-
    ment of Conflict." *Contemporary Psychoanalysis* 40, no. 2 (April 2004): 197–237.
Stuss, D. T. and D. F. Benson. *The Frontal Lobes.* New York: Raven Press, 1986.
Tave, Stuart. *Some Words of Jane Austen.* Chicago: University of Chicago Press, 1973.
Thrailkill, Jane F. *Affecting Fictions: Mind, Body, Emotion in American Literary Realism.*
    Cambridge, MA: Harvard University Press, 2007.
Tomalin, Claire. *Jane Austen: A Life.* New York: Alfred A. Knopf, 1997.
Tramo, Mark Jude. "Music of the Hemispheres." *Science Magazine* 291, no. 5501
    (January 5, 2001): 54–56.
Trimble, Michael, M.D. *The Soul in the Brain: The Cerebral Basis of Language, Art, and
    Belief.* Baltimore: The Johns Hopkins University Press, 2007.
Turner, Mark. *The Literary Mind.* Oxford: Oxford University Press, 1996.
Von Hartmann, Eduard. *Philosophy of the Unconscious.* Translated by William Chat-
    terton Coupland. London: Kegan Paul, Trench, Trubner, & Co., 1893.
Wiltshire, John. *Jane Austen and the Body.* Cambridge: Cambridge University Press,
    1992.
Wittgenstein, Ludwig. *Philosophical Investigations.* Translated by G. E. M. Anscombe.
    Oxford: Basil Blackwell, 1958.
Wood, James. "The Heroic Consciousness of Jane Austen: The Birth of Inwardness."
    The New Republic (August 17 and 24, 1998): 25–28.
———. *How Fiction Works.* New York: Farrar, Strauss, Giroux, 2008.
Woodward, William R. and Mitchell G. Ash, eds. *The Problematic Science: Psychology
    in Nineteenth-Century Thought.* New York: Praeger, 1982.
Woolf, Virginia. *To the Lighthouse.* Foreword by Eudora Welty. New York: Harvest/
    HBJ, 1981.
Young, Robert. *Mind, Brain, and Adaptation in the Nineteenth Century.* Oxford: Oxford
    University Press, 1990.
Zahavi, Dan. "Beyond Empathy: Phenomenological Approaches to Intersubjectivity."
    Journal of Consciousness Studies 8 (2001): 151–67.
Zeki, Semir. "Art and the Brain." *Journal of Consciousness Studies* 6 (1999): 76–96.
———. "Artistic Creativity and the Brain." *Science* 293 (2001): 51–52.
———. *Splendors and Miseries of the Brain: Love, Creativity, and the Quest for Human
    Happiness.* West Sussex, UK: Wiley-Blackwell, 2009.
Zeman, Adam. *Consciousness: A User's Guide.* New Haven, CT: Yale University Press,
    2002.
Zola, S. M. "The Neurobiology of Recovered Memory." *Journal of Neuropsychiatry
    and Clinical Neurosciences* 9 (1997): 449–59.
Zunshine, Lisa. *Why We Read Fiction: Theory of Mind and the Novel.* Columbus: The
    Ohio State University Press, 2006.

INDEX

THEORY AND INTERPRETATION OF NARRATIVE

James Phelan and Peter J. Rabinowitz, Series Editors

Because the series editors believe that the most significant work in narrative studies today contributes both to our knowledge of specific narratives and to our understanding of narrative in general, studies in the series typically offer interpretations of individual narratives and address significant theoretical issues underlying those interpretations. The series does not privilege one critical perspective but is open to work from any strong theoretical position.